The Best of the Independent
Rhetoric and Composition Journals

The Best of the Independent Rhetoric and Composition Journals
Series Editor: Steve Parks

Each year, a team of editors selects the best work published in the independent journals in the field of Rhetoric and Composition, following a competitive review process involving journal editors and publishers. For additional information about the series, see http://www.parlorpress.com/bestofrhetcomp.

THE BEST OF THE INDEPENDENT RHETORIC AND COMPOSITION JOURNALS

2010

Edited by Steve Parks, Linda Adler-Kassner, Brian Bailie, and Collette Caton

Parlor Press
Anderson, South Carolina
www.parlorpress.com

Parlor Press LLC, Anderson, South Carolina, USA

© 2011 by Parlor Press. Individual essays in this book have been reprinted with permission of the respective copyright owners.
All rights reserved.
Printed in the United States of America

SAN: 254-8879

Library of Congress Cataloging-in-Publication Data
Application in Process

Cover design by David Blakesley.
Printed on acid-free paper.

Parlor Press, LLC is an independent publisher of scholarly and trade titles in print and multimedia formats. This book is available in paper and digital formats from Parlor Press on the World Wide Web at http://www.parlorpress.com or through online and brick-and-mortar bookstores. For submission information or to find out about Parlor Press publications, write to Parlor Press, 3015 Brackenberry Drive, Anderson, South Carolina, 29621, or email editor@parlorpress.com.

Contents

Introduction   *vii*
    Stephen J. Parks, Linda Adler-Kassner,
    Brian Bailie, and Collette Caton

Across the Disciplines *2*

    Writing in Central and Eastern Europe: Stakeholders
    and Directions in Initiating Change   *3*
       John Harbord

Community Literacy Journal *26*

    Street Sex Work: Re/Constructing Discourse
    from Margin to Center   *27*
       Jill McCracken

Composition Forum *48*

    Sustaining Writing Theory   *49*
       Amy M. Patrick

Composition Studies *70*

    An Inconvenient Tool: Rethinking the Role of
    Slideware in the Writing Classroom   *71*
       Laurie E. Gries and Collin Gifford Brooke

Computers and Composition *92*

    Recovering Delivery for Digital Rhetoric   *93*
       James E. Porter

JAC *132*

    Pass It On: Revising the *Plagiarism Is Theft* Metaphor   *133*
       Amy Robillard

The Journal of Teaching Writing *164*

    Freewriting and Free Speech: A Pragmatic Perspective   *165*
        Janet Bean and Peter Elbow

Kairos *186*

    Speaking with Students: Profiles in Digital Pedagogy   *187*
        Virginia Kuhn, with DJ Johnson and David Lopez

Pedagogy *194*

    Remediating the Book Review: Toward Collaboration and
      Multimodality across the English Curriculum   *195*
        Christine Tulley and Kristine Blair

Reflections *228*

    Engaging Community Literacy through the Rhetorical
      Work of a Social Movement   *229*
        Christopher Wilkey

    Interview with Bonnie Neumeier   *258*
        Christopher Wilkey

Writing on the Edge *270*

    Everything Was Going Quite Smoothly Until
      I Stumbled on a Footnote   *271*
        David Bartholomae

    About the Editors   *285*

Introduction

*Stephen J. Parks, Linda Adler-Kassner,
Brian Bailie, and Collette Caton*

Any anthology that announces itself as offering the "best" clearly needs to explain its intent, its theory, and its rationale. From the outset, then, we want to acknowledge the inherent difficulty of defining the "best" for a field whose research begins in the classroom, but transverses programs, colleges, communities, and ultimately, national borders. Within such a simultaneously pragmatic and theoretical, local and global context, any research produced will need to address multiple concerns across multiple audiences.

Any collection of the "best," then, should not favor one particular teaching moment or research model, but should represent the dynamic interplay of all these contexts, simultaneously moving across different domains, demands, and decision points. It should present essays that have helped form and inform the debates that mark our current field, as well as suggesting ways to shift and rearrange key terms within rhetoric and composition to allow new knowledge to be created. Nor is such work the domain of print journals only; we have also worked with digitally born journals to ensure their multimedia work could be included, representing how scholarship has been strengthened by the interaction of traditional writing genres, new media, and social networking technology. And it is for that reason that the "book" you are now reading will appear on the Web so that you can see the original digital formats in which some of the essays originated: http://www.parlorpress.com/bestofrhetcomp.

We also believed that any such anthology must emerge out of this sense of collaborative conversation. To that end, we invited any journal that identified as "independent" to select two essays published in the past year. These would be our base set of essays, from which the "best" would be drawn. This process allowed the individual editors of journals to select the work they believed best represented the goals and aims of the journal. Here we wanted to respect their work, their editorial insights. Then, instead of producing an anthology which relied upon our own sense of "best" or even a "select" group of elite readers, we decided to made the selection of essays in this volume an opportunity for a broad discussion amongst the many laborers and scholars in our field – adjunct instructors, graduate students, full time faculty, tenured professors, unionized and non-unionized workers; individuals who saw their primary identification as writing program administrators, scholars, writing center tutors, or classroom teachers. (Our one failing in this regard was not having a community college or two year faculty labor pool represented, a failing we hope to correct for the future editions.)

Working with four institutions, representing different student and teaching populations, we established reading teams who ranked the essays according to a set of opening criteria:

- Article demonstrates a broad sense of the discipline, demonstrating the ability to explain how its specific focus in a sub-disciplinary area addresses broader concerns in the field.
- Article makes original contributions to the field, expanding or rearticulating central premises.
- Article is written in a style that, while based in the discipline, attempts to engage with a wider audience or concerns a wider audience.

Each reading group was asked to rank the essays on a scale of 1-4, indicating which work best met the criteria. At each moment, however, we also encouraged the readers to expand our criteria. For that reason, the rankings began to intimate how institutional location affected one's reading – graduate students looking for essays that provided both theory and practice; adjunct faculty looking for discussions of labor and teaching; writing program administrators looking for strategic insights on practice. And, as you might expect, many group participants used their multiple locations as individuals, members of particular heritages, and institutionally located workers to inform their collective decisions.

It is from this collaborative and collective process, then, that the essays in this volume were chosen. To us, then, they are the "best" because they reflect the decisions made by a broad cross-section of those active in our field's classrooms, programs, and institutions. The selected essays represent how workers in our field chose to best represent the dynamic interchange of ideas and practices occurring in the independent Rhetoric and Composition journals.

This was our intent and theory in putting together this anthology. Our rationale, however, touches upon a slightly different sense of "our field" and how knowledge is produced. Unlike institutionally supported journals, such as *College English*, independent journals often do not have the resources to have a collective visible presence at our regional or national conferences. At those moments when our field "gathers" to represent its important research and scholarship, there is little public space for the work of independent journals. And as a consequence, there is little opportunity to share the insights contained in their publication and to expand their readership base (which for independent journals is often a vital element in their continued existence).

Economics, then, are impacting the sustainability of independent journals. For while certain journals might be able to attend the Conference on College Composition and Communication (4Cs), for instance, conversations with journal editors will highlight how the economics of conferences have led many to lower their profile. Exhibition booths and conference program advertising space are all too expensive. In addition, the economics of college and department budgets have also hindered the profile of independent journals in academic libraries. The recent recession has also hurt the ability of home institutions to offer internal support. All these factors hurt the long-term viability of this important network of scholarly production.

For we would argue that independent journals often serve as the place new ideas are incubated, where theories and projects begin to emerge into programmatic focus, and new frameworks for our field are articulated. Read the citation pages in mainstream journals, the bibliographies in recently published books, and you'll see the impact of independent journals: *Across the Disciplines, Community Literacy Journal, Computers and Composition*, and others. Very often these journals are part of the intellectual underpinnings that support the publications featured at the conference. They are an integral part of the conversation in our field. Their ability to remain vital and visible, however, is under increasing pressure.

A principle rationale for this collection, then, is to increase their visibility – to highlight some of the important work in Rhetoric and Composition that for economic reasons may not have reached a broad audience in the field. And it is important to note that the profits from the book that you are now reading will collectively support independent journals in Rhetoric and Composition securing space at 4Cs. Your purchase of the book, then, is also a contribution to increasing their visibility in the conversations that mark or field.

Before moving onto the essays featured in this book, however, we hope you will take a moment to read this partial list of individuals who have helped organize or participate in our reading groups. Their willingness to volunteer time, actively discuss, and help assess the work speaks to the spirit of collaboration and conversation which marks the "best" of our field. For this help and support, we want to express our sincerest gratitude: Phil Alexander, Noelle Ballmer, Mashey Bernstein, Samantha Blackmon, Jennifer Bray, Marilee Brooks-Gilles, John Catalini, Ljiljana Coklin, Collin Craig, James Donelan, Kiffen Dosch, Tim Dougherty, Auli Ek, Letitia Fowler, Lorna Gonzalez, Jeff Grabill, Leslie Hammer, Nicole Howell, Kellie Jarvis, Dawnelle Jager, Jennifer Johnson, Cristina Kirklighter, Ben Kuebrich, Emily Legg, Justin Lewis, Kevin Mahoney, Madhu Narayan, Kathryn Navickas, Ty O'Bryan, Kathy Patterson, Staci Perryman-Clark, Patty Pytleski, Enrique Reynoso, Cissy Ross, Jennifer Sano-Franchini, LaToya Sawyer, Kelly Simon, Madeleine Sorapure, Kathleen A. Swift, W. Kurt Stavenhagen, Adam Strantz, Don Unger, Edward Williams, Gina Vallis, Roy Vallis, Molly Voorheis, Melissa Watson, and Michael Wojick.

Finally, we want to express our gratitude to Dave Blakesley, Parlor Press, for supporting this project's aims of having funds generated by sales go to support independent journals.

THE BEST OF THE INDEPENDENT
RHETORIC AND COMPOSITION JOURNALS 2010

ACROSS THE DISCIPLINES

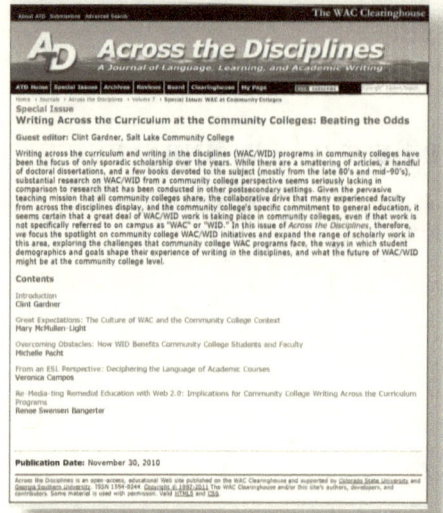

John Harbord's article appears in the special issue of *Across the Disciplines* on "Writing Across the Curriculum at the Commpunity Colleges: Beating the Odds," edited by Clint Gardner. On the Web at http://wac.colostate.edu/atd/community_colleges/index.cfm

Across the Disciplines is a peer-reviewed journal dedicated to publishing the best scholarly work in interdisciplinary writing, WAC/WID, and communication across the curriculum. The journal (originally called *Language and Learning Across the Disciplines*) began publication in 1994 and merged with the online journal *Academic.Writing* in 2004 under its current title. It is now a part of the WAC Clearinghouse site, hosted by Colorado State University. *Across the Disciplines* receives an average of 4,500 hits a day. In 2009, the journal recorded more than 1,700,000 hits by scholars, students, and other users who visited its site.

"Writing in Central and Eastern Europe: Stakeholders and Directions in Initiating Change" by John Harbord

This article investigates the development of writing initiatives in Central and Eastern Europe and the former Soviet Union, an area where prior to 1989, writing in universities played a very minor role. Using data gathered from eight institutions that currently have writing programs of some sort, Harbord identifies three typical paths writing initiatives have taken, showing how such initiatives have often resulted in writing being taught largely in English as a second language, while the teaching of writing in local languages has been widely neglected. Harbord provides a detailed, insightful analysis of how developing writing programs can be impacted by language politics, institutional histories, and cultural norms.

Writing in Central and Eastern Europe: Stakeholders and Directions in Initiating Change

John Harbord

Abstract

This paper investigates the development of writing initiatives in Central and Eastern Europe and the former Soviet Union, an area where prior to 1989, writing in universities played a very minor role. Using data gathered from eight institutions that currently have writing programs of some sort, I identify three typical paths writing initiatives have taken. I show how the identity of the stakeholders involved in the introduction of such initiatives has resulted in writing being taught largely in English as a second language, and the teaching of writing in local languages has been widely neglected. Finally, I discuss possible measures to remedy this situation.

It is an aim of the CCCC National Language Policy "[t]o support programs that assert the legitimacy of native languages and dialects and ensure that proficiency in one's mother tongue will not be lost" (1992). While such a national policy focuses by definition on the US, where English is the principle language of the state and education, it should be even more self-evident that the great global power and reach of the English language should not repress the legitimacy of local languages or endanger *academic* literacy in other countries, where English is *not* the national language. This is not always obviously the case. Indeed, writers such as Phillipson (2001) and Skutnabb-Kangas (1999) have broadly argued that commercial, capitalist, post-imperialist forces drive a machine the main objective of which is to eradicate as many as possible of the world's languages from as many spheres as possible – including academe – to the benefit of English.

While much of the debate that Phillipson and Skutnabb-Kangas contribute to focuses around the teaching of English to speakers of other languages, the teaching of writing/composition* outside English-speaking contexts has received rather less scholarly attention. Much of the recent discussion on the "internationalization" of writing focuses on the internationalization of US WAC initiatives to other English-speaking contexts (eg. Monroe 2002, Emerson et al. 2002, Anson, forthcoming) or ensuring the rights and representation of speakers of English as a second language (e.g. Canagarajah 2002, Lu 2004). Indeed Zegers and Wilkinson argue that the internationalization of education *de facto* "implies education through English" (2005, 1). The issue of introducing or promoting writing and writing support in students' own languages or in the state language of education has received rather less attention at international level. An exception to this, Donahue (2009) has pointed out that in France, for example, a strong theoretical tradition exists that not only provides a foundation for writing, but indeed may be a source of scholarship from which US practitioners can learn, in other words that internationalization can entail movement of ideas in directions other than from the US outwards. The same is true to an extent of several other Western European countries (cf. Bräuer 2002 regarding Germany), where writing is used extensively in education and where writing support in one form or another not necessarily resembling US models is growing.

This is much less true, however, of Central and Eastern Europe and the former Soviet Union (hereafter referred to as "the region" or CEE/fSU), where the development of writing as a taught subject is relatively new. Indeed until 1989, in most countries in the region there was effectively 'no writing' in the sense that not only was writing not taught, it was only rarely used as a form of assessment or student activity in university courses, other than in the form of note-taking during lectures. Until then, the principle form of assessment in this part of the world was by oral exam. There was often a piece of writing prior to graduation referred to as a 'thesis', or in the Soviet Union as a 'referat' – but it was typically a summative literature review, the purpose of which was to demonstrate the student had completed and understood a certain

---

* I use the term "composition" reluctantly, as it is deeply rooted in the US context of liberal arts education, and for a reader from outside the US, at least, contains heavy connotations of first steps in essay writing. To the extent that they exist, European initiatives tend to use the word "writing".

amount of reading. It was largely assumed that students' ability to write this piece depended on their knowledge of the studied texts, not their writing skills. In keeping with the pattern of 'continental' writing described by Rienecker and Stray Jørgensen (2003), writing was seen as an inherent ability one either had or didn't; there was no perception of the need to teach it, not least because it only became important once one had left the role of student and become a professional academic.

The fall of communism saw a huge influx of all things western into the countries and the education systems of the former communist block, a trend – and an ensuing regional-transnational conflict – that Zimmerman (2007) has outlined admirably from the point of view of women's and gender studies. Writing initiatives also began to appear in various forms, however, to date there has been no analysis of how these initiatives developed or why, or any consideration as to whether their development has been optimal.

As Donahue (2009) has lamented, the process of internationalization in writing studies is largely a process of transfer from the US to the rest of the world (see also Canagarajah 2002, 44). As in any case of transfer of ideas from the centre to the periphery, those ideas may be *transplanted* into the new context with little effort to adapt them, or indeed with every effort to preserve their 'purity' from local corruption – one of the origins of Zimmermann's regional-transnational conflict. Alternatively, they may be *translated*, that is, consciously or unconsciously, the original idea may be reshaped to suit the local context or culture and owned by the users in that context. The interests of the stakeholders involved in any process of academic innovation, both locals and outsiders, inevitably determine to a large extent how that innovation develops, consolidates and is institutionalized, or not. Because writing is a part of language, because ideas about writing come from countries where the dominant language is English, because the stakeholders from the center are often concerned with the promotion of English as such (cf. Phillipson 2001), because those stakeholders rarely speak the languages of the periphery and therefore communicate with those who speak English, namely teachers of English as a foreign language, for all these reasons, the internationalization of writing is complicated in particular ways that merit further investigation.

In this paper, I argue that the identity of the stakeholders involved in the introduction of writing initiatives in the region has led to an internationalization whereby although the use of written tasks for assessment in local languages is gradually beginning to increase, academic writing is taught only through English. I suggest that in many situations this is suboptimal. I identify three typical developmental paths of writing initiatives in the CEE/fSU region and draw conclusions about the nature of their development, showing how the identity of the initiators impacts on the nature of transplant or translation. Finally, I discuss the challenge of implementing effective writing initiatives in local languages.

Profile of the Initiatives

The present research draws on data formally gathered from eight writing initiatives in six countries,* supplemented with personal knowledge and informal data from my work as a consultant with universities in the region. These eight are not the only writing programmes in the region, indeed many state university English departments offer some form of English writing courses. Writing programs in American-style universities in Europe are rather fewer. Examples of the third group I identify, initiatives started by local academics, are very rare.

It is beyond the scope of this article to give a full overview of all eight initiatives investigated, nor indeed is this my purpose. For this reason, in this section I focus mainly on one US-style university, Central European University (CEU) with brief comparisons to other similar institutions. I then discuss more broadly the second group, state university English departments. Finally I focus particularly on two of the three initiatives started by local faculty.

US-Style Universities

I define a US-style university as one where, as well all courses being taught in English, the university will have some of the following: US accreditation, US charter, US-style curriculum, US grading system, a liberal arts approach, and some faculty from the US. Central European University is a graduate university of social sciences found-

---

* Central European University and Szeged University, Hungary; Lithuanian Christian College University and Vilnius University, Lithuania; Tbilisi State University, Georgia; Babes-Bolyai University, Romania; Comenius University, Slovakia; and Lviv University, Ukraine. Semi-structured questionnaires sent to program coordinators or directors were followed up with e-mail correspondence.

ed in 1991, with some 1540 current registered students in fifteen departments ranging from International Relations and Environmental Sciences to Legal Studies and History. The language of education is exclusively English, and the university is accredited by the Middle States Commission on Higher Education; more recently it has also become accredited by the Hungarian state. Both the student body and faculty are of very diverse origin. The former comprises 97 different nationalities, with largest single national group (Hungarians) accounting for only 20%, followed by Romanians (17%), the USA (6%), Russians (5%), Serbians, Georgians, Bulgarians and Ukrainians (4% each) and Germans, Turks, Slovaks and Azerbaijanis (2% each). The nearly 250 faculty come from 33 different countries, notably Hungary (40%), North America and the UK (20%), and Germany (8%), as well as France, Romania and Austria. While the diversity of CEU is especially strong, the Lithuanian Christian College (LCC) University and the American University in Bulgaria also exhibit very international student and faculty profiles. The main difference between CEU and these two institutions is that the former is a graduate university while the latter offer only undergraduate studies.

CEU, like other 'American model' universities (cf. Anson forthcoming, Schaub 2003), is based on the idea of exporting US-style education to the rest of the world, and writing has been part of that almost since the founding of the university, for several reasons. First, about 90% students are not native speakers of English and therefore are expected to have problems coping with education in English, including writing. Secondly, the lack of writing as an assessment form in the region prior to 1989 meant that students had little experience of formulating ideas in writing even in their own language, and had difficulties completing the assignments their often US-educated professors set them. A consultancy commissioned by the university in 1996 marked a shift away from general English language teaching and a focus on specialized writing support, though the 'Language Teaching Center' was not renamed 'Center for Academic Writing' till 2003. Many of the staff of the Center have backgrounds in applied linguistics and ESL rather than English literature or Rhetoric.

The support offered by the Center for Academic Writing combines taught writing courses, individual writing consultations and collaboration between writing center staff and faculty in the disciplines both to help students meet their expectations and to guide faculty in providing the most effective and explicit assignments. In this sense, it fits the model that is often called writing support, which is characterized by two features: (1) specialized writing instructors take responsibility for the teaching of writing rather than faculty in the disciplines, and (2) these instructors work closely with faculty in the disciplines rather than independently, as is usually the case with first year composition courses. In this sense, CEU again differs significantly from the American University in Bulgaria, which adheres closely to a first year comp model, but to a much lesser extent from LCC University, which changed four years ago from a first year comp approach to a more writing-in-the-disciplines approach, responding to perceived needs.

State University English Departments

It may be that significant differences existed between universities within and across the countries of the former communist block prior to the advent of communism, however, my own extensive experience in communist Hungary, Bulgaria, Soviet Estonia and Czechoslovakia suggests that communism was remarkably powerful in eliminating differences in university education not only between institutions but between nation states. One Czech academic, reading in 1991 my master's dissertation on reforming English teacher training in Estonia, written in 1990, commented that the weaknesses of the (Soviet) Estonian university education system were identical to those of the Czechoslovak system, in spite of the completely different history of the two countries prior to World War II.

From 1989 onwards, the British Council and various US organizations, including Fulbright, USIS and some US universities, were extensively involved in promoting the transfer of ESL teaching methodology, and somewhat later of writing as a part of English for academic purposes. During the 1990s there was scarcely a state university in Central Europe that did not have a British Council English language teaching specialist posted to its English department to assist in curricular reform. Being directly or indirectly involved in this process for four years in Bulgaria, Estonia and the Czech Republic, my assessment is that communication between these experts, who were seen and saw themselves as a team, revealed many similarities across institutions and very few differences. Where there were differences, these were typically the product of individual personalities that dominated English departments, whether these were more receptive or resistant to change. It is also true to an extent, in all disciplines, that flagship universities (such as Moscow State University and Baku State University) were and are highly conservative, while smaller, less influential universities (eg. the Azerbaijani University of Languages) have been much more keen to reinvent themselves and embrace innovation.

In the English departments of these state universities where foreign experts were active, like in the US-Style universities, teaching was generally in English, though certain mandatory general courses unconnected to the study of English were and still are taught in the official state language. Writing was a part of the teaching of English as a foreign language – that is, students were seen as being taught to write *English*, not to *write* as such. Composition, as it is understood in the States, was therefore not really identifiable in the early stages. Even now, because of the greater influence of the British Council, academic writing tends more to draw on theoretical approaches associated with applied linguistics, such as genre analysis (cf. Swales, Johns, Hyland), while concepts such as WAC and WiD are little known. Of the universities I examined, only Lviv in Ukraine possesses a writing center, principally as it was set up through collaboration with the University of Oregon. I am not aware of writing centers in any other state university English departments.

Initiatives in State Universities Outside English Departments

The three final initiatives I examine – Comenius University in Bratislava, Slovakia, Babes Bolyai University in Cluj, Romania and the Centre for Social Sciences at Tbilisi State University in Georgia – have all been significantly influenced in their development by Central European University. In Bratislava and Cluj, writing programs were set up by CEU graduates; in Tbilisi, I made several consultancy visits to help set up writing programs, working with local academics and administrators. Because of CEU's focus on the social sciences, all three initiatives are run by academics with backgrounds in these disciplines. In Bratislava, the language of the academic writing course, which is taught at graduate level, is English. While the university does offer some other graduate courses in English, notably as part of this graduate program, the official language of the university is Slovak. Babes Bolyai, which was the object of a merger of a Hungarian language university and a Romanian language one during the communist period, operates in several languages, offering 105 specializations in Romanian, 52 in Hungarian, 13 in German and four in English (Babes Bolyai 2009). The academic writing course was initially taught in Romanian, as its founder, political scientist Romana Careja is a Romanian speaker, though since 2006 it has been offered both in Romanian and in English. At Tbilisi State University Centre for Social Sciences, an academic writing course was initially introduced into the graduate program in English, as students were required to write a final research project in English. Subsequently an undergraduate writing program in Georgian was initiated. The syllabus and theoretical underpinning of courses in all three universities is heavily influenced by the approach at CEU, in that it is largely driven by genre analysis and writing in the disciplines.

The Interaction of Language and Change

Two interrelated issues can be identified across the region: choice of language, and the identity of the initiators of change. Because of their educational, disciplinary and cultural background, agents of change who introduce academic writing courses in the local language do so in a rather different way from those who introduce English writing courses. I discuss the implications of this below.

Choice of Language

Rarely have academic writing courses been *literally* translated into other languages, Babes Bolyai (Romanian), and the Tbilisi undergraduate course (Georgian) being the only ones I am aware of (I recently learnt of the existence of a basic composition course taught in Russian to first year economists at Samara University of Aeronautics but have not been able to learn more). In American-style universities, English is the official language of the institution and the language that permits internationalization, allowing these institutions to draw students from beyond the borders of the nation state they are located in – a requirement that is essential to their mission and usually to their financial survival. In state institutions, most writing programs are housed in English departments due to the history of methodological innovations in English as a foreign language. External stakeholders' interests thus led to the institutionalization of writing as a part of English language teaching. In the case of the British Council, this is very much a matter of policy in that it is part of the Council's role to "promote the UK as a global centre for education, knowledge, skills and creativity [and to] build relationships that strengthen the UK's position in these areas" (British Council 2009; see also Phillipson 1992, 2001).

So why did writing happen in the students' own language in Tbilisi and Cluj? The most obvious reason, particularly in Tbilisi, is that such writing as students needed to do as part of their courses (and my recent communication with Georgian academics suggests this is increasing) was in Georgian. As most students outside English departments have a very low level of English proficiency, this is inevitable, and even if students did master English it would be somehow perverse to teach them in English in preparation for writing in Georgian. In some countries in the former Soviet Union, even in English departments, many students enter undergraduate studies with a proficiency in English barely adequate to follow a meaningful writing course in that language. In Cluj, with the improving level of students' English, since 2006 the course has been offered both in Romanian and English, the latter for the benefit of those students who take courses taught in English and those who plan to continue their studies in English-medium universities, and there has been significant interest in this option. Whether this will lead to a decline in the popularity of the Romanian course remains to be seen.

The second reason that contributed to the setting up of writing programs in the local language is less immediately obvious, namely that the initiators were not teachers of English but in both cases social scientists. (In Tbilisi, I as consultant supported this plan, and inadequate student English made the alternative impossible, but in other cases, a consultant might tip the scales against the instincts of the local initiators.) This brings us to the second point, namely the impact of the initiators on the development of writing projects.

Initiators and How They Work

As mentioned above, by far the most common initiators of writing programs are 'foreign experts', both in the case of American-style institutions, and in most state university English departments. In state universities, these foreign experts are typically teachers of English as a foreign language, though in the case of LCC and Lviv they were US writing specialists with an English literature/Rhetoric background.

My research suggests that programs initiated by 'foreign experts' are more likely to experiment with a range of western approaches.

LCC University changed several years ago from a liberal arts first year composition approach to a more WID approach (Jen Stewart, personal communication, July 2006). Vilnius English department also experimented with 'new rhetoric', process writing and genre-based approaches (Laima Erika Katkuviene, personal communication, May 8, 2008). My informant at Szeged justified the approach there by drawing on writing theory (E. Barat, personal communication April 8, 2008). CEU has adapted its approach to its European, graduate context, developing a theoretical underpinning for its way of working (cf. Harbord 2003). The people who teach in this context are informed about writing theory and are able to adapt and translate ideas.

In Slovakia, Romania and Georgia, the instigators of writing initiatives are social scientists. In all three cases, these are alumni or faculty of the institution who have studied at American universities, in the case of Bratislava and Cluj, at CEU. They return home with the desire to set up social science programs comparable to the ones they have been through, and they see academic writing as a necessary part of that, so students can do the writing assignments. What is interesting is that apart from the literal translation into the local language, these people do not adapt courses to the local context, they transplant them. The current teacher in the Cluj program, Cosmin Marian put it tellingly:

> ...our department had in the past visiting or Fulbright professors that used to teach this course ... They developed a pattern and... I try to stay as close with the models that are accepted in the academic and research community in political sciences as possible (personal communication April 2, 2008).

In other words, the agenda here is the preservation of the purity of the model from possible local dilution or corruption. One of my master's students who studied at Cluj before coming to CEU commented, 'the syllabus is the same, just in Romanian'. This similarity is not entirely surprising, given that Romana Careja, the founder of the initiative, studied at CEU eleven years ago and was taught academic writing by me personally. On leaving CEU, Romana expressed a desire to set up a writing program in her home university on her return, which she must have done directly, as the program at Cluj has been in existence for ten years. The syllabus at Babes Bolyai would thus appear to be a carefully preserved version of her course syllabus at CEU.

One could claim, and the argument has been made by Peter Dral, co-initiator of the program in Bratislava, that the courses taught there and in Cluj, based on the CEU model, which is informed by both WID and genre theory, and specifically tailored to the needs of social scientists, do not need rethinking or adaptation to the local context (personal communication April 11, 2008). Certainly, the students who receive the course in Bratislava are very similar in profile to those who come from Bratislava to Budapest to take the same course as part of an MA in a social science at CEU. This may be true; however, there remains a hazy boundary between social scientists' assessment that a course may not need adapting, or indeed *should not* be adapted to the local context (see Marian above), and their own questionable ability to adapt syllabus and teaching methods effectively in keeping with best practices in the field of writing theory. The team of social scientists I worked with developing the writing program in Tbilisi did indeed lack confidence regarding teaching methodology and curriculum design, and did not feel qualified to adapt these. They hoped that I as 'expert' would give them or at least help them design the ideal course that they would then teach indefinitely according to my instructions.

TEACHING ENGLISH OR TEACHING WRITING?

In the light of the above discussion, two closely related issues emerge: whether and how to deal with the transfer of writing courses into local languages, and who is the best equipped to teach such courses.

Teaching in the First Language: Transferring Skills or Transplanting Culture?

Particularly for countries like the Netherlands, Scandinavia and to a lesser extent Germany, where students entering university generally already have a solid command of English, Zegers and Wilkinson's (2005) arguments about plurilingualism and the value of English education may hold, and in such countries, it may make some sense to teach academic writing in English. However, much of the world is not yet in the position of the Netherlands; in many parts of the world not only the majority of students but even the majority of academics have a very limited mastery of English. Quite apart from Skutnabb-Kangas's "ecology of languages paradigm" which sees "multilingualism and linguistic diversity" as a desirable alternative to "capitalism [and] transnationalisation" driving the domination of English (in Phillipson 2001, 193), there are three less political and more rudimentary reasons why in such countries academic literacy should be taught in the students' first language, or at least in a language that students master fully.

First, there is nothing more disheartening and incapacitating than trying to express sophisticated thoughts in a language where limited proficiency makes one's ideas appear childish and trivial. Second, trying to master academic writing in a language one speaks poorly blurs the boundaries between problems with lower-order concerns (inadequacy of vocabulary and grammar) and the higher-order concerns that writing courses are usually concerned with, such as logic and clarity of thinking and expression. This conflation of English teaching and writing teaching perpetuates the naive belief that problems in writing are due to inadequate mastery of vocabulary and grammar. It thus brings the teaching of writing under the remit of those whose business is the teaching of English, with all the cultural-imperialist implications that Phillipson raises. At the same time, it promotes a product-oriented model of writing teaching (cf. Jordan 1980) which ignores most recent scholarship on process and genre, and confines the teaching of writing largely to the selection of the right words and phrases to "plug in". While some more recent pedagogical efforts have also focused on plugging in the right words (e.g. Graff and Birkenstein 2005), most scholarship on composition concedes that there is rather more to the matter than that.

Finally, and connected to both the above, teaching writing in an inadequately mastered language frequently confines the syllabus to basic issues, such as paragraph structure, simply because students' language competence does not permit them to tackle more complex issues. This is the main weakness of the writing program developed by US foreign experts at the English Department of the Azerbaijani University of Languages. Because the students' mastery of English is very limited, the syllabus mainly addresses paragraph-level and sentence-level issues. If the course were taught in Azeri, it is very likely that more sophisticated and more macro issues could be addressed. Indeed anyone who engaged with the idea of translating the course into Azeri would very quickly see that it is in reality an 'English course' and one that is little adapted to local needs in writing. In sum, while English is the lingua franca of the international academic community, before students become fully fledged members of that community, to adapt slightly Barbara Seidlhofer's words, "[Teachers] should naturally always make themselves understood with the language which is best understood by all those involved" (University of Vienna 2009).*

If writing is a transferable skill, following the logic above it would be best taught in a language one masters, then transferred to a language one masters less well. But is writing in fact a transferable skill? A great deal of literature has focused on the topic of contrastive rhetoric and the differences of academic writing in different cultures (cf. Connor 1996, Galtung 1988) which might cause sever problems in transfer across languages. My own students have also described the occasional undesirable consequences of over-zealous transfer of writing conventions from English into their mother tongue.

We can, however, reasonably make the assumption, as Bräuer (2002) does in importing the US model of the writing center to Germany, that many features of best practice that we are concerned with – such as the effective scaffolding of assignments, including clear instructions, a recognizable audience and purpose, adequate and constructive feedback and opportunities for revision and improvement – are not language specific any more than biology or business studies are language specific. Indeed, there is in some countries of the region a tradition akin to that in China, as mentioned by Townsend, whereby culture dictates a greater personal responsibility on the part of the teacher to help the student individually outside class time than may be typical in the US (2002, 140).

Once we come to the issue of genres and conventions of writing, these will indeed be culture-specific, though research I have conducted in the framework of another project with bilingual academics suggests that the conventions of English academic writing are increasingly influencing academic writing in other languages. In spite of this, one piece of evidence to hand does demonstrate the transferability of writing skills, albeit in the opposite direction. A recent survey of one cohort of CEU alumni (as part of US reaccreditation) assessed the transferability of skills from MA academic writing courses to the world of work and paid academe, eighteen months after graduation. The survey also asked whether skills that students had learnt in *English* writing courses at CEU had subsequently been of use *in their first language*. Of

---

* Original German: "SprecherInnen (speakers) sollen sich natürlich immer mit der Sprache verständigen, die von allen Beteiligten am besten verstanden wird." My translation.

those who responded, 74% said that these writing courses *had* helped them write in their first language (41% claimed 'considerably'). The fact that the writing course at CEU is strongly influenced by genre and WID theory makes it unlikely that students who claimed to be able to transfer skills to their own language were referring exclusively to the non-language-specific skills of drafting and revising.

If writing skills can indeed be transferred from English to the first language, it is not unreasonable to assume that they can also be transferred in the other direction. The transfer may not work the same way in both directions, and further research is needed on this subject. However, much of the very extensive pedagogy of English for Academic Purposes assumes that the transfer of cultural habits in writing from the mother tongue will influence (by implication negatively) students' writing in English. It is entirely logical to assume that if the cultural habits were similar to those of English because comparable principles of writing had been taught, the transfer would be both possible and positive.

If we do transplant concepts and structures of teaching writing from English to other languages, we need to move with caution to avoid the accusation of cultural imperialism (cf. Canagarajah 2002). At the same time, we should not automatically assume that local faculty or administrators will be opposed to innovation. During a consultancy visit to Prishtina University in Kosova in 2000, I was surprised at the view expressed by Xhavit Rexhai, a professor in the English department. He felt Kosova needed to import "the English model" of writing into Albanian because teachers of Albanian language and stylistics were conservative and had rigid, old-fashioned ideas about good writing focusing on elaborate, complex syntax (Xhavit Rexhai, personal communication, April 2000). Since then, I have heard similar views expressed about teachers of the national language – a mandatory subject in most former communist countries – in Georgia and Azerbaijan. The impression is that teachers of local languages are seen and often see themselves as guardians of the pure language, which may be under threat either from less cultured dialects or from foreign influence, in the past Russian, today more likely English. Nora Mzavanadze, a PhD student I interviewed for another project, described such a course at Vilnius University. The course 'Language Culture' is mandatory for all undergraduates and is seen by students, in her words, as a "pain in the ass". It is not concerned with how to argue or how to write research but with how to avoid "barbarisms", which she described as including the use of wrong grammatical cases or word forms associated with low prestige regional dialects that might "resemble Latvian more than Lithuanian" (personal communication, March 29, 2009).

While one may wish to express mild alarm at such stigmatization of non-standard varieties of language, it is not my purpose here to question the claim that the elegant use of a language to convey finer emotions, whether through verse or prose, is a part of national cultural heritage worthy of preservation. The same, however, is not automatically true of academic writing, not least because in academic writing the focus is more on the message and less on the form. While Galtung (1988:38) has suggested that play of words and grammatical reversals are a key feature of some academic cultures, the *main* purpose of research writing in the social sciences in most languages remains the creation of new knowledge, not dazzling the reader with verbal repartee.

Social scientists, in contrast to teachers of the national language, seem rather less concerned about cultural heritage and more interested in obtaining effective tools for doing their job. Which culture these tools come from appears less important to them. Marine Chitashvili, the distinguished Georgian psychologist who founded the Centre for Social Sciences at Tbilisi University, framed this very well when I raised concerns about imposing the norms of English academic writing on Georgian. She said:

> Georgian doesn't have its own culture of academic scholarship. The way we have written until now is the Russian way, which was imposed upon us as part of the Russian empire in the 19th century and the Soviet empire in the 20th. We have the choice to keep the Russian way of writing which is not ours, or exchange it for the Anglo-American way of writing, which is also not inherently Georgian (personal communication May 22, 2008).*

I have heard similar views expressed by other Georgian social scientists. It seems then to be a defensible position for those who seek to bring writing to the region – comparable to that adopted by Holliday (2005, 14) in the context of the debate on teaching English as an in-

---

* She did, when I asked permission to quote her, ask me to add that her comments in no way apply to Georgian fine literature, which has a heritage of fifteen centuries.

ternational language – that the experience and strategies developed for teaching writing in English may be valuable tools that those from other cultures are at liberty to use in teaching writing in their own language in the ways they see fit to meet their needs, so long as we do not impose those models or preach their superiority. Once learners are in a context where they are learning to write for an English-speaking community, for example an American university, we may urge them to respond to their American readers' expectation by conforming to certain norms, but so long as they are operating in their own language, we have to respect that norms may differ, and that while local teachers of writing may well want to build on the long experience of writing teaching in the US, they will know best what to build on and how.

What I am suggesting is that we need to separate the teaching of writing from the teaching of English, whether English as a foreign language or English literature. Writing (or composition, or whatever the most appropriate correlate term in the relevant language may be) as a subject of study in its own right may provide a tool which is useful and relevant in other cultures. Tying writing to the English language, or worse to any aspect of Anglo-American culture, ties it to a bunch of cultural assumptions and associations that make it more problematic to implement without treading on cultural toes and getting caught up in Zimmermann's regional-transnational culture debate.

Who Does the Teaching?

The practical question remains as to who should have the job of teaching writing courses in local languages in the region. Three groups present themselves; none is without problems. The first is teachers of the local language. Unlike the situation in Germany, where teachers of German language and didactics are described as good potential partners in introducing writing (Bräuer 2002, 70), the support of indigenous departments of local languages and stylistics in the region is less clear. These teachers, as described above, currently have a different agenda and a very traditional training. Not only would they need significant retraining, but they would be likely to retain emotional attachment to their former views. Equally importantly, most of them do not speak English and thus have no direct access to US scholarly literature on writing. These two obstacles cannot be overcome without serious investment and restructuring.

The second option is teachers of English as a foreign language. This group has two advantages: they have more up-to-date methodological training, and more importantly, they are able to read the literature on writing theory in English, or to receive training in the US/UK. On the down side, they are *English* teachers. This makes it harder for them to dissociate themselves from Anglophile cultural baggage, both in terms of how they are seen by others and how they see themselves. It also lowers the face validity of their professed ability to do the job, as they are not formally qualified in the area they propose to practice. To the extent that writing courses are embedded in the disciplines, they, like the previous group, also suffer the weakness that Hansen and Adams (2010) point out, namely that they lack any more than the most superficial disciplinary knowledge, including knowledge of what preferred genres look like.

The third group of candidates are teachers of the discipline, that is, social scientists. Both the effective initiatives so far in the region that teach writing in the local language are taught by social scientists. To jump to the conclusion that faculty in the disciplines are the best candidates to teach writing courses, however, would be hasty. In all the social-science-driven initiatives (Romania, Georgia and Slovakia) the teachers gleaned their knowledge of writing teaching from (former) ESL teachers, in that they either followed writing courses at CEU or else employed a consultant from CEU. In other words, they are teaching something they themselves have (recently) learnt as students, not something they are formally qualified to teach, a state of affairs that, as discussed above, renders them less able to judge how and when to adapt their teaching or their syllabus to local contexts and needs. Particularly in Georgia, a trend also appeared that may be familiar to those working in WAC contexts in the US. Social scientists often feel that teaching writing is neither their area of expertise nor their real business. They not only feel on safer ground with their own discipline (cf. Hansen and Adams 2010), but also that teaching writing as a subject is rather a low-prestige task. In my own university until recently, some departments employed their own academic writing instructors. These people had a background in the relevant discipline, but were almost always very junior in the department, and once they had climbed up the career ladder a little were keen to offload this burden on someone else. Interviews I carried out in a number of US universities in early 2009 suggested a similar response from some US faculty in the disciplines. In this regard, the development of writing in the region might more effectively concentrate on getting faculty in the disciplines to use writing effectively in their courses, whether for assessment or writing to learn (cf. Gottschalk and Hjortshoj 2004) rather than asking them to teach writing courses.

As Bräuer (2002, 76) suggests for Germany, the most effective solution is likely to be achieved by these three groups working together to develop and institutionalize writing initiatives. Faculty in the disciplines have an important role because they are the ones who set the writing that matters, and they will need to work with writing teachers to ensure the genres set match as closely as possible those used in the discipline (Hansen and Adams 2010). As regards the actual teaching of academic writing, however, the question is who is most easily and quickly retrained. I think ironically, in the *short term*, the people to retrain are the English teachers. The region is littered with people in NGOs and government organizations who used to be English teachers and have changed career. This is partly because English teaching offers such dismal career prospects in this part of the world, but also because proficiency in English is a valuable professional tool that often makes such people more adaptable and open to the opportunities of a globalized world. They need to understand, however, that they are retraining and refocusing certain skills they possess so as to do a different job, not just switching employers.

In the longer term, however, some teachers of the local language need to be retrained into the service of teaching writing. By 'some' I mean that rather than trying to redirect the discipline of local language teaching and stylistics into being something else, an approach that challenges the authority of that discipline, a number of teachers should be seduced away from the profession and employed in the service of supporting faculty in achieving the writing goals of their curriculum. In other words, the teaching of writing proper should not be turned over to existing departments of local language and stylistics as their domain; rather support courses should be created where the goals are dictated by the instructors in the discipline whose work is being supported.

Given the heritage of the Soviet system, where many countries have a range of ancillary courses at undergraduate level that are perceived as lightweight and irrelevant, a model that introduces writing in the form of non-discipline-related first year composition is likely to lead to its relegation to the ranks of 'language culture', 'national folk history' – burdensome irrelevancies students plod (or sleep) their way through because their elders and betters have deemed it to be for their good. Writing specialists, whether originally local language teachers or English teachers, need to learn how to work in close partnership with faculty in the disciplines, a tradition that hitherto has been largely absent in the region, where any form of inquiry by a colleague into one's work has traditionally been regarded with suspicion. Faculty and writing specialists need to see themselves as two halves of a team that prepares writers in the discipline, a re-visioning of academic roles that is perhaps one of the most difficult goals to achieve.

Most faculty in the disciplines will have limited experience in using writing in the classroom, or may not use it effectively: concepts of genre and process are both usually extremely vague, if they exist at all, and where writing assignments are set, they are often one-draft pieces on vague questions that are easy to plagiarize because they mostly involve knowledge telling. Writing teachers will therefore need to become WAC advisors who simultaneously provide help and expertise in the design and scaffolding of written assignments as well as in the use of writing-to-learn activities, but at the same time listen carefully to faculty's expertise on what kinds of writing need to be mastered in the discipline and how these might look (cf. Hansen and Adams 2010).

Conclusion

In this article I have shown how the introduction of writing initiatives into in CEE/fSU region has been driven by international stakeholders whose agenda, explicitly or implicitly focuses on the teaching of writing in English. The development of writing initiatives in local languages has been largely neglected, with the consequence both that the resource of writing to learn remains untapped, and students from the region outside the discipline of English literature continue, when they do learn English, to come into the international education system unprepared for the challenge of writing.

While considerable caution needs to be exercised in translating WAC and WID to local contexts that are very different to the US, very many aspects of best practices in writing are not, or need not be, language-specific. The introduction of writing into the curriculum of universities in the region can best be achieved by a collaborative effort between retrained teachers of English, refocused teachers of local languages and faculty in the disciplines. WAC/WID programs in the US have a valuable role to play in providing input through those local individuals (mostly ex-English teachers and faculty) who have access to that input via English. However, just as translating US WAC to other English-speaking contexts needs considerable caution and rethinking (McLeod 2002, Emerson et al. 2002), when it is to be translated into other languages proportionally more caution, rethinking and discussion with local stakeholders is required to ensure that models and approaches are effectively translated to fit the local context and needs.

References

Anson, Chris M. (forthcoming). Worldwide composition: Virtual uncertainties. *Teaching Writing in a Globalized World: Remapping Composition Studies*, ed. Daphne Desser and Darin Payne.

Babes Bolyai University. (2009) About BBU: The multicultural character. Retrieved April 16, 2009 from http://www.ubbcluj.ro/en/despre/multicultural.html

Bräuer, Gerd. (2002). Drawing connections across education: The Freiburg writing center model. *Language and Learning Across the Disciplines* 5(3), 61-80

British Council. (2009). Creating opportunities worldwide: Creative knowledge and economy. Retrieved April 15, 2009 from http://www.britishcouncil.org/new/

Canagarajah, Suresh. (2002). *A geopolitics of academic writing*. Pittsburgh: University of Pittsburgh Press

Conference on College Composition and Communication. (1992). CCCC Guideline on the National Language Policy, Retrieved April 15, 2009 from http://www.ncte.org/cccc/resources/positions/nationallangpolicy?source=gs

Connor, Ulla. (1996). *Contrastive rhetoric: Cross-cultural aspects of second-language writing.* New York: Cambridge University Press.

Donahue, Christiane. (2009) "Internationalization" and composition studies: Re-orienting the discourse. *College Composition and Communication* 61(2), 212-243.

Emerson, Lisa, MacKay, Bruce R., Funnell, Keith A. and MacKay, Marion B. (2002). Writing in a New Zealand tertiary context: WAC and action research. *Language and Learning Across the Disciplines* 5(3), 110-133.

Galtung, Johan. (1988). *Methodology and development.* Essays in methodology 3. Copenhagen: Christian Ejlers.

Gottschalk, Katherine and Hjortshoj, Keith. (2004). *The elements of teaching writing.* Boston: Bedford/St. Martin's.

Graff, Gerald and Birkenstein, Cathy. (2005). *They say/I say: The moves that matter in academic writing.* New York: W.W. Norton

Hansen, Kristine, & Adams, Joyce. (2010). Teaching writing in the social sciences: A comparison and critique of three models. *Across the Disciplines, 7.* Retrieved March 3, 2010 from http://wac.colostate.edu/atd/articles/hansen_adams2010.cfm

Harbord, John. (2003). Minimalist tutoring: an exportable model? *Writing Lab Newsletter 28*(4), 1-5.

Holliday, Adrian. (2007). *The struggle to teach English as an international language.* Oxford: Oxford University Press.

Jordan, Robert. R. (1980). *Academic writing course.* Glasgow: Collins.

Lu, Min-Zhan. (2004). An Essay on the work of composition: composing English against the order of fast capitalism. *College Composition and Communication 56*(1), 16-50.

McLeod, Susan H. (2002). WAC in international contexts: an introduction. *Language and Learning Across the Disciplines 5*(3), 4-10.

Monroe, Jonathan. (2002). Global cultures, local writing: The Cornell Consortium for Writing in the Disciplines. *Language and Learning Across the Disciplines 5*(3), 11-27.

Middle States Commission on Higher Education. (2010). Home Page. Retrieved February 3, 2010 from http://www.msche.org/.

Phillipson, Robert. (1992). *Linguistic imperialism.* Oxford: Oxford University Press.

_____ (2001). English for globalisation or for the world's people? *International Review of Education, 47*(3-4), 185-200.

Rienecker, Lotte & Stray Jorgensen, Peter. (2003). The (im)possibilities in teaching university writing in the Anglo-American tradition when dealing with continental student writers. In Lennart Björk, Gerd Bräuer, Lotte Rienecker and Peter Stray Jorgensen (Eds) *Teaching Academic Writing in European Higher Education* (pp.101-112). Dordrecht: Kluwer Academic Publishers.

Schaub, Mark. (2003). Beyond these shores: An argument for internationalizing composition. *Pedagogy 3* (1), 85-98.

Skutnabb-Kangas, Tove. (1999). Linguistic diversity, human rights and the "free" market. In Miklós Kontra, Robert Phillipson, Tove Skutnabb-Kangas & Tibor Várady (Eds). *Language: A right and a resource. Approaching linguistic human rights* (pp.187-222). Budapest: CEU Press

Townsend, Marty. (2002). Writing in/across the curriculum at a comprehensive Chinese university. *Language and Learning Across the Disciplines 5* (3), 134-149.

University of Vienna. (2009). Die Rolle von Englisch in einem multilingualen Europa. Retrieved May 13, 2009 from http://forschungsnewsletter.univie.ac.at/index.php?id=49653&tx_ttnews[tt_news].

Zegers, Vera, and Wilkinson, Robert. (2005). Squaring the pyramid: internationalization, plurilingualism, and the university. Conference on bi- and multilingual universities, Helsinki, Finland. Retrieved March 3, 2010 from http://www.palmenia.helsinki.fi/congress/bilingual2005/presentations/zegers.pdf

Zimmermann, Susan. (2007). The institutionalization of women and gender studies in higher education in Central and Eastern Europe and the former Soviet Union: Asymmetric politics and the regional-transnational configuration. In: *East-Central Europe/L'Europe du Centre-Est: Eine wissenschaftliche Zeitschrift 33* (1–2), thematic issue: "Social history in East Central Europe," 189-214.

COMMUNITY LITERACY JOURNAL

Community Litearcy Journal is on the Web at http://www.communityliteracy.org/index.php/clj/index

We understand "community literacy" as the domain for literacy work that exists outside of mainstream educational and work institutions. It can be found in programs devoted to adult education, early childhood education, reading initiatives, lifelong learning, workplace literacy, or work with marginalized populations, but it can also be found in more informal, *ad hoc* projects. For us, literacy is defined as the realm where attention is paid not just to content or to knowledge but to the symbolic means by which it is represented and used. Thus, literacy makes reference not just to letters and to text but to other multimodal and technological representations as well. We publish work that contributes to the field's emerging methodologies and research agendas.

"Street Sex Work: Re/Constructing Discourse from Margin to Center" by Jill McCracken

We nominated Professor McCracken's article for inclusion in *The Best of the Independent Rhetoric and Composition Journals 2010* because we think it exemplifies some of the powerful and productive capacities for combining rigorous scholarship with real, genuine, and meaningful community work. McCracken's ethnographic case study "argues that the material conditions of many street sex workers—the physical environments they live in and their effects on the workers' bodies, identities, and spirits—are represented, reproduced, and entrenched in the language surrounding their work." Her analyses of those materials conditions and language provides both a method and a challenge for further research in community literacy and ethnography.

Street Sex Work: Re/Constructing Discourse from Margin to Center

Jill McCracken

"She's a prostitute, addict, and abuser, but she's a mom and he misses her"

"Prostitution wrecks neighborhood"

"Casualties of the Street"

"A Way Out for Prostitutes"

[Headlines from newspaper articles about prostitution/street sex work]

Abstract

Newspaper media create interpretations of marginalized groups that require rhetorical analysis so that we can better understand these representations. This article focuses on how newspaper articles create interpretations of sex work that affect both the marginalized and mainstream communities. My ethnographic case study argues that the material conditions of many street sex workers—the physical environments they live in and their effects on the workers' bodies, identities, and spirits—are represented, reproduced, and entrenched in the language surrounding their work. The signs and symbols that make up these "material conditions" can be rhetorically analyzed in order to better understand how interests, goals, and ideologies are represented and implemented through language. My analysis reveals that journalists highlight particular material conditions through the inclusion and omission of words and themes that serve to highlight particular material conditions related to street sex work, a practice that influences the readers' perspectives of sex work as a whole. I offer suggestions for making different language choices that subvert these disempowering ideologies.[1]

WHORE, PROSTITUTE, SEX WORKER, SACRED PROSTITUTE/NEW AGE PRIESTESS

Marginalized populations—those on the margins, the sidelines—serve to reinforce the acceptable mores of the mainstream. Examining how marginalized communities are constructed not only reveals the underlying beliefs that support these representations, but simultaneously illuminates what aspects of the mainstream are valued and in turn require the creation of the marginalized. For those readers who are unfamiliar with the myriad types of "sex work,"[2] a quick overview of such categories may prove useful. Sex work is defined as any commercial sexual service performed in exchange for material compensation. This category includes activities that are both legal (exotic dancing, phone sex, burlesque, adult pornography) and illegal (any activity that involves a face-to-face direct exchange of stimulation for commercial gain). Street sex work is illegal in the United States and involves those persons who solicit sex on or near the street as opposed to using telephones, the Internet, or other referral systems.[3]

My research centers on the language surrounding what is commonly referred to as "prostitution" or street sex work, that is, people who exchange sex for money, drugs, or other gain. Because newspaper articles largely inform laypersons' views on sex work, I examine this public discourse to gain a better understanding of how street sex workers and their related material conditions—the physical environments they live in and their effects on the workers' bodies, identities, and spirits—are represented within the community. My analysis reveals that journalists include and omit words and themes, thereby highlighting particular material conditions and situations. This practice influences the reader to view street sex work as a problem of individual choice and responsibility.

I use an ideological rhetorical analysis, by which I mean, rhetorically—the study of how language shapes and is shaped by cultures, institutions, and the individuals within them— ideologically—the identification and examination of the underlying belief systems contained within the language. Consider the words *whore, prostitute, sex worker*, or *sacred prostitute/new age priestess*. We can interrogate the ideologies and ethical systems found in these words in order to better understand how street sex workers' identities are created and can be created differently. The word choice of *prostitute, sex worker*, or *victim of sexual exploitation* is continually debated and ultimately reflects the speaker's moral and political standpoint regarding the discourse subject's agency and position in society.[4]

I draw on Barry Brummett's concept of quotidian rhetoric in order to provide an alternative perspective on sex work. In *Rhetorical Dimensions of Popular Culture*, Brummett defines quotidian rhetoric as:

> the public and personal meanings that affect everyday, even minute-to-minute decisions. This level of rhetoric is where decisions are guided that do not take the form of peak crises [. . .] but do involve long-term concerns as well as the momentary choices that people must make to get through the day. [. . .] People are constantly surrounded by signs that influence them, or signs that they use to influence others, in ongoing, mundane, and nonexigent yet important ways. (41)

Brummett argues that the function of quotidian rhetoric is carried out through *appropriational* manifestations of rhetoric, or that which is most appropriate in a given situation. Therefore, people, in general, are relatively "less consciously aware that the management of shared meanings is underway," which means they are "less likely to take or assign responsibility for a rhetorical effort" (42). Because appropriational rhetoric is *participation in* as much as it is the *production of* the management of meaning, ultimately, individual responsibility for both is less clear. Examining sex-worker identities and their surrounding material conditions through this lens offers insights into how these representations influence attitudes about sex work while contributing to the growing body of knowledge that is examining the rhetoric of the "everyday."

Research Site & Methods

From 2005 through 2007, I researched women[5] who work on or near the street in primarily heterosexual work environments exchanging sex for money or drugs in an undisclosed city in the Southwest. "Jemez"[6] has a metropolitan population of approximately 1,000,000, and, because Jemez is located relatively closely to the border of Mexico, illegal immigration and trafficking issues are also prevalent. Similar to many other cities throughout the country, Jemez is a "typical" environment for prostitution. The initial questions that led me to this study were:

1. How are women who exchange sex for money or drugs represented in the newspaper media surrounding street sex work in Jemez?
2. What tropes recur in these representations?
3. What ideologies are embedded in these texts about these women and their work?

This article presents a portion of my analysis surrounding community literacy and newspaper media representations.

Drawing on the three primary newspapers in the Jemez community—*The Jemez Daily*, *The Jemez Weekly*, and *The State's Daily News*—I analyzed ten years of newspaper articles in order to offer the most comprehensive viewpoint of how sex work is framed and represented. My initial library search for terms commonly associated with sex work—*sex work, sex worker(s), prostitute(s),* and *prostitution*—led me to scan/read approximately thirteen hundred (1300) articles. Because my goal was to examine how local sex work, specifically street sex work, is represented and discussed in the community, throughout my searches and subsequent analysis I included only the articles that specifically mentioned local sex work and issues related to sex work in the community. Within my corpus there were a total of 490 articles that mentioned or were specifically about local sex work.

Sex Work vs. Street Sex Work. Once I had determined if an article dealt with sex work, I then placed it in one of three categories: street sex work, non-street sex work, or illegal sex work in general. This delineation between street and non-street sex work is also one that many researchers make (see Chapkis, *Live Sex Acts*; Leigh, "Prostitution"; Nagle, *Whores*; Porter and Bonilla, "Drug Use"; Weitzer, *Sex for Sale*). The third category, illegal sex work in general, was created to include articles related to all illegal sex work that don't mention street sex work specifically.

Within these three categories, 91% (444) of the articles focused on street sex work, 8% (39) focused on non-street sex work, and 1% (seven) of the articles focused on the laws and penalties relating to illegal sex work in general. Based on this simple categorization, it is easy to see why the picture most commonly considered by the layperson is that of *street* sex work. The increased emphasis in the media on human sex trafficking—a commercial sex act that is induced by force, fraud, or coercion, or in which the person induced to perform such acts has not reached eighteen years of age—is also increasingly conflated with street prostitution and the material conditions of exploitation, another reason why the public is more likely to picture street sex work when sex work is mentioned in any context (*Victims of Trafficking and Violence Protection Act of 2000*).

MATERIAL CONDITIONS AND STREET SEX WORK

After searching, compiling, reading, coding, and categorizing all of the articles according to the themes that I saw emerging from the articles, I then analyzed these articles as they related to the material conditions of sex workers' lives. As I explain above, I define material conditions as the physical environments surrounding street workers and their effects on the workers' bodies, identities, and spirits. For example, material conditions would include the aspects commonly associated with street sex work, such as drug use and sexually transmitted diseases, and they would also include how these conditions shape both the experiences of street workers and the perceptions of street workers by the general public. The material conditions of street prostitutes' lives cannot be mapped out in their entirety as they differ substantially based on location and personal circumstances, but some of the primary considerations include social status, control and power over and within working conditions, experiences of and adjustment to the work, arrests, drug use and risk of HIV/AIDS, and inherent issues with and responses to prostitution. I borrow from Wendy Chapkis's categories in her article "Power and Control in the Commercial Sex Trade," expanding on her categories based on my own analysis of the central issues most publications deal with surrounding street sex work. The above categorizations also interact to cause more oppression of and difficulty in the lives of women and men who exchange sex for drugs or money.

THE DATA: RHETORICAL AND IDEOLOGICAL ANALYSIS

After the initial categorizations between sex work in general and street sex work, I further categorized the articles according to their individual subject matter. These subcategories are outlined in the table below:

Table 1. Categorization of Newspaper Articles from 1997-2006 by Individual Subject Matter.

Subcategory	Articles
Historical perspectives on sex work	7
Violence against street sex workers	8
Disease transmission via sexual contact or intravenous drug use	8
In-depth coverage of sex work	12
Legal cases peripherally involving street sex workers	38
Arrests of sex workers and their clients	43
Articles about the local community where street sex work was mentioned but was not *the* central focus	328

Within this article I analyze the underlying assumptions and ideological frameworks contained in the twelve articles within the ten-year period examined whose stated purpose is to provide an in-depth exploration of street prostitution, including its causes, consequences, and possible solutions. I then draw conclusions based on comparisons of this analysis and offer suggestions for a re-*construction* of the problems and solutions that surround street sex work. Comprising slightly more than 15,000 words, these articles include nine full articles written by newspaper reporters, two letters to the editor, and one editorial written by a newspaper columnist.

Who Gets to Speak?

One way to understand how street sex workers are presented to the public is to examine each article's focus and who is given a voice within each one.[7] As outlined in the table below, I divided these articles into categories based on who gets to speak within them.

Seven of the twelve articles focus on penalties for prostitution, plans to decrease prostitution, and a planned diversion program for men and women arrested for prostitution.[8] None of these articles include interviews with or mention of specific prostitutes or johns. They do include the voices of city councilmen and women, police officers, attorneys, residents, neighborhood association leaders, business owners, activists in the sex-worker movement, senators involved in the proposed and contested bills regarding penalties for prostitution, the governor, and program directors of programs designed to help prostitutes and provide diversion services, along with statistics regarding the number of women in street prostitution, number of arrests both locally and in other areas, proposed laws, and research from nationally known researchers involving street prostitution.

The remaining five articles are in-depth explorations of street prostitution and organizations that work with women on the street. They include interviews with and information about specific street sex workers or prostitutes. Specifically, ten women who are or were actively working as prostitutes are quoted directly, paraphrased, or discussed in some detail. Of these ten women, three are dead, purportedly as a result of being prostitutes, three are—at the time of publication, at least—current prostitutes, and four were former prostitutes who had changed their lives, are actively involved in helping others to remove themselves from prostitution and their lives on the street, and are represented as role models for those still working in prostitution. Of these former prostitutes, one had become the director of a diversion program in another city for women arrested for prostitution. All ten of the women were cited by either their real or street names. Only one of these five articles includes interviews with and specific information about the johns or clients who employ street prostitutes—one who is famous and not local and two who are local and anonymous.

Table 2. Who Gets to Speak? Article's Focal Point Based on Twelve Articles that Focus on Street Sex Work from 1997-2006.

Article's Focal Point	Voices Included	Information Included
Penalties Diversion Programs Strategies to decrease prostitution	City councilmen and women Police Attorneys Residents Neighborhood association leaders Business owners Activists	Statistics Number of Arrests Research

Article's Focal Point	Voices Included	Information Included
In-depth exploration of street prostitution	Three women who have died Three women who are currently exchanging sex at the time of publication Four women who are former "prostitutes" who are currently helping others to leave prostitution One male solicitor who is famous and from out of town Two male solicitors who are local and anonymous	Personal information Quotations Descriptions of experiences

Based on this subset of articles, when looking at proposed solutions and penalties regarding street prostitution, the public hears from lawmakers, enforcers, and the general public, but not those who are directly participating in these crimes and are subject to these laws, ordinances, and penalties. In one article that addresses proposed penalties on owners of places where prostitution occurs, the owners are interviewed and given a voice in order to express how this proposed ordinance would potentially affect them, but again, those directly participating in prostitution are not included. From this perspective, a reader might conclude that it is only necessary to hear from those on the law-making and enforcement side of the policy—in terms of how it will affect a neighborhood and its residents, and in some cases the business owners—because these are the only people who are given a voice in terms of proposed plans and solutions. The men and women who participate in acts of prostitution are directly or indirectly silenced when matters of policy are discussed and are only given a voice when the subject matter of the article is an in-depth look at prostitution and the programs created to "help" prostitutes.

The voices of the men and women engaged in these acts are silenced further still when concerned citizens who are only marginally involved in sex-work issues are nonetheless asked to offer their opinions for print. This trend is also consistent within the hundreds of articles contained in the larger corpus of articles. In very few cases were the women and men who were directly involved in exchanging sex asked to express their opinions about the laws and penalties surrounding street prostitution.

These choices have implications for the reader's perception of street workers and street prostitution as a whole. Removing the reader from the lived experiences of those participating in these activities when their political, legislative, and criminal attributes are discussed, while simultaneously providing an up-close and personal understanding of street workers' lived experiences when the issues of personal choice and experience are explored, creates a distinction whereby the responsibility lies in the hands of the individual making these choices, rather than in the community that is responding to these issues systemically and legislatively.

REPRESENTATIONS OF PROSTITUTES AND JOHNS

The types of questions that are asked of those interviewed in the articles construct and constrain the answers that are given. In order to better understand what type of information was elicited and how the individuals are thereby constructed, I analyze the types of questions asked of both the women/prostitutes and men/johns. From this analysis, I create several categories to help track the types of information solicited from those interviewed and include them in Table 3 below.

I briefly outline the following categories and then explain how these categories relate to the representations of prostitutes and johns in the corpus as a whole. The categories include whether the interview participant is anonymous or named in the article; their current relationship status with significant others and children; their reasons for and length of time participating in prostitution; their histories with illegal substance abuse; the length of time and/or cause of incarceration; their status as a victim of physical or sexual assault; and the presence of a physical description specifically related to drug use.

Table 3 Representations of Prostitutes and Johns. Information Solicited from Women/Prostitutes and Men/Johns based on twelve articles from 1997-2006 that focus on Street Sex Work.

Information Solicited	Women/ Prostitutes	Men/ Johns
Source is anonymous; Interviewee was not asked or did not provide name		X
Current relationship status (married, significant other, live-in, etc.)		X

Information Solicited	Women/ Prostitutes	Men/ Johns
Children currently live with participant		X
Children are removed from the home	X	
Reasons for participating in prostitution	X	X
Length of time participating in prostitution	X	
Description of drugs used and patterns of drug use	X	
Length of time using drugs and/or treatment for drug addiction	X	
Length of time and cause for jail/incarceration	X	
Physical and/or sexual assault status	X	
Physical description based on drug use	X	

The Men/Johns. Within this corpus, only one article focused on the men or johns who chose to participate in prostitution. Within this one article, two men are interviewed and quoted. Mike is a "lonely" man because his marriage ended over ten years ago, but he never thought his "search for comfort" would land him in jail. [9] He is described as "just wanting to talk" and "to be with somebody for a little bit." Mike states that he's "not just a pervert." The second man quoted in the article is Tommy, a mechanic who "lives with his girlfriend and their year-old daughter" who says he's "satisfied with his love life." Nonetheless, he stopped to proposition a woman standing on the side of the road, although he says he doesn't know why. Later, Tommy suggests that his choice has "probably something to do with men." These are the only two examples of men who purchase sex the reader sees within this corpus. Although the men are definitely portrayed as responsible for their actions and are obviously choosing to participate in acts of prostitution, they are also portrayed as somewhat confused and pathetic.

The Women/Prostitutes. The descriptions of the women are quite different from those of the men. For example, Rebecca is "tired of working the streets"—as her "harsh history" includes six years as a prostitute and twice as long as a heroin addict. She says she was "looking for a legitimate job, but didn't have any luck." She doesn't know if it's her past, but "it's hard to get a job." She goes on to say, "I'm trying as hard as I can." Similarly, Sandy was "dragged under by drugs and knows of no way out." She thinks of trying to create a new life for herself, but she "doesn't know where to begin." And again, "life on the streets and on drugs is all that she has known for several years." Both of these women are described as long-time drug users who are trying to get out of street work but aren't able to due to their circumstances.

In addition to not knowing how to get out, the women are also described as becoming involved in prostitution due to their desperation or as a way of taking care of themselves. For example: "Desperate for cash and with little forethought other than getting well, she turned her first trick—selling her body for quick money"; "Prostitution was her method of survival"; and "I didn't consider it prostitution. I was taking care of myself—I didn't have to beg or steal or depend on someone else." Within this corpus, women become involved in prostitution because they are leaving abusive home lives, either as children or adults, and/or due to their involvement with drugs.

In general, the rhetoric related to prostitution and drugs consists of either 1) the women get hooked on drugs and then end up selling themselves in order to support their habits, or 2) they turn to drugs or their drug use escalates in order to provide a mental escape from prostitution. Within these articles, prostitution was their means of supporting themselves and is portrayed as a "choice" these women make to survive.

Based on the above analysis, I present the following comparisons: The johns commented on their relationship statuses and why they participated in prostitution, whereas the prostitutes were not asked about or did not discuss their relationship statuses. The women were asked how long they had worked as prostitutes, whereas the men were not asked how long they had been paying for prostitutes. The women were asked about the length of time and treatment for their use of drugs, whereas the men weren't asked if they had used, were currently using, or had been treated for drug addiction. The women discussed their length of time in jail or prison, whereas the same information was not provided about the men, except for the fact that both men were experiencing their first arrest for prostitution. The men were asked questions that focused on their reasons for participating in prostitution: There is no overriding narrative about the men's lives related specifically to prostitution, drugs, or jail/prison.

And finally, the women were asked if they had been victims of physical or sexual abuse or assaults, whereas the men were not asked if they had been victims of or had victimized others sexually or physically. The articles also included physical descriptions of the women's skin due to drug use ("arms showing scars of track marks left by needles"; "her face is pocked because, while under the influence of drugs, she picked at imaginary bugs"; and "pock marks scar her shoulders where she punched needles into her skin"[10]). Based on the information provided, the reader envisions the physical description of the women/prostitutes but not necessarily the men/johns.

There is a much greater focus on the negative aspects of the women's/prostitutes' lives than the men's/johns' lives. While the women are depicted as having lives ravaged by addiction, abuse, and social ostracism, the men are depicted as lonely or unfulfilled, but essentially harmless to both themselves and their community. The descriptions don't denote the quality of the men's skin in the same way that the women's skin is identified: they are regular, everyday guys who don't wear the physical signs of drug use and its correlation to the exchanging of sex for money or drugs for everyone to see. Unlike the sex workers themselves who are physically marked and clearly identified, their clients are anonymous in both name and appearance. The women/prostitutes and their paths are revealed and made public, while the men/johns remain unknown. The women/prostitutes are also much more in the spotlight in terms of their actions, both past and present, that led them to participate in prostitution, whereas the men's/johns' motives and history are vague.

AVAILABLE PATHS: PAST AND FUTURE

According to the newspaper media in Jemez, the pathways the street workers have traveled as well as those paths available to them in the future are limited. As I stated above, five of the twelve articles are in-depth explorations of street prostitution and organizations that work with women on the street. All of these articles focus on women who are currently using or have a history of using drugs, have been sexually and physically abused as children or as adults by johns, have been in jail/prison on charges ranging from drug paraphernalia to manslaughter, and are vulnerable to diseases and general violence. These women include those who currently work as street prostitutes and want to leave, those who had previously worked and were victims of violent crimes resulting in their deaths, and those who left prostitution and offer a message of hope to others.

Four of these articles focus on street prostitutes who have since left this environment and now work with and inspire others to leave street prostitution. Through personal strength and programmatic support, four women found their way out of prostitution and are now active role models and work to help others who are involved with drugs and prostitution. One article focuses on Casa Segura,[11] a program that works with street prostitutes, and two women are interviewed and describe their current statuses in detail. The first woman is unsure of her options, wants to leave prostitution and drugs, but is not sure if she'll be able to. The second street worker talks about her history of prostitution and now works with Casa Segura in order to help others get out of prostitution. Only one of the five articles includes the voices of street workers who are currently working as prostitutes, and these women are unhappy and want to leave this work. This same article also includes the stories of three prostitutes who were found beaten and killed—violence that was attributed to their work as street workers.

In all of the above stories, the women who are working on the street want to leave prostitution. Of course, the reader doesn't hear from those who are dead, but it can be assumed that these women would prefer to be alive over being beaten, raped, and killed because of their choice to be involved with prostitution. In four out of the five articles (80%), the reader is offered a message of hope that individual street workers are able to remove themselves from street prostitution and work to help others do the same. Only in two cases does the reader see women working as prostitutes who do not necessarily plan on leaving prostitution, but who say they would like to leave and are worried about their futures. And because these messages saturate the newspaper media, the public associates these stories with all women who work in street prostitution, and most likely all people who work in sex work in general.

SOLUTIONS: PERSONAL CHOICE AND RESPONSIBILITY

One of the stated purposes of the in-depth articles is to explore potential solutions to the "problem" of prostitution. By emphasizing the personal choices made by the women involved in prostitution, the newspaper articles construct the *individuals* as the source of the problem, which constrains the potential solutions. When we reframe the problem, we see different solutions.

Ironically, the story is one of "escape" that hinges on personal choice. The women are portrayed as becoming involved in prostitution because they are desperate—to escape from an abusive home life, to support a drug habit, or to support themselves in general. And yet once involved in prostitution, it is up to the individual women to choose to remove themselves from this "lifestyle." As stated in the articles: it is up to them to "choose drugs on the street over a new lifestyle"; there are "options that exist to help prostitutes break their cycle of danger and despair, but the choice is up to them whether they will change their lifestyle"; and "it is up to them if they want to change their lifestyle." Within these statements lies the assumption these women *should choose* to change their lifestyle, that there are programs out there to help them change their lifestyle, but ultimately it is their *personal* choice to change or not.

This construction simultaneously positions the women as prisoners or captives of the drug and prostitution lifestyle while also agents of their own change. The focus is on the individual—individuals make choices, they escape prostitution and drugs, and they become role models and provide hope, both for those who are still in prostitution and want to find their way out and for the general community who wants to find solutions to prostitution. This focus on the individual encourages the public to view prostitution as an individual's problem, rather than one that society as a whole might be responsible for.

This framework is one that makes sense in the United States where individualism, self-reliance, and the ideology of "pulling oneself up by one's bootstraps" pervade mass culture. And yet this focus becomes ironic and contradictory in an analysis of the newspaper rhetoric concerning street sex workers: prostitutes shoulder the harshest blame for the evils of sex work, while johns are allowed to shirk their collusion in the same transactions; prostitutes are celebrated for their eventual choice to leave prostitution, but no celebratory voice is ever given to their initial (and in many cases, life-saving) choice to enter into prostitution; and prostitutes are commended for their strong will in leaving the sex trade while virtually ignoring the deep and damaging socio-economic roots that make prostitution a viable option for desperate women in the first place. The newspaper articles do not focus this much attention on the men who have chosen to purchase sex—they are assumed to be nowhere near as desperate as the women, perhaps because they are paying rather than receiving money for sex. But readers never learn their histories as intimately as they do the prostitutes', nor are they considered the primary problem. Within this corpus the problem is framed as one that primarily involves drug use and focuses on the women who choose to participate in these activities. The reader's attention is not brought to focus on the cycle of abuse, both as children and as women, that many of these women have been subject to, nor the perceived need for drugs that many of these women feel, nor the issues of poverty and difficulty supporting oneself and perhaps one's children also. This framing of the intimate details of these women's lives accompanied by the message of personal choice and responsibility then encourages the public to view the prostitution "problem" as one that can be solved by the individual, and, more specifically, by the individual prostitute.

Conclusions: Language and Systemic Responsibility

Based on these articles, first and foremost, when prostitution is mentioned, it is street sex work that is primarily the focus of the attention. Within the subset of my corpus that specifically gives voice to prostitutes and johns, I found that when an in-depth look at prostitution is offered, the participants in the trade are included, but when penalties, laws, and plans to decrease prostitution are discussed, neither the prostitutes' nor the johns' perspectives are included; instead, the reader hears only from police, social service agency leaders, lawyers, and legislators.

Therefore, when the public does hear from these women, it is only in response to in-depth articles about prostitution rather than about neighborhood plans to rid the area of or penalties for prostitution. When the articles focus on policy and programs for women involved in prostitution, the women are silent, as are their customers. They aren't interviewed or asked what they think of the programs and penalties and how these programs or penalties might affect their lives. Readers hear from those working to implement the programs and policies, such as city council leaders, police officers, attorneys, and neighborhood association leaders. They hear from researchers about the problems associated with prostitution, residents and workers who live and work in the areas where prostitution is more visible, and local business owners and neighborhood association leaders who believe prostitution is decreasing the value of their properties and businesses. In two articles, sex-worker activists and sex-worker activist organizations are also mentioned—in one article briefly as an aside, and in another a more in-depth description of the organization and the issues surrounding sex-work activism is given.[12] As a whole, the johns receive the least amount of attention in terms of biographical detail and the reasons for their participation in prostitution, while the prostitutes receive the greatest amount of exposure, especially about their drug use, criminal pasts, jail time, and statuses as victims of violence.

Finally, the "problem" of prostitution is represented largely as one of personal choice and responsibility. Although the women may have entered prostitution due to desperation and the need for survival, the articles focus on women who have made choices to get "help," change their "lifestyle," and are no longer involved in prostitution. These women are represented as heroes and role models for others who are still involved in prostitution. This same attention is not paid to the johns who are no longer involved in purchasing sex. The framework of personal choice and responsibility encourages the public to focus on the individual, and specifically on individual women, as the solution to the "problem"; larger systems of poverty, abuse, and violence are not considered.

Within these articles a number of messages about street prostitution are clear. The focus on the individual woman prostitute both diverts attention from and maintains mainstream systems of hierarchy and power. When the individual street worker is presented in the spotlight, her role is to show how other individuals can take responsibility for themselves and change—on an individual basis. The systems (poverty, abuse, violence) that have contributed to these problems are not questioned, nor is attention placed on the individual man/customer who also perpetuates and maintains this system. These relationships between the men and women, the selling of sex, the state's role in that sale, its status as illegal, and the advantages of selling sex over other choices—none of these issues are questioned, critiqued, or even acknowledged. The construction of the woman and her role in the "problem" of prostitution maintains the system in which prostitution exists—or even thrives—by placing the public's attention on the individual and the choices it expects her to make.

Not only applicable to street workers, this construction of the individual nature of street prostitution contributes to the public's understanding of other marginalized groups. How can we as readers of our newspapers, teachers, citizens in our communities, and perhaps advocates for social justice "read" these literacy practices? Not only must we demand more realistic community representations, but these representations must include the voices from the community—most specifically those that are most directly impacted by the legislation, policies, and movements toward the eradication of this "problem."

We must also consider these issues from alternative perspectives. How might the women and men who sell sex be experts—working with legislators, neighborhood association leaders, social service agents, etc.—to resolve community conflicts, share resources, and address individual needs? One example of an organization that does indeed draw on the expertise of sex workers is the Sex Industry Worker Safety Action Group (SIWAG) in Vancouver, Canada, a collaborative action group that "connects police, sex industry workers, and community organizations to address the safety concerns of sex workers" ("SISWAG-Outline")[13]. See online site "Community Resources for Sex Work and Public Policy" for additional resources (http://www.stpt.usf.edu/mccracken/research/sexwork/community_resources).

And finally, we need to implement systemic changes that would prevent individuals from being in a position where this "choice" is the only available one. If the spotlight were placed on the system, —what responsibilities and choices would be revealed? Rather than constructing the individual worker and even her customer as those on the margins and thereby responsible for creating change, the discursive and practical emphasis should be placed on the systems that are not successfully providing support for members of our communities.

Let's review the headlines quoted at the beginning of this article, all of which were found in local papers. Consider how they might be re-written to shift the focus from the individual to systemic issues, including the voices and perspectives of those who are the primary subjects of the articles.

Table 4. Newspaper Article Headlines Revised to Shift the Emphasis from the Individual to the System.

Original Headline	Revised Headline
She's a Prostitute, Addict, and Abuser, but She's a Mom and He Misses Her	Poverty, Abuse, and Inequality Fail Woman, Leaving her Son without a Mother
Prostitution Wrecks Neighborhood	Women and Men on the Street Offer Solutions for Improved Neighborhood Safety
Casualties of the Street	Poverty, Unemployment, and Violence Create Casualties, Leaving Them on the Street
A Way Out for Prostitutes	Women and Men Shed Light on Complicated Subjects: Sex Work and Society

The above headline revisions should reflect a new focus within each article that would shift the perspective, the questions asked and answered, and the voices included, which would provide a re-vision of how the problems and solutions are constructed and understood.

This shift will require collaborations with the people who are trained to create these kinds of texts. Given the current state of newspaper decline and as the definition of what a newspaper is continues to evolve, now is the perfect time to effect this type of change. Community and social justice advocates can assist in conversations between these marginalized groups and newspaper reporters/writers/editorial boards to develop means for more realistic community representations that, based in the voices of the marginalized groups, provide more just interpretations and frameworks through which to view the material conditions that surround these people's lives.

Notes

1. This study received IRB approval, a Department of Health and Human Services Confidentiality Certificate, and meets the CCCC "Guidelines for the Ethical Conduct of Research in Composition Studies." I want to thank Julie Armstrong and Morgan Gresham, who provided substantial feedback on earlier drafts of this essay, as well as my anonymous *CLJ* reviewers, who pushed me to make my argument and examples stronger.

2. I call attention to the terms commonly used to describe the activities of exchanging sex for drugs or money, such as "sex work" and "prostitution" by placing them in quotations in order to show that these terms are political and place the people who practice these activities in predetermined places, often based on the political and moral stance of the speaker. For readability, I place the words in quotations when I first use them. Throughout this article I use the term *sex work* to describe these activities based on my own perspective that these activities are forms of labor that people perform for remuneration.

3. In undertaking this research, my primary concern is not about justifying a particular view of people who exchange sex for money or drugs in terms of decriminalization, legalization, AIDS, health issues, violence, racism, sexism, or any of the other myriad issues that are involved with and are products of these types of transactions.

4. For example, those people who tend to position themselves in opposition to sex work use the words *prostitutes* and *victims of sexual exploitation* to refer to women who exchange sex for money or drugs. Their choice of language underscores their own belief and argument that these women are victims rather than agents making an occupational choice. And then there are sex workers and sex-worker advocates who believe that many sex workers are agents who freely choose this occupation and use the term *sex work/er* to reflect this belief and argument. Although complicated by many scholars, the "victim" versus "agent" status of the subject of the discourse holds fast in many debates, yet neither "victim" nor "agent" does the person justice. This dichotomy is far too simplistic to define any one individual or group of people in general, especially when it comes to people who are working in an area so fraught with the moral and political ideologies surrounding sexuality, gender roles, commerce, and social relationships. See Chapkis, Farley, and Weitzer for examples and explanations of these terms.

5. Analyzing issues surrounding male and transgendered sex workers and alternatively identified sexualities in sex work is beyond the scope of this project. These issues are extremely important to consider in an analysis of sex work, and yet trying to include them in this analysis would complicate the study by involving those ideologies and discriminations that arise when concepts of gender and sexuality beyond the "mainstream" are involved.

6. Not its real name. In order to maintain anonymity of the people I interviewed for other parts of my research, I am not at liberty to reveal the location of my research site. Therefore, any indicators of personal identities or geographic locales—including the titles of local newspapers—have been changed.

7. Rather than continuing to use my language of choice, at this point I use the actual language included in the articles in order to provide the reader with a more seamless picture of the language and context found in the corpus.

8. Within these articles all of the people who exchange sex are women and all of the people who purchase sex are men. There is no mention of men who exchange sex or women who purchase sex. Although men also exchange sex on the street for both male and female clients, there is no mention of these transactions in this corpus.

9. This quotation is a paraphrase of the actual quote in order to maintain anonymity, but the key terms such as *comfort* and *loneliness* are those actually used in the article.

10. These excerpts are not exact quotations from the newspaper articles in order to preserve anonymity, but they are written very closely to the actual language used.

11. In order to maintain anonymity of my research site, the name of this organization has been changed.

12. In order to maintain anonymity of the people I interviewed for other parts of my research, I am not at liberty to reveal the names of the organizations mentioned in these articles.

13. See online site "Community Resources for Sex Work and Public Policy" for additional resources (http://www.stpt.usf.edu/mccracken/research/sexwork/community_resources).

Works Cited

Brummett, Barry. *Rhetorical Dimensions of Popular Culture*. Tuscaloosa: U of Alabama P, 1991.

Chapkis, Wendy. *Live Sex Acts: Women Performing Erotic Labor*. New York: Routledge, 1997.

---. "Power and Control in the Commercial Sex Trade." *Sex for Sale: Prostitution, Pornography, and the Sex Industry*. Ed. Ronald John Weitzer. New York: Routledge, 2000. 181-201.

Farley, Melissa. "'Bad for the Body, Bad for the Heart': Prostitution Harms Women Even if Legalized or Decriminalized." *Violence Against Women* 10.10 (2004): 1087-1125.

Leigh, Carol. "Prostitution in the United States: The Statistics." *Gauntlet* 1 (1994): 17-18.

McCracken, Jill. *Community Resources for Sex Work and Public Policy*. 2009. <http://www.stpt.usf.edu/mccracken/research/sexwork/community_resources>. January 22, 2009.

Nagle, Jill, ed. *Whores and Other Feminists*. New York: Routledge, 1997.

Porter, Judith, and Louis Bonilla. "Drug Use, HIV, and the Ecology of Street Prostitution." *Sex for Sale: Prostitution, Pornography, and the Sex Industry*. Ed. Ronald John Weitzer. New York: Routledge, 2000. 103-21.

Sex Industry Worker Safety Action Group (SIWSAG). "SISWAG-Outline." White Paper. 2009. 30 July 2009. <http://vancouver.ca/police/diversity/2009/SISWAG-outline.pdf>

United States Government. *Victims of Trafficking and Violence Protection Act of 2000.* 2000. <http://www.state.gov/documents/organization/10492.pdf>. January 20, 20, 2010.

Weitzer, Ronald John, ed. *Sex for Sale: Prostitution, Pornography, and the Sex Industry.* New York: Routledge, 2000.

COMPOSITION FORUM

A journal of pedagogical theory in rhetoric and composition

Volume 21
Spring 2010

Composition Forum and this article are on the Web at http://compositionforum.com/issue/21/sustaining-writing-theory.php

Composition Forum is a peer-reviewed journal for scholars and teachers interested in the investigation of composition theory and its relation to the teaching of writing at the post-secondary level. The journal features articles that explore the intersections of composition theory and pedagogy, including essays that examine specific pedagogical theories or that examine how theory could or should inform classroom practices, methodology, and research into multiple literacies. *Composition Forum* also publishes articles that describe specific and innovative writing program practices and writing courses, reviews of relevant books in composition studies, and interviews with notable scholars and teachers who can address issues germane to our theoretical approach.

"Sustaining Writing Theory" by Amy M. Patrick

Amy Patrick's "Sustaining Writing Theory" demonstrates *Composition Forum*'s unique focus on the intersections of composition theory and practice, as well as the journal's commitment to interdisciplinary research and scholarship. The article provides a sophisticated study of writing theory, sustainability studies, and the implications of these two related conversations to composition pedagogy. As the author suggests, the essay seeks to "open discussion about a theory of writing that is sustainable and sustains writing practice across a variety of areas." In doing so, the article helps to expand our discipline's conversations by drawing upon scholarly work from a range of disciplinary perspectives. The editorial team at *Composition Forum* has selected this essay because it theorizes practice in an insightful and provocative way, and we are pleased to have it represent the scope and focus of the journal.

Sustaining Writing Theory

Amy M. Patrick

Abstract

This article examines ways in which the fundamentals of both writing studies and sustainability studies overlap and complement each other, ultimately moving toward a theory of writing that not only is sustainable, but that also sustains writing practice across a variety of areas. For example, in order to be sustainable, both writing and geographical communities must consider several elements in any decision or employed strategy. Both writing (the act and the teaching of it) and sustainability studies are localized, regionally specific. Key to the argument's theoretical positioning is the role of technology and technological innovation in both a community and a classroom in terms of inhibiting and facilitating sustainability and communication.

In his March 2009 Conference on College Composition and Communication address, Sidney Dobrin critiques the field of writing studies, and ecocomposition in particular, for focusing too much on students in the classroom and program management and not enough on writing itself. Indeed, much writing in the field today would fall under the category of "show and tell" or of quantitative studies of classroom behaviors and students' end products. Dobrin notes that when he and Christian Weisser co-edited the book *Ecocomposition: Theoretical and Pedagogical Approaches* (published in 2001), they predicted ecocomposition would grow and move forward in dynamic ways. Yet the field's development has not followed this projection. Dobrin maintains that, if the field of writing studies is to grow in dynamic and innovative ways, it will be through the development of new theoretical perspectives on writing itself; furthermore, he suggests that the point of this growth can and should come from the developing subfield of ecocomposition.

Ecocomposition has been defined in several ways; the most common definitions center around writing about place and writing in place—for some, this simply means nature writing; for others, this means covering environmental issues as content in the writing classroom. However, ecocomposition encompasses much more complexity and subtlety than these interpretations suggest, and its scope extends beyond the writing classroom. In his 2005 article "From Environmental Rhetoric to Ecocomposition and Ecopoetics: Finding a Place for Professional Communication," M. Jimmie Killingsworth notes the limitations of reducing any kind of communication, discourse, or pedagogy to a slogan or bullet points (359). In his critique, Killingsworth aims to "guide a revived ecological pedagogy and research program" and, specifically, to both problematize and extend aspects of ecocomposition and its implications for technical communication (360). As Dobrin and Weisser note, "Ecocomposition must be about more than simply bringing nature writing texts to the writing classroom; it must be about the act of producing writing" (587). Drawing on Dobrin, Killingsworth suggests that "writing takes place" (364). I argue here that it takes more than that—to be effective, writing must consider the complete multidimensional context (sociohistorical, economic, etc.) that includes place at its core. Merging sustainability studies and writing studies has the potential to produce very nuanced theories of writing production and dissemination from which both administration and pedagogy can greatly benefit, in turn benefiting our students in first-year writing, in professional writing, and across the curriculum.

Here, I examine the ways in which the fundamentals of both writing studies and sustainability studies overlap and complement each other, in order to open discussion about a theory of writing that is sustainable and sustains writing practice across a variety of areas. To do so, I engage the history of ecocomposition, connect central elements of sustainability studies that parallel and are relevant to writing studies, and address the implications of sustainable writing theory for research, pedagogy, and our own writing practices.

Engaging Ecocomposition: Expanding Specialties, Theorizing Practice

To engage the history of ecocomposition, it is helpful to review some of the main trends—their strengths and limitations. One of the important, yet limiting, developments in ecocomposition has been the approach most individuals take to focus on subjects and genres that could be classified as "environmental." This trend reflects the focus of literature in environmental rhetoric, as well as an assumption that professional communicators need to be concerned with environmental considerations only if they work in an environmental field (Killingsworth 360). Thus, as Killingsworth notes, "[t]he professionalization of the environment leaves us thinking that only certain groups are touched by ecological concerns and the interest in place" (361). This treatment of ecocomposition, by limiting the focus to the topical, also limits the sense of who is and should be thinking about the environment. Citing Kenneth Burke, Killingsworth notes that such a belief is problematic because the compartmentalization leads specialists—scientists and technical communicators—to believe "they can live in a constant state of denial about their responsibility for their research and their inventions" (362). I argue that the same is true of any professional communicator and of writing students: the sense that this is specialized or even an academic exercise excuses accountability beyond literature or the classroom. A sustainable writing theory must incorporate this accountability into the practice and teaching of writing.

In summarizing the ecocomposition approach that emerged with scholars Sidney Dobrin, Christian Weisser, and Derek Owens, Killingsworth remarks:

> For them, ecology becomes something more than a set of themes that occupy the attention of a special group of authors and texts. Instead it appears as a component in every text—the writer's realization of spatial limits and contexts, a concern with the place that any text occupies in the world. It also becomes a model for how authors and readers join in a web of discourse clearly anchored in the roots and soil of earthly life. The ecocompositionists want to know where as well as how and why writing works. (364)

An ecocomposition further informed by sustainability studies considers, as equally critical as ecology, the impact of economic considerations, social considerations, and even technological innovations on discourse and community.

As Killingsworth observes, "[e]cocomposition encourages us to start with the question of place: Is it really the same experience to use a computer in New York and in Beijing?" (365). No. But *why?* Not just for ecological and geographical reasons—social factors, economic factors, and both receptiveness to technological innovation and the use of different innovations all distinguish the experiences as well. Especially in a world where technological innovations allow us to operate in "sites" with no rootedness in place, it is easy to ignore ecological concerns and even the social concerns of our immediate, physical communities. Yet as Killingsworth notes, "[v]irtual reality fails when the roof leaks, the machine breaks, the network goes down, and real life intrudes. The mind wakes up and finds itself attached to a body, and the body is made of the earth's own clay" (367). We need to be able to cope with challenges and crises in our immediate, physical communities in ways that aim to sustain those communities. In order to do so, we need to consider in our writing a balance between global and local thinking, and we need to be conscious not only that an audience exists for our writing but also of who that audience might be, what they value, and how their context relates to and differs from our own. Killingsworth observes, "[a]ny attempt to act globally probably entails an imposition of overextended local thinking. Thus it is essential that we understand the local elements of our own products and visions before we assume their universal applicability" (369). As teachers, we need to frame global and local considerations for audiences and contexts in ways that draw on and demonstrate implications beyond the classroom.

For professional communication classes, Killingsworth suggests developing a "place-conscious, ecopoetically informed pedagogy" (370). He notes that this does not require an ideological affiliation with an environmental position but rather a more comprehensive and sensitive perception of the role of place in writing and social engagement (370). While Killingsworth moves toward theory building, he ultimately ends in pedagogical advice by adapting Derek Owens's work in ecocomposition to professional communication. Thus, his revised pedagogy is still practice-based, without articulating in clear terms the larger theoretical framework from which the pedagogical practices emerge—a framework that helps us understand how and why the practice supports and enhances the act and process of writing itself.

Such frameworks are suggested by Marilyn Cooper in her essay "The Ecology of Writing" and Margaret Syverson in her book *The Wealth of Reality: An Ecology of Composition*. Cooper moves toward developing a theoretical framework at the intersection of sustainability and writing studies. She critiques the cognitive process model of writing, suggesting that it is problematic because it frames the writer as isolated from the communities within which she operates (366). To counter this, Cooper cites pedagogical approaches such as collaborative brainstorming, debates, and group work as pushing beyond this notion, arguing that there is "a growing awareness that language and texts are not simply the means by which individuals discover and communicate information, but are essentially social activities, dependent on social structures and processes not only in their interpretive but also in their constructive phases" (366). Thus, in her essay, she proposes an ecological writing model grounded in the belief that individuals, through writing, are continuously engaging webs of dynamic social systems (367).

Applying an ecologically informed approach to writing theory gives us one way to understand "how writers interact to form systems: all the characteristics of any individual writer or piece of writing both determine and are determined by the characteristics of all the other writers and writings in the system" (368). While this model is an encouraging step forward that contributed to the evolution of ecocomposition in productive and innovative ways by suggesting the dynamic connections between systems, it does not address in depth the degrees of how and why these systems are connected. It does not adequately acknowledge, for example, that all parts in a system are different and rarely act the same or even the same way twice. Moreover, ecological science alone cannot provide all the explanations. While this model addresses engagement in and with the environment (broadly conceived), it does not address a sense of responsibility to engage, nor does it directly provide a way for addressing the specific social, economic, and technological factors within the larger environment or context.

Drawing on complex systems theory, Syverson argues that writers, their audiences, and their writing form complex systems, defined as "self-organizing, adaptive, and dynamic" (4-5). She sees composing as an ecological system and proposes "an ecology of composing" (2). Understanding the dimensions of complex systems and applying this kind of analysis to writing studies research may help us understand how and why people write what they do, but it does not tie the process back to its actual function within communities. For example, examining aspects of the psychological dimension of composing and reading in the writing studies complex system may reveal information about an individual or group of individuals that is crucial to bringing social equity to the classroom because it allows us to understand how our students learn, but a sustainable theory of writing actually requires us to take this step for the good of our students in the first place. While complex systems theory may provide the how, sustainability provides the why and the motivation. In addition, we can pay attention to the physical-material dimension of the complex system of composing, which helps us to recognize the physical and material factors impacting our production and reading of writing, but sustainability pushes us to question how these materials themselves facilitate or hinder not only the act of writing but also the cumulative effects of the words and their physical, material production. What quantitative study and knowledge of complex systems theory allows us to produce about the composing process is useful, but it does not directly contribute to a more sustainable society by itself because it is not tied to a particular ethical code of being in the world.

Citing Cooper and others, Dobrin and Weisser outline two branches of ecocomposition—ecological literacy and discursive ecology—and advocate theories and pedagogies that combine the two (581). While the former stresses raising ecological awareness among students, the latter "asks students to see writing as an ecological process, to explore writing and writing processes as systems of interaction, economy, and interconnectedness" (581). Ecocomposition informed by sustainability not only combines the two, but it also asks writers to consider in those systems and processes the equally critical dimensions of social equity, economic stability, and technological innovation, at the same time looking to the goals of sustainability as a way to understand and be effective in the engagement of writing itself.

SUSTAINABILITY STUDIES IN CONTEXT AND WRITING STUDIES IN THEORY

In an effort to connect central elements of sustainability studies that parallel and are relevant to writing studies, I do not want to discuss what or how to teach as much as understanding the phenomenon of writing and communication itself in its full dimensional context, so that we can adapt our teaching and our writing to fit specific communities and purposes. While we draw on ecological concepts in modeling and examining the environment-culture relationship, sustainability breaks both environment and culture out into economy, social justice, politics, ideology, spirituality, ecology, place (natural, constructed, and imagined as Dobrin and Weisser define it), and technology. By raising awareness of the multiple contextual layers that inform and produce writing in a way that reflects our global and local contexts, a sustainability theory of writing has the potential to allow for not only a temporal and spatial move beyond crisis in and through writing but also an engagement with and an understanding of ways in which other problems and crises—genocide, political unrest, terrorism—are connected to ecological, social, economic, spiritual, and technological contexts. As Dobrin and Weisser point out, ecocomposition should extend beyond nature discourse to include "the relationships between discourse and any site where discourse exists" (573). Sustainability studies thus expands ecocomposition, allowing us to examine and apply the complexity of the whole writing situation, as it reflects the complexity of communities.

In order to be sustainable, both writing and geographical communities must consider several elements in any decision or employed strategy, from audience or community to historical and cultural context and the impact on both. Both writing (the act and the teaching of it) and sustainability studies are localized, regionally specific. Writing pedagogy, to be effective, must be student-specific—yet in a way that fits the larger classroom community. Workplace writing and disciplinary writing are no exception. In writing studies, then, we talk about rhetorical strategies, a consideration of situation or context, audience, and purpose or authorial intent. In sustainability studies, the areas of ecological integrity, social equity, and economic stability, respectively, parallel the rhetorical situation in writing.

In order for a piece of writing to be successful, the writer must consider the situation or context—cultural and sociohistorical, for example—just as the community planner or business owner must consider the ecological integrity of a specific biological or bioregional community—its historical and contemporary identity—in order to create a sustainable community or business plan. Likewise, a writer must be concerned with audience in order to achieve the desired response—the writer must work toward common ground with her audience, just as the individual or group concerned with sustainability must consider what will best achieve or preserve social equity in a particular community. The writer must also be concerned with accessibility—how clear is the writing (in content and form) to a particular audience, and how available in terms of both media presentation and dissemination.[1] The writer's concern with purpose or intent parallels sustainability's concern with economic stability, for both involve making a connection between point A and point B: what the writer wants/needs, what the audience wants/needs, and what each side is willing to give or take to most effectively and—often, efficiently—achieve that common ground. Writing, as with the economy, involves selling or persuasion. Writers must also be concerned with the idea of usability, which falls within the realm of social equity but also economic stability because it is concerned with effectiveness, access, and efficiency. The concept of intellectual property, through its commodification of ideas and assignment of ownership, is an element of writing that can be considered in both social and economic terms as well.

To be socially equitable and effective in the writing classroom, teachers must consider students' learning needs, which requires a consideration of cultural background and learning style. Attention must also be given to marketability and effectiveness (in terms of writing skills) and to context in a specific way—for example, is the course online, face-to-face, or hybrid? Is it a first-year writing class or a graduate professional writing seminar? Is one teaching in a private liberal arts college or a community college? All of these things, just like the social, economic, and environmental considerations of sustainability, must be considered in writing, administration, and the teaching of writing in order to be sustainable.

Developing a theory of writing based on sustainability is a way to articulate what many of us already are doing, in many ways, in our classrooms and our own writing, and supports the ways in which a writer successfully adapts, functions, and innovates in a dynamic society by engaging critical thinking, judgment, and communication. However, there is one element that I believe needs to be added to the sustainability model that complements and reflects what is happening in writing theory as well: technology. One of the most widely cited models of sustainability is the three-legged stool model, which considers the balance of ecological integrity, social equity, and economic stability (Dawe and Ryan). This model is greatly contested, but nonetheless is the most commonly considered, especially in light of the often-quoted goal of sustainability from the 1987 Brundtland Commission Report: "meeting present needs without compromising the ability of future generations to meet their own needs" (WCED). Arguments have been made for other considerations, including education, futurity, public participation, and spirituality (Orr; Dawe and Ryan; Edwards; Palmer, Cooper, and van der Vorst). I would argue that technology, though often cited—and rightly so—as problematic with respect to sustainability, needs to be a distinct element of the model because the balance between tradition and technological innovation in any community, from the classroom to the corporation, is critical, determining the sustainability of any larger plan, process, or strategy.

Following Everett M. Rogers's definition, "an innovation is an idea, practice, or object that is *perceived* as new by an individual or other unit of adoption" (11; emphasis added). The extent to which an innovation will be accepted by an individual or community and the amount of time and effort acceptance or adoption requires is determined by five factors: relative advantage the innovation holds over its predecessor; compatibility with the audience or user's values, needs, and experiences; complexity; trialability; and observability or visibility in terms of results (15-16). In terms of environment, society, or even a piece of writing, success depends not only on the ability to meet the economic, social, and ecological needs of that community or context; an innovation or text's sustainability will never be realized if it is not accepted by the individuals affected.

Technological traditions and innovations thus create a critical dynamic not only in physical communities but also with writing in physical and intellectual ways. Physically, new writing technologies must be diffused acceptably to be effective. Intellectually, writers often seek to communicate and diffuse innovations through their writing. According to Rogers, "Diffusion is the process by which an innovation is communicated through certain channels over time among members of a social system" and "[c]ommunication is a process in which participants create and share information with one another in order to reach a mutual understanding" (6). Thus, "[w]hen new ideas are invented, diffused, and are adopted or rejected, leading to certain consequences, social change occurs" (6). This connects well to Killingsworth's observation that writing "is not simply a way of thinking but more fundamentally a way of acting" (373). As our writing technologies develop and change—consider, for example, texting, social networking, and other new media and genres for writing—individuals' abilities to engage their communities and meet both their needs and the needs of future generations are determined by their knowledge of and comfort with particular technologies.

In order to sustain the writing communities of our classrooms, we need to innovate. We need to understand how writing happens and how the engagement of different modes affects our students' instructional needs and our instructional possibilities and opportunities so that we all effectively engage our social worlds. At the same time that we are compelled to innovate, we cannot forget the needs and concerns of students for whom more traditional technologies and classroom spaces represent a comfort zone from which they will not willingly part. Yet the classroom is not the only place where this shift takes place. Richard Coe maintains, "[a]s long as we are socializing students to observe, think, and express themselves in particular modes, therefore, we may well choose modes which will be particularly useful in today's (and tomorrow's) world" (233). Such modes today include an increasing number of electronic and online genres; and therefore, what students learn and engage about writing must be connected to these evolving modes.

But writing in this world also means engaging moral as well as technical issues. In his book *Technology and the Contested Meanings of Sustainability*, Aidan Davison states, "current crises in ecological systems and in development strategies demand fundamental technological change" (ix). In addressing what sustainability means and how we get there, Davison believes we must engage both technical and moral questions, reflecting on "our moral experience and our technological practice" (ix). Thus, Davison seeks to "reconfigure the meanings of sustainability as prompts for open-ended questions that focus our attention on the nature of moral experience in our technological world" (5). How do we modify our pedagogy to become more sustainable? How do we help students to write sustainably? By asking questions (of what we read, what we write, and what and how we teach) that engage the intersection of ecological, economic, social, technological, and moral concerns.

Specific Implications, Further Connections, and Professional Practices

Much of what we already do in our classrooms—innovations and directions of development over the years—contributes to the sustainability of both communities and our students' writing, including service and experiential learning, peer feedback, one-on-one conferences, and specific, localized writing assignments. Yet a theoretical merging of sustainability and writing studies provides a guiding framework, allowing us to build on previous developments in writing studies and other disciplines to adapt to new cultural and technological contexts. Just as I believe it is important to ask: "What will help my students learn?" I believe it is also important to ask: "What will help my students contribute to a sustainable world now and in the future?" As teachers of writing and administrators of writing programs, we have marked influence on our students' professional and social development, and therefore, the responsibility to direct (without imposing ideology) that influence in ways that benefit not only our students, but also their communities and ours.

Most of us have written a statement of our teaching, or perhaps administrative, philosophy at some point in our careers—many of us have written and re-written that philosophy, influenced by theory and practice. Why? They demonstrate our own pedagogical and administrative profiles, to be sure. They also provide a level of transparency, a way to assess if what we are doing in our classrooms and writing programs reflects what we profess to believe. The philosophy and the practice should dance together. When one strays from the other or neither suits the changing context, accommodations—innovations, even—must be made. If these philosophies truly guide our teaching and administration, then a consideration of how to connect what we do to sustainability should develop there and move outward even as it also generates in the classroom. Conscientiousness, awareness of the connection between philosophy and practice is important, just as conscientiousness about our beliefs on the environment, social justice, and so forth inform, or should inform, our citizenly actions. One does not profess to prioritize the health of the environment, for example, and then strew plastic bags and polystyrene across neighborhoods and landfills. One starts, perhaps, with buying energy efficient light bulbs, carrying reusable grocery bags. It is not changing the world in drastic ways—though that would be a fine thing—but it is practice connected to a philosophy, and the two should reinforce each other and coevolve.

So too with our philosophies and practices at both the classroom and program levels, and that is at the very core of a sustainable theory of writing: conscientious application and practice tied to beliefs and knowledge about how the world works, what facilitates communication in that world, and what might sustain that world in positive ways for the future. A theory of writing grounded in the tenets of sustainability recognizes that it is critical to know why we do what we do in our writing and in our daily and professional lives: to be able to trace practice back to its origins in order to move forward and adapt successfully to new situations, environments, crises, and technologies. For example, why do we encourage peer feedback in the classroom? Why do we allow students to submit more than one draft of a piece of writing? Perhaps we want to raise students' awareness of audience as a real, tangible thing (which it is, as they will learn professionally). Perhaps we want them to broaden their perspectives by engaging the perspectives of others and negotiating those shared and disparate values, interpretations, and beliefs. Perhaps we want them to recognize the dynamic nature of communication as it plays out in the evolution of a written text so that they can harness what is useful in that engagement and apply it to later situations. Only in recognizing those origins can we then modify and adapt the practice to meet the needs of both students and communities.

To further connect sustainability and writing studies—that is, to move toward the beginnings of a sustainable writing theory—I draw on the works of Coe and Nedra Reynolds. In his 1975 article, Coe recognizes the need for not only a new way to teach writing, but a new rhetorical approach to communication. He critiques traditional rhetorical modes as "inadequate" to the complexities of contemporary discourse and issues because they "divide wholes into smaller units to be discussed individually or serially" (232). His critique is similar to Killingsworth's critique of how we study workplace situations, using a synecdochal versus holistic or comprehensive approach (372). Coe's 1975 observation is still true today: "many contemporary problems, especially our ecological difficulties, result in part from our using this [traditional Western] logic inappropriately" (232). Coe therefore proposes eco-logic, which, unlike traditional rhetoric, actually seeks to understand situations in their wholeness by following the ecological principle "that meaning is relative to context" (232-33).

It is important to note here that in using metaphors drawn from ecological concepts, we must do so in full awareness of their limitations and even distance from ecological science as practiced and theorized today. Dana Philips, in *The Truth of Ecology*, notes, for example, that the ideas of a connected web of life and holism have been found to be deeply problematic when it comes to ecology, neither recognizing the reductive ways in which ecological science often necessarily operates nor the complexity individual elements bring to any system (60-69, 75). Simply put, these concepts are limiting and just do not fit the complexity of the science. In his book *Ecocriticism*, Greg Garrard, like Philips, cautions against the appropriation by fields such as ecocriticism and ecocomposition of ecological terms "without any acknowledgment of change in use or qualification of meaning" (27). Though Philips does not address the field of writing studies or ecocomposition in his critique, it is important, when using ecological science and concepts to inform writing theory, to recognize, as Philips suggests, the difference between analogy and metaphor and to point out the limitations of outdated and current ecological concepts when applied to writing studies (76). Just as we cannot look at elements in isolation from the system, we cannot understand them as systems without also recognizing them as individual elements. With these qualifications in mind, I argue to expand rather than invalidate Coe's point.

Like Coe, Reynolds advocates a consideration of context in its complexity. Drawing on work in cultural geography, Reynolds notes, "[w]here the work of ecocomposition looks mostly to the natural world, cultural geography focuses on the interaction of the social and the built environment, but the idea of *inhabitance* is crucial to both geographical or ecological theories of writing" (4). Like other ecocompositionists, Reynolds believes the idea of place is central to writing theory. Place can be understood on so many levels, from physical, concrete, and scientific to emotional, abstract, and philosophical. All of these perceptions impact communities. Thus, it can no more be overlooked in a discourse of writing studies than of sustainability studies.

Reynolds contends that the link between the act of composing and context, place, or environment is clear, explaining, "[M]emory and place, location and argument, walking and learning, are vitally and dramatically linked in our personal histories and personal geographies. Places evoke powerful human emotions because they become layered, like sediment or a palimpsest, with histories and stories and memories" (2). Maintaining ecological integrity is crucial to sustainability and requires an understanding of the history and dynamics of a place, just as helping our students to write effectively requires awareness of our contexts and theirs. As writers and audiences, we react, respond, and innovate from a grounding in some *place*. Reynolds argues that theories of writing (like theories of communication and literacy) and, I would add, theories of sustainability, need to demonstrate a keen, multi-layered conception of place or environment.

But there is another side to this, and that is that those of us who teach writing are also, ourselves, writers. When we reflect on our own writing, the path that leads us as individuals to negotiate written text, what philosophy or beliefs guide our writing practices? To what extent do we share that with our students? How close to or far from what we teach is what we do? How do we better align the two? Reynolds recognizes that students "are often transient residents of learning communities" (3). Thus, they differ from us markedly in the classroom environment where we often remain, watching them come and go each semester. And their writing practices, their individual paths and the contexts they bring not only to their writing but also to the classroom, are circumstantially different from ours.

Reynolds describes the phenomenon well when she asserts, "[f]inally, as teachers are faced with students from whom they feel distant, either by age or experience, race or languages, or different access to power, it's important to find common ground, shared spaces of concern, and topics of interest. We share with students and colleagues the everyday realities of material conditions and physical spaces of campuses and towns, buildings and streets" (7). When we feel as if our students leave our classrooms having retained nothing they learned about formatting a paper, citing research, developing a thesis, or eliminating comma splices, we need to ask ourselves how we can teach writing in a way that sustains beyond the classroom—spatially and temporally—with this transient audience. Recognition of common ground is vital to productive discourse in sustainability studies because different stakeholders are often prioritizing different values. Solutions and compromises thus require common ground on which to build. The same is true for writing studies. What common ground do we share with our students in terms of place, experience, values? Where do we differ? Considering what we share and where we differ socially, economically, ecologically, and technologically can open up fruitful lines for discourse that lead to writing that reflects and affects the complex dynamics of the worlds in which we and our students actually live our daily lives.

On the other hand, recognition of differences and celebration of diversity are also important to fostering productive discourse and sustainability, whether the discourse takes place in the writing classroom or a stakeholder meeting. Coe explains that our communications usually occur "in the context of a set of expectations about 'normal' response" (235). We are not always aware of this, especially when we engage individuals or communities who come from similar social and/or cultural backgrounds and therefore "have been socialized to make the same choices that we ourselves make" (235). Thus, Coe emphasizes that meaning is contingent upon context, and this is as true in the world of sustainability discourse as it is in the world of the writing classroom. Maintaining diversity is key to sustaining healthy communities, and recognizing diversity is key to moving toward sustainable solutions. Helping our students to understand the ways we and they perceive relationships to individuals, communities, the ecological, social, economic, and technological world around them—consciously or unconsciously—is thus crucial to our engagement with them as writers. A writing theory informed by sustainability requires writers to recognize both pattern and difference and how they function in the context of particular communication situations at levels that begin locally and extend to the global.

In addition to recognizing patterns and differences, a sustainable theory of writing asks teachers and scholars to reflect on the social equity of writing practices and pedagogy, as well as the ways in which the writing practices and conventions we teach are exclusionary. As Reynolds notes, "[i]n composition studies, it's important to understand the ways in which writers feel alienated from certain discourses or institutional practices, or why new forms of reading and writing are so difficult" (6). This issue is one with which we are all familiar: How do we reach particular individuals in our writing communities? How do we contribute to the sustainability of their own ability to navigate the discourses of our classrooms and their individual environments? By answering these questions, we can begin to address the implications of a sustainable writing theory for research, pedagogy, and our own writing practices.

We ask students to follow rules; we teach them conventions and genres. Yet, Reynolds warns, "[w]e are so intent on figuring out where the borders lie and who can cross them that we may be neglecting the places *constructed by* those borders" (6). If we consider our writing communities as geographic communities in which writing and communication are pivotal, we need to consider elements of what is socially equitable, what preserves the ecological (or contextual) integrity of that community, and what will promote economic stability as individuals and groups within that community operate locally and engage other communities. How, in turn, does the writing taking place, there, then extend to impact the sustainability of our individual geographic and cultural communities? In other words, how can we model in writing theory the frame of practice for our social, professional, political, and geographic environments?

Writing—the teaching and practice of it—exists in a complex system of theory and practice that engages a number of contexts (or environments) and entities (individuals, groups, audiences). Recognizing the ways in which each is connected to the others is crucial to moving toward more sophisticated, dynamic models of writing and theories of writing that fit the communication needs and problems of our current worlds. As we move toward increasing connectivity through technological innovation and globalization, we also contend with increasingly complex environmental, economic, and social challenges on a global scale that often require a kind of glocalization to be addressed sustainably. As technology develops and changes at increasingly faster intervals, as the geography of the world ceases to be a barrier and intercultural collaborations and clashes increase and lead to both benefits and tensions between the global and the local, we need to adapt as well, and we need to prepare our students to do so. While the concept of sustainability is vague and imperfect and its goals are perhaps vague and arguably unattainable, the pursuit of them follows a particular ethical and logical path that invokes a series of questions we can also ask about any communication situation. A writing theory informed by sustainability studies allows for a new level of complexity and variability in navigating the communication situations of our dynamic and increasingly globalized world.

I believe discourse at the nexus of sustainability and writing studies can lead to language that is effective in this and many other ways. Are there ways we can teach the personal narrative assignment that better prepare students to not only engage that world but also contribute to the sustainability of the global and local communities to which they belong? Are there ways we can foreground peer review so that students recognize its implications and parallels to the professional and social world in which they will continue to evolve as writers? How can we frame the annotated bibliography so that it is more than an academic exercise for an academic genre? Many individuals, to be sure, are already doing these things. But not all. And if we cannot tell students the why, how can we expect them to be on board with the what and the how? They need to understand the system to be able to negotiate writing their ways into and through it. That understanding should include an understanding of certain elements as they relate to writing and global and local contexts, including rhetorical situation and socio/cultural/historical context and ecological integrity; audience and social equity; persuasion, intellectual property, and economic stability; and technology.

Reynolds suggests, and I agree, that our current age (into the foreseeable future) requires new metaphors for space and place that move beyond linear and bounded concepts to reflect emerging technologies and dynamic populations (5). Technological innovations have changed not only how we perceive and define places, but also how and with what we write. As an example of the inadequacies of current metaphors in practice, she discusses the idea of drafts in an age when most composing is done with computers. Indeed, most teachers of writing are familiar with the difficulty of having students show significant revision between drafts. This does not mean they are not revising—it means that revision is harder to snapshot because it takes place "on screen in a more fluid, spatial medium that doesn't lend itself very well to 'frozen' representations" (6). How do we innovate metaphors and pedagogies to make the nuances of the act of writing more visible given these technological modes in order to raise our students' awareness of the environments in which they write and to help us help them?

When we consider writing contexts in terms of the elements of sustainability as vital to a community's success, we have an adaptable model on which to build pedagogy and practice. In order to help our students, it is productive to envision discourses as places with the same needs and elements vital to their sustainability as physical places and geographical communities. Writing theory informed by sustainability studies emphasizes what Coe describes as "systemic interrelations instead of analytic separations" (237). This kind of rhetoric is not only adaptable, guided more by principles than rules, but it also allows us to create meaningful discourse about the complex ecological, social, economic, and technological contexts in which we must act and write on a daily basis.

As technological innovations generate more varied modes of communication with different opportunities and limitations, we need a writing theory that can adapt with the modes without compromising the integrity and effectiveness of writing itself. Who is to say, for example, that our written language will not become more symbolic of rather than transcriptive of spoken language? What if texting becomes standardized and conventional for all nonverbal modes of communication? Writing may still be taught, but the ways in which we approach practice and pedagogy will have to adapt accordingly. We want to avoid both the extremes of Newspeak and Babel.

Writing pedagogy is not just about teaching our students models for good writing—it is about teaching them to think critically, to innovate ideas through the engagement of texts and the world, and to articulate them effectively following certain principles and using the available technological means for communication to the best effect, just as sustainable solutions in our physical environments require a merging of contextual knowledge, guiding principles, and innovation.

Conclusion

I am not saying that a sustainability theory of writing or writing practice should preach ideology or particular political views—one need not be an environmentalist or liberal, nor encourage students to be such. But there is nothing one-sided about the very real concern that we are perpetuating a world that may not be able to sustain itself into the future, and that we are teaching writing—a tool for communicating, for effecting change and moving societies forward—in this world. Effective writing is successful because it engages these elements, just as a successful plan for the future of a community must engage the elements of ecological integrity, social equity, economic stability, and technological innovation.

So, what principles might guide a sustainable writing theory? Though I agree with Killingsworth in his assertion, quoted earlier in this essay, that a discourse should not be reduced to bullet points, for the sake of clarity, I will do just that. Thus, my position is that a sustainable writing theory should consider:

- ecological, economic, social, technological, and moral accountability in the practice, study, and teaching of writing;
- the impact of ecological, economic, social, and technological innovations on individuals' writing and discourse communities generally in terms of both processes, development, and outcomes;
- the phenomenon of writing itself as grounded in place (defined broadly in its multidimensional complexity);
- classroom practice as continuously and directly connected to local and global communities, including real possibilities for student writing in writing classes and across disciplines to effect change within communities;
- ongoing adaptation of pedagogy and genres to the learning, cultural, and spatial needs and contexts of individuals and communities over time;
- accessibility and usability for a particular community in any piece of writing, which includes asking who has access and who is excluded and what factors (medium, content, etc.) enhance or impede access and use.

The challenge now for theorists of writing and sustainability is to develop all of these individual points so that a fully formed sustainable writing theory can emerge.

Note

1. In their book *Ecospeak: Rhetoric and Environmental Politics in America*, Killingsworth and Palmer demonstrate the importance of accessibility of writing to social equity and empowerment, noting several ways accessibility is achieved in writing, "including informative headings; topic sentences; thumbnail essays and narratives; active-voice sentences and strong action verbs; concrete and familiar vocabulary; carefully selected, low-density tables and charts; and other graphical devices to enhance readability" (254).

Works Cited

Coe, Richard M. "Eco-Logic for the Composition Classroom." *College Composition and Communication* 26.3 (Oct 1975): 232-37. Print.

Cooper, Marilyn M. "The Ecology of Writing." *College English* 48.4 (Apr. 1986): 364-375. Print.

Davison, Aidan. *Technology and the Contested Meanings of Sustainability*. New York: State U of New York P, 2001.Print.

Dawe, Neil K., and Kenneth L. Ryan. "The Faulty Three-Legged Stool Model of Sustainable Development." *Conservation Biology* 17.5 (2003): 1458-60. Print.

Dobrin, Sidney I. "Post-/Ecocomposition." Becoming Ecocomposition. Conference on College Composition and Communication. San Francisco, CA. 13 March 2009. Featured speaker.

———. "Writing Takes Place." *Ecocomposition: Theoretical and Pedagogical Approaches*. Eds. Christian R. Weisser and Sidney I. Dobrin. New York: State U of New York P, 2001. 11-25. Print.

Dobrin, Sidney I. and Christian R. Weisser. "Breaking Ground in Ecocomposition: Exploring Relationships between Discourse and Environment." *College English* 64.5 (May 2002): 566-89. Print.

Edwards, Andrés R. *The Sustainability Revolution: Portrait of a Paradigm Shift*. Gabriola Island, BC: New Society P, 2005. Print.

Garrard, Greg. *Ecocriticism*. New York: Routledge, 2004. Print.

Killingsworth, M. Jimmie. "From Environmental Rhetoric to Ecocomposition and Ecopoetics: Finding a Place for Professional Communication." *Technical Communication Quarterly* 14.4 (2005): 359-73. Print.

Killingsworth, M. Jimmie, and Jacqueline S. Palmer. *Ecospeak: Rhetoric and Environmental Politics in America*. Carbondale: Southern Illinois UP, 1992. Print.

Orr, David W. "Four Challenges of Sustainability." *Conservation Biology* 16.6 (2002): 1457-60. Print.

Owens, Derek. *Composition and Sustainability: Teaching for a Threatened Generation*. Urbana, IL: NCTE, 2001. Print.

———. "Sustainable Composition." *Ecocomposition: Theoretical and Pedagogical Approaches*. Eds. Christian R. Weisser and Sidney I. Dobrin. New York: State U of New York P, 2001. 27-37. Print.

Palmer, Jason, Ian Cooper, and Rita van der Vorst. "Mapping Out Fuzzy Buzzwords—Who Sits Where on Sustainability and Sustainable Development." *Sustainable Development* 5 (1997): 87-93. Print.

Philips, Dana. *The Truth of Ecology: Nature, Culture, and Literature in America*. New York: Oxford UP, 2003. Print.

Reynolds, Nedra. *Geographies of Writing: Inhabiting Places and Encountering Difference*. Carbondale: Southern Illinois UP, 2004. Print.

Rogers, Everett M. *Diffusion of Innovations*. 1962. 4th ed. New York: The Free P, 1995. Print.

Syverson, Margaret A. *The Wealth of Reality: An Ecology of Composition*. Carbondale: Southern Illinois UP, 1999. Print.

[WCED] United Nations World Commission on Environment and Development. *Our Common Future: Report of the World Commission on Environment and Development*. Oxford: Oxford UP, 1987. Print.

Weisser, Christian R., and Sidney I. Dobrin, eds. *Ecocomposition: Theoretical and Pedagogical Approaches*. New York: State U of New York P, 2001. Print.

"Sustaining Writing Theory" from *Composition Forum* 21 (Spring 2010) Online at: http://compositionforum.com/issue/21/sustaining-writing-theory.php

© Copyright 2010 Amy M. Patrick. Licensed under a Creative Commons Attribution-Share Alike License. For more information, see http://compositionforum.com/editorial-policy.php.

COMPOSITION STUDIES

Composition Studies is on the Web at http://www.compositionstudies.uwinnipeg.ca/index.html

In publication since March 1972, *Composition Studies* holds the distinction of being the oldest independent journal in the field of rhetoric and composition. Composition Studies is an academic journal dedicated to the range of professional practices associated with the field: teaching college writing; theorizing rhetoric and composing; administering writing related programs; preparing the field's future teacher-scholars. Currently *Composition Studies* is the only periodical in writing studies to cross international borders, moving from Texas to Winnipeg, Canada in 2010. The current editor is Jennifer Clary-Lemon.

"An Inconvenient Tool: Rethinking the Role of Slideware in the Writing Classroom" by Laurie E. Gries and Collin Gifford Brooke

In "An Inconvenient Tool: Rethinking the Role of Slideware in the Writing Classroom," Laurie E. Gries and Collin Gifford Brooke reconsider the affordances of slide presentation software—PowerPoint—as an important technology for writing and design. Using the presentation method of Pecha Kucha as a model, they advocate teaching students to work within presentation constraints (e.g., 20 slides each displayed for 20 seconds) as a means of constructing arguments, rather than simply delivering completed ones. This important resituating of "the presentation" enables students' visual thinking, promotes authentic dialogue in the classroom, and can revitalize student work throughout all stages of the composing process.

An Inconvenient Tool: Rethinking the Role of Slideware in the Writing Classroom

Laurie E. Gries and Collin Gifford Brooke

Every so often, a technology will saturate the market to the extent that the name of the product becomes a stand-in for the technology itself, like Kleenex or Xerox. While it belongs to the broader genre of slideware,[1] Microsoft PowerPoint is perhaps the best example of software that has achieved that level of ubiquity. Despite Apple's Keynote, the Presentation Editor within Google Docs, Zoho Show, and others, the visual display of sequential slides (most typically during an oral presentation) has become synonymous with PowerPoint. Although it has achieved this level of popularity, PowerPoint is also considered by many to be synonymous with mind-numbing boredom, painful expository bullet points, and the overexposure of the Microsoft clip art library. That is, PowerPoint may be used widely, but it is just as widely disparaged, and often used only begrudgingly. For all of the success PowerPoint has achieved as a piece of software, it has inspired an equal amount of dismay in dimly lit classrooms, boardrooms, and conferences across the world.

To imagine, then, that a PowerPoint presentation might win an Academy Award sounds absurd, like someone receiving a Pulitzer Prize for a five-paragraph theme. And yet, in 2007, *An Inconvenient Truth*, the documentary based upon Al Gore's slideshow about global warming, received two Academy Awards (for best documentary and best original song). By the time the film was released, Gore himself estimated that he had delivered his presentation more than a thousand times; combined with the worldwide success of the documentary, this suggests that millions of people have seen this single slideshow, and presumably acted upon the message it was designed to support. Nancy Duarte explains in *slide:ology* that Gore "has done more than any other individual to legitimize multimedia presentations as one of the most compelling communication vehicles on the planet" (86). While the rehabilitation of slideware may seem a negligible benefit when compared to the political and environmental impact of *Inconvenient Truth*, we would argue that the success of Gore's documentary is merely the most visible example of a larger movement towards a re-legitimation of PowerPoint and slideware more broadly. This movement has emerged, in part, by redefining the terms according to which we think about multimedia presentations. As we discuss below, PowerPoint has been articulated as an inferior information technology, incapable of the kind of information density possible with other media. Industry professionals like Duarte and Garr Reynolds, however, refuse to engage this critique of PowerPoint on those terms, seeing it instead as a rich environment for the practice of multimedia rhetoric, as opposed to information delivery.

In rhetoric and composition, we are more likely to hold to the former position, seeing slideware as a necessary evil at best. Although we in the academy hold different goals and motives, our opinions of presentation software have generally run parallel to those of the business world. It is time that we reconsider our received opinions regarding slideware, and listen closely to the new voices (and visions) of presentation and design experts. After all, some of the leading thinkers in technology-related fields, such as Lawrence Lessig and Steve Jobs, are among slideware's most dynamic presenters. Others such as Daniel Pink are encouraging us to make more room for creativity in our thinking, suggesting that critiques of PowerPoint may not provide us with the whole story when it comes to considering slideware. We argue below that when used in dynamic, inventive ways, slideware can become an integral and productive part of our pedagogical and technological repertoires. We believe it is time to set aside our mistrust and disdain for software like PowerPoint and consider carefully how it might aid us in the teaching of writing. Using the presentation format Pecha Kucha as a model, we offer productive reasons and ways to reconfigure the role of slideware in the composing process. Slideware design and delivery can play a creative and inventive role in our students' making of writing.

THE RISE AND FALL (AND RISE?) OF POWERPOINT

Because we have generally accepted the terms of the PowerPoint "debate" as it has played out in public discourse—going so far sometimes as to teach Edward Tufte's and others' critiques of the software—it is worth reviewing that debate, and understanding the values implied there, before we explore slideware's specific application in the classroom. Understanding how professionals like Reynolds and Duarte are positioning slideware can provide us with useful guidance as we consider it for adoption.

In part, the return to slideware is a response to the public backlash against PowerPoint that followed its meteoric rise to popularity. In a 2001 *New Yorker* article titled "Absolute PowerPoint," for example, Ian Parker claimed that PowerPoint "is software you impose on other people" (76). Parker details PowerPoint's success, its presence at the confluence of factors like the changing structure of industry in the 1960s and 1970s, the emergence of affordable personal computers in the 1980s, and the fear that most people have of public speaking. "Because PowerPoint can be an impressive antidote to fear," Parker explains, "there seems to be no great impulse to fight th[e] influence" of PowerPoint itself, or of the templates supplied with the program (78). There is an unevenness to Parker's treatment of PowerPoint in the article, however—an uncertainty about whether or not the ubiquity of PowerPoint is worth taking seriously. On the one hand, he explains that PowerPoint

> has a private, interior influence. It edits ideas. It is, almost surreptitiously, a business manual as well as a business suit, with an opinion—an oddly pedantic, prescriptive opinion—about the way we should think. It helps you make a case, but it also makes its own case: about how to organize information, how much information to organize, how to look at the world. (76)

Implied in Parker's more serious descriptions is the question of whether any software should play as large a role as PowerPoint seems to in the shaping of our ideas. And yet this question alternates throughout with amused accounts of the "joke" of the Auto-Content Wizard, product development being driven by marketing departments, a housewife driving her children to tears with slideshows about "domestic harmony," and the infamous PowerPoint translation-parody of the

Gettysburg Address. Despite both anecdotal and empirical evidence of PowerPoint's effect on information and subsequent audience judgments, one has the impression from Parker that to take PowerPoint too seriously would result in becoming the anonymous user who admits "I caught myself planning out (in my head) the slides I would need to explain to my wife why we couldn't afford a vacation this year" (78).

If there is some ambivalence to Parker's account of PowerPoint, there is none in Edward Tufte's scathing critique of the software, his 2003, self-published essay, "The Cognitive Style of PowerPoint: Pitching Out Corrupts Within." The cover visual for his essay is instructive: Tufte adds several thought and speech balloons to a picture of Stalin Square in Budapest, with comments like, "There's no bullet list like Stalin's bullet list!" and "For re-education campaigns, nothing is better than the Auto-Content Wizard!" The humor of these additions is strained at best; underlying it is a strong sense of disapproval, if not outright contempt, for PowerPoint, and the core of Tufte's argument is deadly serious. In what is perhaps the conceptual centerpiece of the essay, Tufte places on two facing pages a single slide from the NASA slideshow that preceded the 2003 explosion of the space shuttle Columbia. The slide is surrounded by several paragraphs of Tufte's detailed commentary critiquing the "festival of bureaucratic hyperrationalism" (10) represented there. Each slide in the presentation, according to Tufte, contains "4 to 6 levels of hierarchy," provides no continuity from slide to slide, and ultimately serves to complicate and obscure what are already difficult technical issues. Eventually, Tufte cites the Columbia Accident Investigation Board's report in support of his own conclusions "that the distinctive cognitive style of PowerPoint reinforced the hierarchical filtering and biases of the NASA bureaucracy during the crucial period when the Columbia was damaged but still functioning" (12). It would perhaps be a stretch to blame the Columbia disaster on PowerPoint, but, as Tufte makes clear, not much of one. "The language, attitude, and presentation tool of the pitch culture had penetrated throughout the NASA organization, even into the most serious technical analysis, the survival of the shuttle" (12). Whether or not we want to go so far as to blame the presentation tool, Tufte is clear that PowerPoint had a marked effect on the communications of the organization and fatal consequences for the crew of the Columbia. Tufte's claims circulated well beyond the traditional audience for such analysis; his condemnation of PowerPoint was not only covered by

Wired but by Sunday's *New York Times Magazine* under the headline "PowerPoint Makes You Dumb." Tufte's essay has also appeared in countless classrooms, an archetypal critique of the problems of uncritically adopting and using software.

As a result of his critique's ubiquity, if there is one person who has done more to shape the academy's attitude towards slideware, it is probably Tufte. But it is worth considering in more detail the perspective compositionists have endorsed. In one sense, Tufte is an obvious ally for writing teachers; as he explains, "Serious problems require a serious tool: written reports" (14). Although an abbreviated form of Tufte's essay appeared in *Wired* with the headline "PowerPoint is Evil," his broader argument is not that PowerPoint is essentially wrong, but rather that print writing is more important than we sometimes imagine. In the case of Columbia, information was circulating, as well as decisions made that were based upon that information, in a form inappropriate to the detail and sophistication needed. The second major argument that Tufte offers in his essay has to do with information density and PowerPoint users' tendency to compromise density in favor of readable font sizes, copious negative space, and meaningless clip art. Given the criterion of information density, Tufte finds PowerPoint wanting on almost every level. The "simple tables" permitted by slides are compared with John Graunt's 1662 "Table of Causalities," which, as Tufte explains, would have required 155 slides to present what Graunt accomplishes in a single page. Standard injunctions about the number of bullet points per slide and words per line reduce potentially complex topics to the diction of first-grade reading primers. In short, Tufte explains, "The PP slide format has the worst signal/noise ratio of any known method of communication on paper or computer screen" (26). As a discipline devoted, in many ways, to the "signal," it is unsurprising that we would find these arguments persuasive.

There have been a few challenges to Tufte's conclusions, however, worth considering; one such appeared from Donald Norman, whose work on design qualifies him easily as a peer of Tufte's. In a 2004 interview with Cliff Atkinson, Norman lays out the ideas that would later turn into an essay, "In Defense of PowerPoint," published at his own website. In that essay, Norman describes Tufte's conclusions as "nonsense;" he argues that the NASA slides, however poorly executed, reflected similarly mistaken findings on the part of the engineers. "The fault is with the findings, not with the slides . . . they highlighted the information they thought important and minimized the parts they thought not important. That is the absolutely proper way to present a set of recommendations" ("In Defense"). Norman's broader point is that information density is a standard more appropriate to the reader than the listener, and that "the speech giver should really develop three different documents:" personal notes, slides, and handouts, each designed to meet different goals as part of a presentation. From a disciplinary perspective, Norman qualifies Tufte's argument in an important way: information density is not a context-independent value. This doesn't necessarily invalidate Tufte's critique, nor does it absolve poor presentations of any responsibility. But it should prompt us to think about those contexts where PowerPoint might actually be appropriate and, used well, a platform that can enrich the role of design and delivery in our writing pedagogies. As design takes a more central place in composition pedagogy, the PowerPoint renaissance that has occurred in the business and design world in recent years challenges us to consider the role of slideware more seriously.

Matters of Slideware Design

As evident in a growing number of articles and textbooks in our field, design has a growing influence in composition pedagogy; Richard Marback refers to it in a recent issue of *College Composition and Communication* as a "centripetal interest" for our discipline (398). In a 2001 *Philosophy and Rhetoric* article, Richard Buchanan suggests we can think of design as "the human power of conceiving, planning, and making products that serve human beings in the accomplishment of any individual or collective purpose" (qtd. in "Design" 191). To think of design, then, as "styling of appearance of products," Buchanan argues, is a serious misconception of what the work of designing entails (194). Like rhetoric, design is an art of forethought, whose work occurs deeply in the act of invention, arrangement, and production. Design, like rhetoric, is a productive act of making.

Anne Wysocki and Dennis Lynch's handbook, *Compose, Design, Advocate*, is perhaps the most explicit in articulating the important function of design can play in the writing classroom. While acknowledging that the discipline of composition has always been closely linked with rhetoric, Wysocki and Lynch point out that because of changes in communication technologies, particularly the digital, thinking about design has become especially pertinent. As Wysocki and Lynch point out, the fields of composition and rhetoric and design share similar concerns—"both are concerned with audiences and with how audiences respond to what we make" (5). Yet, design also differs from composition and rhetoric in that design is more concerned with: a) the material and creative process of composing; b) testing the audience's experiences with the products; and c) the future functions of the product once it enters into circulation. Such concerns, Wysocki and Lynch note, have the potential to enhance our students' composing processes as they learn to anticipate and consider the responses their artifacts might invoke in the daily lives of their audience.

Students also, and perhaps most importantly, learn to consider which different media are most appropriate to use in achieving their rhetorical goals. Because PowerPoint has gotten a "bad rap" in recent years from figures such as Tufte, the innovative and rhetorical potential of slideware is often overlooked. Contemporary designers, however, make a strong case as to why slideware presentations should take a more important role in the writing classroom. The design of slideware cannot only enhance our students' abilities to think creatively about problems that matter, but also to communicate clearly in designs that matter. In addition, slideware design makes use of whole- mind aptitudes, which many argue are needed to communicate successfully and persuasively in today's global arena.

Nancy Duarte's book *slide:ology: The Art and Science of Generating Great Presentations* is one text that makes a strong case for thinking about slideware as an innovative writing technology that can boost our students' creative thinking. Duarte—the designer behind *An Inconvenient Truth*—situates PowerPoint at the tail end of a long history of visual storytelling that begins nearly 2,000 years ago with the oldest cave painting found to date in Lascaux, France. Duarte rejects Tufte's argument that PowerPoint reduces the analytical quality of presentations and weakens verbal and spatial reasoning. Instead, she suggests that PowerPoint can be a productive visual aid for generating innovative ideas and communicating creatively, clearly, and effectively for a given audience. As evidence, in *slide:ology* Duarte illustrates how PowerPoint design is revitalizing the role of multimedia presentations in the business world. Case studies are woven throughout her text to illustrate how creative PowerPoint presentations are not only saving business people from committing "career suislide," but also enhancing the production and reception of presentations performed by today's most innovative thinkers. At intellectual gatherings such as the highly prestigious TED and PopTech conferences, the innovative role of slideware is certainly pervasive, giving rise, in many people's opinion, to some of the most compelling media presentations ever produced.

In *slide:ology* Duarte offers composition teachers and students a useful framework for thinking about the development process of slideware as a "presentation ecosystem" constituted by an interdependence of innovative ideas, effective (rhetorical, in essence) delivery, and visual design (11). Too often, visual design in composition classrooms is simply thought of as an act and sign of "academic decorum" (George 25). Students, in other words, use visual design to demonstrate their attention to document design. In slideware, this act translates to mere concern with representation. *slide:ology* demonstrates how visual design is actually a highly conceptual and creative communicative act that can help students solve problems by generating new ideas. For instance, by sketching ideas and creating diagrams to communicate abstract ideas in their slide presentations, students can find relationships between information that leads to new insights and generates deeper understanding between audience and presenter. In *slide:ology* the creative process of designing slides is positioned, in other words, as not simply the representation of ideas but rather the generation of ideas. In this sense, slideware becomes an important means of invention, dispelling notions of slideware simply as a means of delivery.

Garr Reynolds's book *Presentation Zen,* in conjunction with its active accompanying website, also offers composition teachers and students a fresh outlook on the productive possibilities afforded by slideware design. Garr Reynolds is a leading consultant in presentation design and delivery for Fortune 500 companies around the globe. He conceived the idea for this book after growing frustrated by the ubiquity of poorly designed and difficult-to-understand presentations riddled with bullet points, crammed text, and egregious clip art. Reynolds calls such poorly and thoughtlessly designed slide presentations "slideuments," which he claims are created more from a desire to save time rather than generate effective presentations. Reynolds argues that PowerPoint as a tool is not to blame, however. If used to create simple, balanced, and beautiful designs in conjunction with a well-crafted story and delivery style, PowerPoint presentations can be highly effective in achieving one's communicative goal(s). Unlike the conventional demonizations of PowerPoint by Parker, Tufte, and others, Reynolds argues and illustrates that PowerPoint is a tool capable of creating intelligent, emotional, and effective communication.

Reynolds's book offers students an "approach" to slideware rather than a method, one that relies heavily on Zen principles[2] relating to aesthetics, mindfulness, and connectedness. As Reynolds explains, a method of presentation design and delivery might offer a set of design rules to be adhered to by everyone in the same way. In contrast, the philosophical approach of *presentationzen* emphasizes a flexible path to designing and delivering presentations that encourage audience awareness, creativity, and discovery (25). Reynolds's main argument can be essentially wrapped up in one line: *Design Matters to Clear Communication.* Reiterating Duarte's argument that design is not about decoration or ornamentation, Reynolds emphasizes that design is, to a great extent, about making communication as easy and clear as possible for one's viewers (163). Thus, design matters because audience matters—a lesson we cannot impress enough upon our students in the composition classroom. To achieve simple, clear, and effective communication, Reynolds suggests being constantly mindful of the principles of restraint, simplicity, and naturalness: "Restraint in preparation. Simplicity in design. Naturalness in delivery" (7). Such mindfulness, he argues, has the potential to generate innovative and effective communication, especially if it becomes a permanent way of thinking about design and delivery.

The design values embodied in both Reynolds's and Duarte's ideas on presentation and delivery are aligned with contemporary notions about the role of creative thinking and design in effective persuasion. While writing instructors might not typically look to contemporary arguments made about communication offered in best selling business books, such arguments challenge us in productive ways to rethink the relation between slideware design and persuasion. Reynolds's approach, for instance, draws deeply on Daniel Pink's right-brain aptitudes as discussed in *A Whole New Mind.* In composition and rhetoric classrooms, analytical thinking is often the privileged form of knowing that we teach in relation to rhetoric and argument. Pink would argue that such logical, linear, and analytical, or left-brain thinking, skills are no longer sufficient to prepare students to communicate effectively in the "Conceptual Age" in which we presently find ourselves. According to Pink, students need to develop "high concept" aptitudes, which include detecting patterns and opportunities, generating creative and emotional beauty, crafting appealing narratives, and synthesizing unrelated ideas to generate new ones (2). Pink especially emphasizes that it is not enough to make logical arguments in order to persuade. We need to be able to create compelling narratives, which Pink argues is at the heart of effective persuasion. In addition, while analysis is obviously still necessary, the ability to empathize and synthesize, see the big picture, and identify interconnectivity is increasingly becoming important to successful global communication. From a design perspective, these abilities, which are fostered through slideware design, are needed to communicate effectively and create effective presentations in today's professional world.

Arguments about the importance of design to persuasion are also evident in Chip Heath and Dan Heath's principles for communicating ideas that stick. In their book, *Made to Stick,* Heath and Heath argue that "sticky" ideas have six common principles: simplicity, unexpectedness, concreteness, credibility, emotions, and stories. Too often, Heath and Heath argue, presenters suffer from what they call the "Curse of Knowledge"—the condition whereby the deliverer overestimates an audience's background knowledge about the topic at hand. Presenters who suffer this condition often create abstract claims that are perfectly clear to the presenter, but barely, if at all, comprehendible to the audience. Scholars who attend highly theoretical conference presentations in our own field will recognize this curse. Too often conference presentations couched in dense theories and discourse fail to make an impact on an audience, not because their ideas are not smart and important, but simply because the language is too abstract for an audience to absorb in a 20-minute session falling in the midst of a long day of conference-going. Their ideas simply are too abstract to stick. Heath and Heath offer a counterargument to Tufte's claim that PowerPoint has too poor of a signal/noise ratio to be effective or appropriate by arguing for the value of a low signal/noise ratio in slideware presentations. While Tufte would argue slideware lacks the ability to convey complex ideas needed in specific rhetorical situations, Heath and Heath—alongside Reynolds and Duarte—argue that simplifying a message actually amplifies the clarity and effect of a complex message. Heath and Heath suggest avoiding too many statistics or, in our field, too many dense quotes, which often stem from over-attempts to establish one's credibility. In addition, Heath and Heath advocate for surprising the audience and speaking of concrete images to increase the stickiness of a message. Making some kind of emotional connections with our audiences and incorporating an element of story in our presentations are also effective ways to create persuasive messages that audience members will remember.

While such principles for effective communication and persuasion, offered by experts in the design and business worlds, may not seem profound or even new to scholars of rhetoric and composition, these applied principles encourage us to rethink the value of slideware design in our classrooms. Unlike Parker, Tufte, and others who see little value in PowerPoint's ability to generate and deliver innovative ideas, design professionals such as Duarte and Reynolds argue and illustrate that we ought to take slideware more seriously as a creative and intelligent tool. First, integrating slideware into our pedagogy has the potential to enhance certain aptitudes and design perspectives that can make students more effective communicators. Second, if taught as a process, slideware can help bridge verbal, visual, and oral communication skills, which still so often get divorced in much writing pedagogy. Also, in addition to improving our students' chances to make their ideas stick, slideware presentation, as we aim to illustrate in the next section, can especially help students realize and make use of design's inventive affordances. For these reasons, we argue it is time that writing teachers take slideware more seriously in our writing classrooms.

SLIDEWARE IN THE CLASSROOM

Integrating slideware successfully and meaningfully into our classrooms depends on rethinking the role and location of delivery in the composing process and reconsidering the productivity of constraint writing, presentation design, and visual thinking. In rethinking the role of delivery, James Porter and others argue that we need to think about how delivery connects to productive, inventional thinking rather than simply a means to disseminate information. For many of us, such reconfiguration of delivery works against all that we have been taught about the composing process. As Kathleen Yancey notes in her recently published NCTE report *Writing in the 21st Century*, in print-based models of composing, delivery has long been associated with publication or presentation—the final stage of the writing process. The writing process, of course, has been taught as recursive; we all know that invention, style, revision, and arrangement do not happen in chronological order. However, in terms of recursivity, at least in many of our classrooms, delivery by and large has been, and still is, conceived and taught as the final act of the composing process—or in more ecological terms, the final stage in the life cycle of a text. As the final stage, the role of delivery is simply to translate one's print-based arguments into oral, visual, or multi-media form and to present one's final arguments to a broader audience. As such, in writing instruction, John Trimbur argues, "delivery has been an afterthought at best, assigned mainly to technical and professional communication and associated largely with such matters of document design as page layout, typography, visual display of information, and Web design ("Composition" 190). Delivery, in other words, is a "technical issue about physical presentation" rather than a practice of invention (190). It is the final touch we put on our already completed written ideas, one that has little to do with the ideas themselves.

A visualization of presentation or delivery being the "last act" cannot be more palpable than in Ruth Culham and Vicki Spandel's 6 + 1 Trait framework. This model is billed as an assessment method, but it is currently being used all over the nation as a writing instruction method for secondary English education. According to this model, presentation is the "+1," added onto and othered from the list of more core traits of idea development and organization. In addition, presentation is positioned outside the recursive process, which only encompasses pre-writing, drafting, responding, and revision. Such frameworks are reinforced in our college composition classrooms when we assign PowerPoints as the culminating assignment in our curricula—when we ask students to visually and orally express their ideas that they have already thought through, polished, and presented in formal writing assignments.

This truncation of delivery as a final, almost inessential, stage in the composing process positions it as exterior to invention. In Derridean terms, delivery conceived here is a supplement, both in that the role of delivery is created by its opposition to invention and that is it is often seen as an unsuitable substitute for invention. As supplement, delivery cannot be trusted as a core trait (if we want to use that term), nor can it be "trusted" as a productive stage in the composing process with the potential to help students develop creative and analytical thought. Continuing to conceive of and to teach delivery according to traditional print-based models of composing necessarily limits the role that slideware might play in the composing process. Using the presentation format Pecha Kucha as a model, we aim to illustrate how slideware can provide writers with meaningful acts of rhetorical transformation, especially when we permit invention to be constituted by delivery, resituating it to a more productive place in our writing curricula.

Pecha Kucha is a contemporary form of presentation design and delivery[3] revitalizing the role of PowerPoint in the design world. The method of Pecha Kucha entails telling a story in sync with 20 slides, shown for 20 seconds each. As Daniel Pink has described the format, "That's it. Say what you need to say in six minutes and 40 seconds and then sit the hell down." Pecha Kucha derives from the Japanese term for "the sound of conversation" or "chit-chat." As originally conceived by Astrid Klein and Mark Dytham, this presentation format affords designers a brief, but potent, means to share their work in public spaces with other designers. In other words, Pecha Kucha began as a designer's adult version of "show and tell." Since its inception in Tokyo in 2003, Pecha Kucha nights have become a global phenomenon in which professionals from the design, architecture, photography, and other creative fields meet, network, and present their current work in public venues.

In the writing classroom, the Pecha Kucha format has transformative affordances that emerge when slideware is used to construct arguments rather than present *already* composed, written arguments. To a great extent, these features emerge when we ask students to work with format and design constraints. In *The Laws of Simplicity,* John Maeda explains, "In the design world, there is the belief that with more constraints, better solutions are revealed" (qtd. in Reynolds 39). Extending this point, Reynolds also argues, "[C]onstraints and limitations are a powerful ally, not an enemy" (39). Working within constraints with the trust that restrictions can be liberators, Reynolds claims, creates clear and powerful messages (39). In the composition classroom, constrained writing has been under-appreciated. As Jan Baetens explains, we can think of constrained writing as "the use of any type of formal technique or program whose application is able to produce a sense of its making text by itself, if need be without any previous "idea" from the writer" ("Freewriting" 2). A constraint-ruled text is opposed to a text in which an author attempts to articulate an idea that was realized before he or she sits down to write (2). Typically, in the composition classroom, we associate constrained writing with a current-traditionalist approach and thus neglect to explore how constraints can be an important part of the inventive process. Yet, as Baetens make clear, constraints can act as a meaningful imaginative tool if an integrated relationship is created between constraints and the entire production process.

Baetens distinguishes between dissociative and integrative processes of constrained writing. Dissociative approaches ask students to work with one constraint in the production of a text. When constructing a Pecha Kucha, for instance, a dissociative approach would impose one rule students must abide by, such as using two sentences per slide and in conjunction with one image. Working within the confines of a single contrived constraint, students are able to dissociate from the design process to a certain degree. An integrative approach, on the other hand, asks students to work with permanent constraints throughout the whole production of their Pecha Kuchas. Unlike a dissociative model, in an integrative process, constraints have the potential to mutually shape all parameters of the work (Baetens). An integrative approach to creating Pecha Kuchas is encouraged when we ask students to abide by presentation design principles forwarded by Reynolds to tell the story of their 10-12 page first-draft, researched arguments in 6 minute and 40 second Pecha Kuchas. Design constraints are conceived as aesthetic values, rather than rules, to be considered through every step of the production process. For example, students are asked to strive for simplicity, balance, subtlety, elegance, naturalness, and tranquility. These values are achieved by using empty space, relevant elements or information, clear and simple display of information, 2-D rather than 3-D representations, repetition of visual elements, contrast, alignment, etc. These design principles, offered by both Reynolds and Duarte, place constraints on slide design throughout the entire production of Pecha Kuchas. In terms of the oral part of their presentation, students are encouraged to avoid reading from a script, move from behind the podium, keep the lights on, and attempt to make some kind of emotional connection with the audience. While these constraints often intimidate students, we also have begun to observe many students taking risks and generating dynamic presentations. Thus, rather than act as creative obstacles, such integrated interaction with constraints stimulates visual play and innovative presentation design.

Constraints, although difficult to work with, help students create visual presentations that are rhetorically powerful. When positioned as rhetorical strategies, students' design choices help them achieve their communicative goals. Yet even more importantly, the integrated process of working with constraints is transformative, especially when we relocate delivery to the middle of our students composing process. In our critical research and writing courses[4], for instance, students begin by crafting full drafts of a written argument. Students then research for, design, and craft their Pecha Kuchas with the goal of narrating the exigency for their study, their findings, and their current arguments about the topic at hand. Students present their ideas in a Pecha Kucha to the class during a Pecha Kucha Night event. After they present their Pecha Kuchas, and the class discusses them, we ask the students to go back to the page to reconstruct their arguments in light of that discussion. Integrating the design and presentation of Pecha Kuchas *into* the composing process helps students revise their initial print-based arguments, not only in terms of organization but also in the development of ideas. The 20 x 20 slideware format obliges students to identify and emphasize only the most relevant ideas in their longer arguments. In rewriting their final print documents, students often omit material included in their original print arguments when they realize it was not significant enough to include in their Pecha Kuchas. At the same time, students often end up rearranging their final written essays to create a more coherent argument. Constructing Pecha Kuchas helps students understand how their written arguments could be more effectively arranged on the page. As a result of deploying slideware *during* the composing process, rather than as an afterthought, students craft powerful narratives that end up resulting in tighter and sharper arguments on the page.

When finding visuals to include in their Pecha Kuchas, students also often discover new information that extends, complicates, and contradicts their previous arguments. Some students even realize that the original focus of their previous arguments is no longer the main point they want to or need to be focusing on. Students develop new ideas, in other words, by working through the composing process of creating their Pecha Kuchas. In an interview with Nancy Duarte about her work with Al Gore, Duarte explains that Gore was "constantly learning from each presentation and refining his message and his visuals along the way" ("Duarte Design"). Similarly, Pecha Kucha stimulates rhetorical revision of students' initial arguments. The rhetorical revision that slideware can provoke has important inventive implications. Our teaching experience similarly indicates that students often have a difficult time "re-seeing" their work and realizing that much of the revision process is actually an act of letting go and developing new directions for their work. They have a difficult idea time buying into the notion, in other words, that revision is constituted by invention just as invention is constituted by delivery. Asking students to switch modalities in the midst of their composing process to design a multimedia presentation of their argument engages them fully in this process, however. Resituating "presentation" in the composing process can help students work recursively between visual and print, as well as other interactive stages of the 21st century composing process. In effect, through the design and production of slideware, students realize inventive possibilities in their own work that the invisibility of typical print-based writing may not encourage.

It is important to note here that the transformative possibilities afforded by slideware exist only when we take time to teach slideware as a presentation design process, which entails crafting a message, designing a visual story, and thinking through delivery. In teaching slideware, the instructor must do more than simply show students how to operate the software. If our pedagogical focus rests solely on the technical—the mastery of the software's basic features—then much of the potential of slideware will be unavailable to us. Following Reynolds, Duarte, and others, slideware can provide us with an opportunity to teach presentation as a sensitive ecosystem, balanced by attention to content, design, and delivery. In our classes, we devote nearly six weeks or one unit to discuss and implement the innovative design and delivery principles offered in *Presentation Zen* and *slide:ology*. During this unit, the classroom is turned into a studio environment where students are creating storyboards, crafting narrative, using visual search engines, playing with Photoshop, designing visuals, creating handouts, and practicing delivery. Rather than being an afterthought, then, slideware is positioned as a rhetorical strategy and a productive means of invention, persuasion, and revision.

We also find that when we ask students to engage in presentation design, many engage in visual thinking, which often triggers creative potentials not accessed in print-based composition. Visual thinking is as highly unstable in meaning as rhetoric itself. Yet, for our purposes, as Dawan Stanford helps us understand, visual thinking, most broadly, can be thought of as "the use and exploration of images as tools for communication, understanding, creativity, problem solving, and explanation" ("What is"). Visual thinking[5] entails such activities as making and using sketches, diagrams, and graphs to think through abstract concepts, generate ideas, make decisions, problem solve and/or illustrate relations between information. Other activities, among many, include creating tag clouds, concept mapping, and data visualization. Visual thinking, as conceived here, is different than visual rhetorics. As articulated in *Defining Visual Rhetorics,* visual rhetorics, in a broad sense, is most often thought of in two ways: as an artifact that individuals create for communicative purposes and as a perspective or lens employed to study how visual artifacts perform rhetorically (303). Visual rhetorics, we would argue, is just one realm of visual thinking. While visual rhetorics is receiving growing attention in composition studies, visual thinking, in its creative, explanatory, and problem-solving sense, has received little attention in composition and rhetoric.

Our work with slideware in the classroom suggests that many of our students, especially those majoring in the design arts, benefit from stimulating visual thinking to generate productive reasoning, creativity, and communicative fluency. Visual thinking can trigger nonlinear, intuitive, and creative thought processes that often, in turn, unlock modes of thought not accessed via linear, logical thought processes (see Rudolf Arnheim's classic text *Visual Thinking).* When students engage in presentation design and visual thinking during the construction of presentations, students are able to access this creative mode of thought that helps to generate new ways of thinking about their topics. This ability to switch between logical and creative modes of thought, in turn, enhances our students' potential to employ their whole mind to generate compelling arguments. As Eva Brumberger argues, visual thinking is important for helping students move fluidly between and within different modes of thought and communication ("Making," 378). When we prepare students to think verbally, but not visually, Brumberger argues, we "risk producing writers who are visual technicians—writers skilled in visual tools and techniques but lacking what Hocks and Kendrick (2003) referred to such ability as 'fully hybrid eloquence'" (378). Such eloquence entails thinking of visual and verbal modes of communication as complementary and being able to move fluently and creatively back and forth between the two to achieve one's communicative and problem-solving goals. Students training to be professional and technical writers especially need to develop ambidexterity in terms of thought and communication style to succeed in the workplace (Brumberger 2007; Johnson-Sheehan, 2002; Olsen, 1991; Stroupe, 2000). As our field takes on the responsibility to prepare technical and professional writers, we argue that when taught as a presentation development process, PowerPoint offers student opportunities to hone this ability.

At least one other significant affordance also emerges. As the creators of Pecha Kucha explain, "Pecha Kucha is a *real* social network" in which presenters interact with each other's ideas throughout the evening in a casual atmosphere (Dytham and Klein 18). In the composition classroom, because of the typical ways in which we position delivery, students too often think of presentations as formal, final reports of their work rather than opportunities to stimulate casual conversation about their ideas. Assimilating Pecha Kucha events in our classrooms, however, repositions delivery as occasions to share their ideas and learn from peer and instructor responses, especially if we omit the typical, stifled Q & A sessions in favor of opportunities for students to casually discuss each other's work. In post- Pecha Kucha reflections, students claim that their peers' presentations and the subsequent conversations actually provoke new ideas about their own arguments. In effect, students' final written arguments become utterances in Bahktinian terms—responses to and determined by previous utterances. If repositioned in *media res* of the composing process, slideware design and delivery helps students begin to see that their writing can generate a response from an intended viewer. This response may or may not be the one they hoped to evoke; yet, no matter—by hearing the responses and seeing how their own work stimulates dialogue, they come to see how their final compositions act as *utterances* generated as part of and for the purpose of dialogue. A tighter social network of writers, rhetors, and designers is thus created in the classroom community. Students begin to take their own as well as their peers' ideas more seriously.

Conclusion

Despite the universal disdain we hold in writing studies for the five-paragraph theme, no one would suggest that we do without paragraphs themselves in our writing, and yet, this is the curious position that most slideware occupies for us. PowerPoint, Keynote, and the rest are judged by the very worst examples of what they can accomplish, leading us to resist their use in our classrooms. This in turn often means that we spend little time exploring or negotiating the software, either on our own or with our students, and this results in the very types of presentation that we dread. Our failure to take slideware seriously as a writing platform keeps us trapped in a vicious circle, one marked by mediocre presentations and an unwillingness to engage seriously the very tools that might help us improve them. We argue for a pedagogical renaissance of slideware in the writing classroom; coupled with contemporary design theories, slideware has the potential to revitalize student writing at all stages of the composing process. Slideware repositions our students as makers and designers in addition to writers and rhetors.

In the *Nicomachean Ethics*, Aristotle distinguishes among the modalities of knowing, doing, and making, suggesting that each has its own values and criteria by which we measure them. One of the striking things about rhetoric and writing, as well as design, is that they cut across all three. While the earliest days of the process movement attested to our ability to know through writing, and the social turn of the past twenty years has emphasized symbolic action and writing as a form of doing, our recent disciplinary forays into multimedia and networked writing encourage us to recover the third term, *making*, as well. It is not ultimately a matter of choosing one over the others, but rather, critically integrating them in a way that allows all three to inform each other. We would not necessarily suggest that slideware presentations supplant more traditional academic essays, but we have found that, as an element of the process rather than an afterthought, slideware can encourage our students to attend more closely to the ways that they *make* as they write. This sense of design can productively complicate their work, make them more conscious of their choices, and help them to develop a better sense of their own rhetorical effectiveness.

Notes

1. Although for many years, PowerPoint has been synonymous with what we call "slideware," a wide array of applications exists that permit the sequential display of slides. For this reason, in this essay, while we center much of the discussion around PowerPoint, we prefer the broader designation of "slideware."

2. Some scholars may certainly scowl at Reynolds' appropriation of Zen imagery and philosophical principles for slideware design and criticize his

explanation of Zen for its reductive qualities. Yet, from an affirmative perspective, the "Presentation Zen approach" does offer a straightforward and, we would argue innovative, way to reconceptualize the value of PowerPoint.

3. Inspired by Pecha Kuchas, Ignite is a similar presentation genre in which presenters show 20 slides that automatically rotate after 15 seconds, creating a 5-minute presentation. Started in Seattle in 2006 by Brady Forrest and Bre Pettis, Ignite has two parts: an Ignite contest and Ignite talks. Community members can decide on what contest they want to hold and then recruit speakers to present.

4. The Pecha Kucha assignment as discussed in this article has been implemented in several sections of WRT 205 at Syracuse University. WRT 205 is a required critical research and writing course designed to be taken during students' sophomore year. The claims made about the value of resituating presentation and the value of constrained writing in the composing process are based on student reflections, teacher observations, and one-on-one conversations with students. No formal study of this assignment has been conducted. This article grows out of the authors' interest in pedagogical exploration of slideware and delivery in the writing classroom, rather than a report of research findings.

5. For an excellent discussion of visual thinking in relation to communication, see Brumberger.

WORKS CITED

Aristotle. *Nicomachean Ethics*. Trans. and Ed. Roger Crisp. Cambridge: Cambridge UP, 2000. Print.

Arnheim, Rudolf. *Visual Thinking*. Berkeley: U of California P, 1972. Print.

Atkinson, Cliff. "PowerPoint Usability: Q&A with Don Norman." *Socialmedia*. (2004): n. pag. Web. 10 Oct. 2009.

Baetens, Jan. "Comic Strips and Constrained Writing." *Image [&] Narrative*. Oct (2003): n. pag. Web. 15 Oct. 2009.

———. "Free Writing, Constrained Writing: The Ideology of Form." *Poetics Today*. 18.1 (1997): 1-14. Print.

Brumberger, Eva R. "Making the Strange Familiar: A Pedagogical Exploration of Visual Thinking." *Journal of Business and Technical Communication*. 21 (2007): 376-401. Print.

Buchanan, Richard. "Design and the New Rhetoric: Productive Arts in the Philosophy of Culture." *Philosophy and Rhetoric*. 34.3 (2001): 183-206. Print.

Duarte, Nancy. *slide:ology: The Art and Science of Creating Great Presentations*. Cambridge: O'Reilly Media, Inc., 2008. Print.

Heath, Chip, and Dan Heath. *Made to Stick: Why Some Ideas Survive and Others Die*. New York: Random House, 2007. Print.

George, Diana. "From Analysis to Design: Visual Communication in the Teaching of Writing." *College Composition and Communication.* 52.1 (September 2002): 11-39. Print.

Johnson-Sheehan, R. "Being Visual, Visual Beings." In *Working with Words and Images: New Steps in an Old Dance.* Ed. Allen.. Westport, CT: Ablex, 2002. Print.

Dytham, Mark, and Astrid Klein. *Pecha Kucha Night: 20 Images x 20 Seconds.* Tokyo: Klein Dytham, 2008. Print.

Maeda, John. *The Laws of Simplicity (Simplicity: Design, Technology, Business, Life).* Cambridge: MIT P, 2006. Print.

Marback, Richard. "Embracing Wicked Problems: The Turn to Design in Composition Studies." *College Composition and Communication* 61.2 (2009): 397-419. Print.

Norman, Donald. "In Defense of PowerPoint." *jnd.org.* 2004. Web. 10 Oct. 2009.

Olsen, G. R. "Eidetecker: The Professional Communicator in the New Visual Culture." *IEEE Transactions on Professional Communication.* 34 (1991): 13-19. Print.

Pink, Daniel. *A Whole New Mind: Why Right-Brainers Will Rule the Future.* New York: Riverhead Books, 2005. Print.

Parker, Ian. "Absolute PowerPoint: Can a Software Package Edit our Thoughts?" *The New Yorker* 77.13 (2001): 76–87. Print.

Porter, James E.. "Recovering Delivery for Digital Rhetoric and Human-Computer Interaction." 2 Feb 2010. Web.

Reynolds, Garr. *Presentation Zen: Simple Ideas on Presentation Design and Delivery.* Berkeley: New Riders, 2008. Print.

———. "Duarte Design Helps Al Gore "go visual." *Presentation Zen Blog.* 01 June 2006. Web. 10 Oct. 2009.

Stanford, Dawan. "What is Visual Thinking? (definition 1.0)" *Fluidhive Blog.* 8 June 2009. Web. 2 Feb. 2010.

Stroupe, C. "Visualizing English: Recognizing the Hybrid Literacy of Visual and Verbal Authorship on the Web." *College English* 62 (2000): 607-32. Print.

Trimbur, John. "Composition and the Circulation of Writing." *College Composition and Communication* 52.2. (2000): 188–219.

Tufte, Edward. "The Cognitive Style of PowerPoint: Pitching Out Corrupts Within." *The Work of Edward Tufte and Graphics Press.* 6 Sep 2005. Web. 10 October 2009.

———. "PowerPoint is Evil: Power Corrupts. PowerPoint Corrupts Absolutely." *Wired* 11.09 (September 2003): n. pag. Web. 10 Oct. 2009.

Yancey, Kathleen. "Writing in the 21st Century: A Report from the National Council of Teachers of English." Urbana: *NCTE.org.* 2009. Web. 10 Oct. 2009.

COMPUTERS AND COMPOSITION

Computers and Composition is on the Web at http://computersand-composition.osu.edu/

Computers and Composition: An International Journal is devoted to exploring the use of computers in writing classes, writing programs, and writing research. It provides a forum for discussing issues connected with writing and computer use and offers information about integrating computers into writing programs on the basis of sound theoretical and pedagogical decisions, and empirical evidence. Topics include descriptions of computer-aided writing and/or reading instruction, computer use; software development; explorations of controversial ethical, legal, or social issues related to computer use in writing programs; and discussions of how computers affect form and content for written discourse, the process by which this discourse is produced, or the impact this discourse has on an audience.

"Recovering Delivery for Digital Rhetoric" by James E. Porter

James Porter's "Recovering Delivery for Digital Rhetoric" (December 2009) asserts that rhetoric's long-overlooked fifth canon, delivery, must be reexamined and re-theorized for the digital age of composition. Porter suggests a five-part theoretical framework for digital delivery that includes Body/Identity, Distribution/Circulation, Access/Accessibility, Interaction, and Economics. Porter uses this framework to consider how digital-age delivery might change our understanding of rhetorical knowledge as well as enrich the digital invention and composition processes. This article richly illustrates how a consideration of digital writing spaces and traditional rhetoric can be mutually beneficial, not only increasing our ability to theorize and teach digital writing practices but also enriching our understanding of rhetorical theory.

Recovering Delivery for Digital Rhetoric

James E. Porter

Abstract

This article develops a rhetorical theory of delivery for Internet-based communications. Delivery, one of the five key canons of classical rhetoric, is still an important topic for rhetorical analysis and production. However, delivery needs to be re-theorized for the digital age. In Part 1, the article notes the importance of delivery in traditional rhetoric and argues that delivery should be viewed as a form of rhetorical knowledge (techne). Part 2 presents a theoretical framework for "digital delivery" consisting of five key topics—Body/Identity, Distribution/Circulation, Access/Accessibility, Interaction, and Economics—and shows how each of these topics can function strategically and heuristically to guide digital writing.

My aim here is to resuscitate and remediate the rhetorical canon of delivery, which, along with memory, is one of the two neglected canons of the art of rhetoric. Delivery—*actio* or *pronuntiatio* in classical Roman rhetoric, *hypokrisis* in Greek (Lanham, 1991; see also Nadeau, 1964; Connors, 1983; Reynolds, 1996)—was one of the five major classical rhetorical canons, along with invention (*inventio*), arrangement (*dispositio*), style (*elocutio*), and memory (*memoria*). In classical rhetoric and through most of the history of rhetoric, delivery referred to the oral/aural and bodily aspects of an oral speech or performance—i.e., to the speaker's voice (intonation, volume, rhythm) and to bodily movements and gestures. Because delivery came to be associated almost exclusively with speech situations and with functions of the speaker's body (voice, gestures), it seemed less relevant, if not irrelevant, to written composition than the other canons (particularly *dispositio* and *elocutio*). By the time of 20th-century rhetoric theory and composition pedagogy, delivery had effectively disappeared. It is seldom taught, at least as a distinct topic, in departments of writing, English, or communication.

With the emergence and, now, ubiquity of Internet-based communication, it is long past time to revive the rhetorical canon of delivery.

Not your father's Oldsmobile but an updated vehicle, an expanded and retheorized notion of delivery designed for the distinctive rhetorical dynamics of Internet-based communication.[1] "Internet-based communication" is, of course, not a monolithic, well-defined thing: it is a range of media, technologies, rhetorical venues, discourse genres, and distribution mechanisms—everything from online discussion forums to news outlets to academic journals to shopping malls to online museums to simulated game and lifeworld environments to wikis to blogs to social networking services (SNSs), and so on. There are considerable rhetorical differences between a wiki, a blog, an email discussion list, and an SNS—and there are considerable ethical, editorial, and political decisions involved in setting up and maintaining any of these types of forums. We need a robust theory of digital delivery to help us navigate these kinds of rhetorical complexities. Understanding how the range of digital delivery choices influences the production, design, and reception of writing is essential to the rhetorical art of writing in the digital age. Rhetoric theorists need to understand this point, as do HCI (human-computer interaction) designers, technical communicators, digital media developers, etc., as the point pertains in fundamental ways to web-based writing and communication.

My audiences for this article are (1) rhetoric/composition scholars and, more generally, humanist scholars, for whom I would like to highlight the importance of technical knowledge as a legitimate form of humanistic thought; and (2) HCI designers, web authors, and technical communicators, for whom I would like to emphasize how rhetoric theory and critical humanistic thinking contribute value to web-based production and design. Each audience can learn much from the other.

This paper is divided into two main parts. In Part 1, I briefly overview the history of rhetorical delivery in order to position delivery as a *techne*, or art—a move that is important to framing delivery more broadly than it is typically understood. In Part 2, I propose a theoretical framework for digital delivery consisting of five components:

- *Body/Identity* – concerning online representations of the body, gestures, voice, dress, and image, and questions of identity and performance and online representations of race, class, gender, sexual orientation, and ethnicity

- *Distribution/Circulation* – concerning the technological publishing options for reproducing, distributing, and circulating digital information
- *Access/Accessibility* – concerning questions about audience connectedness to Internet-based information
- *Interaction* – concerning the range and types of engagement (between people, between people and information) encouraged or allowed by digital designs
- *Economics* – concerning copyright, ownership and control of information, fair use, authorship, and the politics of information policy

These five components are more than merely subject area domains, abstracted topics, or technical proficiencies. Rather, think of these as the common topics (*koinoi topoi*) of delivery—i.e., categories that operate heuristically and productively across multiple situations to prompt rhetorical decisions regarding production. In short, they help you write. For example, under the common topic of "access," demographic information about your audience's degree of access to broadband Internet should serve the productive purpose of guiding the format you, as a writer or web designer, use to deliver information. Indeed, you might offer multiple formats for audiences with restricted vision (and who are rendering digital information via screen reading programs) or for audiences who have limited (or no) access to broadband connections. If you produce a web page, you should use CSS (Cascading Style Sheets), an approach to web design that separates out formatting elements from informational content to increase accessibility for, for instance, blind persons or persons using handheld devices to read the information.

Technical knowledge about distribution options—i.e., how audiences are likely to access, engage, and interact with information—pertains in critical ways to rhetorical decisions about informational content, design, style, etc. In short, technical knowledge is integral to the art of rhetoric and to the canon of rhetorical delivery in the digital age. As Kathleen Welch (1990) argued nearly thirty years ago, "The fifth canon [delivery]... is now the most powerful canon of the five." Now more than ever.

1. Framing Rhetoric and Delivery as Art (*techne*)

In classical Greek and Roman rhetoric, delivery referred primarily to oral delivery: to making a public speech on political, juridical, or ceremonial occasions. Aristotle did not show much respect for delivery in *Rhetoric*, treating it only briefly (*Rhetoric* 3.1–3.7). He saw delivery functioning "in the same way as acting... a matter of natural talent and largely not reducible to artistic rule," except insofar as it relates to "how things are said [*lexis*]" (Aristotle, 1991, 3.1.7, p. 219). This dismissal of delivery provided the dominant cue for Western thought in regard to the canon: that is, delivery does not require "artistic labors"—ergo, it is not that important.

But Aristotle's students and later Roman rhetoricians afforded delivery considerably more attention, along two lines in particular: (1) emphasizing the role of the body in rhetorical action and (2) stressing the importance of emotional impact. For instance, the author of *Rhetorica ad Herennium* regretted the lack of attention to delivery and argued for its importance: "[B]ecause no one has written carefully on this subject.. and because the mastery of delivery is a very important requisite for speaking, the whole subject, as I believe, deserves serious consideration" ([Cicero, 1981], 3.21.19, p. 191). *Rhetorica ad Herennium* offered specific advice about how voice and body pertain to persuasive impact, noting how different occasions call for different strategies. For example, the rhetor can achieve an emotional effect by using "a restrained voice, deep tone, frequent intermissions, long pauses, and marked changes" ([Cicero, 1981], 3.24.25. p. 201); however, for sustained debate it is better for the rhetor to use "a quick gesture of the arm, a mobile countenance, and a keen glance" (3.25.27, p. 203). Roman rhetoricians such as Theophrastus and Cicero viewed delivery as an important component of emotional—and, therefore, persuasive—effect. In contradistinction to Aristotle, Cicero saw delivery as critical to rhetorical effect, as he discussed in *De Oratore* (1988). Cicero's treatment (3.213-27) acknowledges the important relationship between performance (bodily, tonal) and persuasion (see Sunkowsky, 1959, p. 273).

In *Institutio Oratoria*, Quintilian (1922) provided a detailed discussion of delivery (11.3), focusing mainly on voice and bodily movement: the quality of voice, the position and carriage of the body (including discussion of hands, neck, eyes, head, and, interestingly, dress), as both relate to the emotional force of the oration. Quintilian told us that being overdressed is as bad as being underdressed: "excessive care with regard to the cut of the toga, the style of the shoes, or the arrangement of the hair, is just as reprehensible as excessive carelessness" (1922, 11.3.137, pp. 317, 319). (For a job interview do you wear a tie, a dress versus dress pants, makeup versus none? Should you cover up your tattoos?) But Quintilian's discussion of delivery is not detached from other rhetorical considerations. Quintilian noted the important connection between delivery and the character of the speaker (*ethos*) and the emotional depth and appeal of the presentation (*pathos*). Delivery relates to persuasive force. For example, a demeanor exuding modesty can be persuasive with judges in a legal matter, just as much as "a toga sitting well upon the shoulder" (11.3.161, p. 333) but it only achieves the desired effect if the emotion is sincere, the facts are compelling, and the argument sound: "All emotional appeals will inevitably fall flat, unless they are given the fire that voice, look, and the whole carriage of the body can give them" (11.3.2, p. 245). The point here is that the body is an integral part of rhetorical action. The sincerity of one's commitment and the appropriate coordination of one's thoughts, feelings, and bodily expressions are important to rhetorical effect.

Fast forward to the early Renaissance. In *The Treasure of the City of Ladies* (1405/1985), Christine de Pisan provided a similarly comprehensive perspective on rhetorical delivery—a holistic view of how the princess or "noble lady" ought to conduct herself in court. De Pisan did not carve up the canon like Aristotle did—i.e., she did not distinguish between invention and style, delivery and audience. She did not create an elaborate classification system or outline of the art of rhetoric, nor did she exclude the body from the rhetorical scene. Rather, de Pisan's rhetoric is of a different kind: it focuses on the whole person, covering the speech, the demeanor, the tone, the ethical stance and moral obligation, the dress, and the behaviors holistically. De Pisan's view is an integrated view of rhetoric and the body that we do not often see represented in the Western rhetorical canon, or at least not the academic canon. Until relatively recently, de Pisan's work was not treated as a serious rhetoric treatise because it is not abstract and philosophical (like Aristotle's); it does not proceed via an elaborate classification system. Historically it was dismissed, disregarded, and neglected as a conduct book, a mere etiquette guide, when in actuality it might well be one of the few historical examples we have of a wholly integrated rhetoric, one that considers the rhetoric of the entire person, not only what she says, but how she behaves, dresses, gestures, and, importantly, interacts with others in complex political settings.

The emergence of the printing press in the 15th century represents a key historical shift in the canon of delivery. Elizabeth Eisenstein's highly regarded book *The Printing Press as an Agent of Change* (1979) described the immense impact of the printing press on Western intellectual, scientific, and religious thought. I view Eisenstein's work as an important treatise on delivery: a detailed story about how a mechanical copying mechanism (the printing press) can affect vast rhetorical, political, social, and cultural upheaval. Eisenstein described the revolutionary effects of the printing press in Western European culture during the 16th and 17th centuries. She stopped just short of saying that the printing press *caused* the Protestant Reformation—but not that far short. Not only did the printing press play a significant role in distributing and promoting religious ideas in the 16th century, she pointed out, but the ability of print to collect, perfectly replicate, and widely distribute common sets of mathematical and scientific data enabled yet another revolution, the rapid growth of scientific thought in the 17th and 18th centuries. The technological shift from scribal to print culture was not a mere technical or instrumental shift from one form of delivering knowledge to another. The new form of delivery *changed knowledge itself*; it changed the parameters, procedures, and locus for what constituted religious truth and scientific knowledge; it changed who had the right to create, promote, and distribute knowledge, giving power to a wider range of voices (including voices of religious protest). Eisenstein pointed out that print enabled "typographical fixity... a basic prerequisite for the rapid advancement of learning" (1979, p. 78). "Fixity" was particularly important for the advancement of science, as this enabled the standardization and wide distribution of mathematical and scientific knowledge: "the development of neutral pictorial and mathematical vocabularies made possible a large-scale pooling of talents for analyzing data and led to the eventual achievement of a consensus that cut across all the old frontiers" (p. 269). Print helped both (a) to establish a fixed archive of scientific knowledge and (b) to distribute that knowledge widely. The result was a pooling of scientific knowledge that enabled later discoveries.

But we do not typically use the term "delivery" in connection with the history of print publishing. Delivery as a term was associated almost exclusively with speech, not with print. Delivery was a dominant concern of the much-maligned English elocutionary movement of the 18th century, with its excessive (some might say obsessive) focus on correct pronunciation and usage, as well as with decorum—the correct posture, stance, and gestures of the orator. Some works, like Gilbert Austin's *Chironomia; or the Art of Manual Rhetoric* (1644/1966), even provided elaborate diagrams of how to hold your hands and arrange your fingers in order to make a point. Here is where the art of delivery became degraded. Delivery techniques became disconnected from rhetorical considerations such as emotional effect on audience (as in Quintilian) or ethical and political action (as in de Pisan).

Why rehash this history of rhetorical delivery? Because these past treatments, categories, and classifications, particularly the systems of Greek and Roman classical rhetoric, persist. They have an enduring power and influence over our categories of thought, our systemic classifications, our vocabularies, our ways of thinking about writing, technology, and production.

Let's start with the word "technology"—probably the #1 god term of the digital age—a term carrying considerable historical baggage. That word contains a key concept from classical Greek rhetoric: *techne*. *Techne* is often translated as "art," but we have to understand that term differently from our contemporary notions of art as the aesthetic, imaginative works of "artists." In the classical Greek rhetoric and philosophy of Aristotle and Plato, *techne* represents a kind of knowledge: "first of all, *techne* is a pure knowledge of form or standard" (Wild, 1941, p. 257), a matter of bringing form to material in order to make something. But the made object has a purpose: "the work of each art is accomplished for the sake of something" (Wild, 1941, p. 259). The true artist has a sense of effect as well as of form: what result or outcome will the made object have in the world? *Techne* requires both an abstract knowledge (e.g., of material and of form) and a procedural knowledge (e.g., of application and technique). In short, it requires both theoretical understanding and practical know-how working in tandem. As John Wild (1941) pointed out, Plato distinguished *techne* from *tribe*, "meaningless repetition of practice" (p. 264), i.e., routinized mechanical procedures lacking insight. In other words, in our own vocabularies "technical" should be distinguished from "mechanical."

Rhetoric, as *techne*, is the art of creating discourse, whether speech or writing, to achieve a desired end for some audience. Like all arts, it can be practiced badly or well. It becomes degraded when it is taught or practiced as a set of *mechanical* procedures, rules or formulas to be followed or patterns to be copied. It achieves status as a true art when it is taught and practiced as a form of knowledge involving a critical understanding of the purposes and effects of the art on audiences and the practical know-how to achieve those effects in new discursive situations. To apply this point to digital writing, knowledge only of the mechanics for coding web pages using CSS (Cascading Style Sheets) is not sufficient to the art of web authoring in the digital age. Rather, the writer/designer needs to know how to use these procedures to achieve the desired effect—for example, distributing useful information to readers and doing so in a readily accessible way.

What I see in too many tutorials, manuals, and workshops on web design is a degraded form of rhetoric, i.e., a reduction of the art to routinized procedures, abstracted from context, without the full comprehensive *techne* kind of knowledge, which includes knowledge and understanding about audiences, effects, and choices. That is one kind of fallacy—a type of instrumental fallacy. However, I often see humanist academics committing a different kind of fallacy: dismissing technical knowledge too readily as mindless mechanics or robotic functions, failing to see the importance of technical know-how to rhetorical competency. One cannot be an effective digital writer without knowing both technical procedures and how to deploy them to achieve the desired end. The *techne* for digital rhetoric includes both technical/procedural knowledge and knowledge of audience and effect (Lauer, 2004, p. 49), not merely know-how in the sense of mechanical production skills but rhetorical knowledge as well.

My point in reviewing the role of delivery in historical rhetoric is to recall that the art of rhetoric has traditionally included delivery under its umbrella, although sometimes a diminished version of that canon, not always a robust form. The principal reason to resuscitate delivery is a productive one: a broad conception of delivery can aid invention as well as the design and evaluation of writing. It is of particular importance to audience. A robust canon of delivery should help us think more productively about how we are writing, and to whom, and lead us to make smarter choices as writers/designers, whether we are producing online information or non-digital information.

When rhetoric shifted its focus historically to writing, the canons of delivery and memory became subordinated (see Trimbur, 2000; Jacobi, 2006). By nature of its permanence, writing seemed to have little need for an art of memory. Similarly, delivery was seldom taught per se as an art of composition, because it seemed to be a material, technical, and economic concern more relevant to publishing than to writing per se. Never deemed all that important compared to other canons, delivery had dropped off the map by the late 20th century. Delivery was seldom taught in composition classes[2]; it was certainly not regarded as a subject worthy of research.

Kathleen Welch (1999) argued that the disappearance of memory and delivery was by no means a "benign removal" (p. 144). Rather she saw it as a "rigorous suppression," part of the overall narrowing of the definition of rhetoric to mean, mostly, "attenuated style or language decoration" (pp. 149-150). She pointed out that for many non-Western cultures (for example, Native American culture) memory and delivery are fundamentally important rhetorical canons. The historical impetus toward erasing/suppressing the canons of memory and delivery is a way to subordinate the materiality of writing and the technical side of composition practice—that part of the art that has to do with material cause, with understanding the materials and tools for writing. Welch saw the shift in rhetoric toward textual formalism—i.e., toward a nearly exclusive focus on two or three rhetorical canons (arrangement and style, and perhaps invention)—as an ideological move toward an abstracted, theoretical-philosophical rhetoric that privileges written discourse over oral and visual; that privileges the modes of exposition and formal argumentation over expressive and narrative writing; that privileges logical and disinterested analysis over emotional response; that privileges empirically derived and rationalistic knowledge over ancestral, religious, and cultural knowledge; that privileges the disciplinary domains and methodologies of science and humanism over community or personal experience. This bias works to the detriment of women, people of color, and non-Western cultures (see Welch, 1994). It is a bias that privileges the contribution of the theorist over the practitioner. Reviving the canons of delivery and memory requires reviving skills and forms of knowledge and practice that traditional Western rhetoric and humanistic thought have seldom acknowledged or valued.

2. A Framework for Digital Delivery

My intention here is not to provide a comprehensive theory of digital delivery, but rather (a) to outline what I see as the chief features of that theory—i.e., what I am calling the five *koinoi topoi* of delivery (body/identity, distribution/circulation, access/accessibility, interaction, economics); (b) to provide some examples of how each of these features can assist the art of rhetorical production, particularly the canon of invention; and (c) to cite some representative scholarship in each of these five areas. Much of this canon recovery work has already been done, particularly in the field of computers and composition. In fact, I would dare say that most of the research published in the journals *Kairos: A Journal of Rhetoric, Technology, and Pedagogy* and *Computers and Composition* is related more closely to the canon of delivery than to any of the other canons—although scholars in that field seldom view their work as "delivery." What I am doing here is not so much creating a new theory of digital delivery as I am aggregating and coordinating a well-established body of research and scholarship under the rubric of "digital delivery."

2.1. Body/Identity

The body plays a key role in face-to-face oral delivery, as the classical Roman rhetoricians noted: the body is enmeshed in persuasive effect, particularly emotional impact. "The body" includes a number of features related to your identity—i.e., how you present in terms of gender, race, ethnicity, sexual preference, age, etc. It also includes your "performance"—i.e., your facial expressions, your gestures, your haircut (or absence of hair), your posture, your physical movements, your manner of dress, and your manner of speaking. These bodily features are significantly intertwined with your *ethos* as a speaker. I can achieve one kind of *ethos* by writing a newspaper editorial advocating labor union representation for Wal-Mart employees. However, I can also rhetorically perform in a different way by putting my body on the line: showing up at a pro-union protest in front of a Wal-Mart outlet carrying a sign, collaborating with others in the protest to create a street scene, a performance, that the media might well report—and thereby raise public consciousness about a labor issue. This public performance is also rhetoric: using the body as itself a "text," a delivery mechanism for a persuasive point.

The body does not disappear in virtual space. It is certainly constructed differently, but it is there in all its non-virtual manifestations: gender, race, sexual preference, social class, age, etc. Is it possible to "gesture" or create a bodily action online? Yes, of course, as we well know from the simplest and most well known of all bodily representations in online space: :). The smiley face emoticon is an ASCII textual representation of a bodily act that is used to add nuance to a piece of text. On a more advanced level, when I make an avatar in the simulated world of Second Life I am creating a bodily representation of myself, one that may or may not correspond to my lifeworld self, but one that has a virtual bodily existence. That avatar is my virtual bodily self that, when combined with virtual speech and behavior, results in a rhetorical performance.

Numerous scholars have explored the bodily aspects of virtual space, particularly from the perspective of gender (e.g., Armstrong, 2005; Blair & Takayoshi, 1997; Blair & Takayoshi, 1999; Gerrard, 1997), race (e.g., Banks, 2005), sexual orientation (e.g., Alexander & Banks, 2004; Alexander, 1997; Rhodes, 2004), and ideological disciplining of the body (Selfe & Selfe, 1994; Porter, 2003). Feminist scholars like Gail Hawisher and Patricia Sullivan (1999) and Susan Herring (2001) have pointed out that the Internet is by no means a neutral space where gender is invisible. On the contrary, Internet participants often take their gender identities into digital space with them: they can approximate their lifeworld gender identities, or they can create dramatically alternative identities in those spaces. As Hawisher and Sullivan (1999) discussed in their analysis of representations of women's bodies on web sites, the Victoria's Secret web site represents "the fantasy version of a desirable woman," reproducing "the age-old stereotypical relations among the sexes" (pp. 274-275). The site often portrays women in provocative sexual poses á la the *Sports Illustrated* swimsuit issue to sell products. The Victoria's Secret site embodies the marketing cliché that "sex sells." However, academics' professional sites also attempt to market a product using bodily images, albeit a scholarly "product" using different forms of appeal. The professional web site for the legal scholar Lawrence Lessig (n.d.) (see <http://www.lessig.org>) is based on a professional *ethos* of scholarly competence, personal integrity, and civic concern. Using mainly text and textual highlighting, along with a few photographs (mainly of his book covers) and links (with associated logos) to public action groups like Creative Commons and the Electronic Frontier Foundation, Lessig creates an online persona for himself: the scholar-activist who publishes legal research but who is also invested in civic action pertaining to Internet freedom and digital intellectual property. He includes a photograph of himself standing with his arms folded, in a white shirt with rolled-up sleeves, in a kind of James Dean-like posture exuding nonchalant (but also studious) cool. No suit here, he's not one of "them." Not the stereotyped image of the corporate lawyer, but rather an activist-lawyer-scholar. Compare Lessig's professional web site with that of another scholar, Donna Haraway (n.d.) (see <http://www.egs.edu/faculty/haraway.html>). Haraway's site is a more conventional programmatic web site consisting mainly of descriptive textual information about her current work: her courses taught, her current research interests, information about how to contact her, and her academic credentials and affiliations. She does not feature her upcoming speaking appearances, as does Lessig, or provide interactive tools like blogs and RSS feeds for readers to engage in discussion or to receive updates about her activities. In one early version of her academic site, she provided a photo of herself with a dog, a casual pose of her in blue jeans in a lush wooded setting. It is not the typical academic headshot at all, but a personal picture showing a warm side to her character. On both Haraway's and Lessig's sites, bodily representations are an important supplement to information about their scholarly activity. Chiefly, those representations add a personal touch, using the body to exhibit an attitude that helps to represent each's identity.

These web sites provide static graphic representations of the body (photographs), but in the world of MMOGs or MMORPGs (Massively Multiplayer Online Role-Playing Games), virtual bodies actually *move* in 3D environments— for example, in game worlds like EverQuest and World of Warcraft and in simulated worlds like Second Life. People can create their own avatars and thereby represent themselves in the names they choose, their manner of dress, and their online performances (e.g., how they present in terms of race, gender, and sexual orientation; how they speak). There is a new generation of rhetoric scholars, like Phill Alexander (2007) and Brian Bailie (2007), taking principles of rhetorical and cultural analysis and critique into virtual worlds to understand the nature of the rhetorical dynamic in those worlds; to develop principles for written production within those spaces (e.g., principles for designing characters and for understanding conventions and ethics of the simulated world); and/or to understand the relationship between RL (Real Life) and VR (Virtual Reality).

It is not only the visual body that is recovered in virtual spaces. The speaking body is also recovered, as numerous scholars have pointed out (for example, Halbritter, 2004; Lunsford, 2006; McKee, 2006; Shankar, 2006; Rice, 2006). Voice and aurality are a central concern in digital rhetoric, as the World Wide Web supports multimedia discourse that enmeshes textual, video/visual, and aural elements. In digital spaces we have to consider not only textual presentation but oral performance, the very qualities of voice that were central to classical rhetoric. As VoIP services (Voice Over Internet Protocol) become more prevalent, the speaking voice will become an even more important feature of online worlds and games, and that will add yet another level of complexity to the rhetorical dynamic of such spaces. Will typed textual discourse disappear once VoIP becomes fully integrated? No, but its role in the rhetorical dynamic is certain to change as it becomes intertwined with voice and virtual bodily movement.

The traditional humanist approach to technology draws a firm line between the human and the machine, but this approach fails to appreciate the compelling power of virtual life and communication. A more promising approach, articulated by Katherine Hayles (1999) and others, is the posthumanist approach to technology. This approach begins with Donna Haraway's (1991) notion of the cyborg: a hybrid metaphor that challenges the human–machine distinction and questions conventional body boundaries and notions of the writer as purely human. A posthumanist approach explores cyborgian hybridity, the connectedness between human–machine. Such an approach begins by recognizing that "there are no essential differences or absolute demarcations between bodily existence and computer simulation, cybernetic mechanism and biological organism, robot teleology and human goals" (Hayles, 1999, p. 3). In effect, "we are all ... cyborgs" (Haraway, 1991, p. 150).

The posthumanist approach views the human body and technology as merged in a new hybrid form: the cyborg. If we are thinking in terms of human communication, the cyborg is an especially useful metaphor, as I have previously argued (Porter, 2003). The machines that we use to write and speak are closely merged with our flesh-and-blood bodies, if you think about how we are connected to our cell phones and our computers (and to our cell phones which have become computers), thanks to the development of mobile and wireless technology. The phone/computer can now be with us at all times, even attached to our ears. But we are also typing text messages into those phones. We are also recreating our bodies in cyberspace, as we create characters to represent us (who we are or who we would like to be) and rhetorically perform in virtual space. In 1990 our online rhetorical performances were mainly textual, as we typed our communications and sent them via email. The smiley face icon (and its ASCII derivatives) was our limit for bodily/facial expression. By 2000 the World Wide Web was pushing us to think more visually about our communications and about how we represented ourselves graphically in photos. And now in the era of YouTube we must think cinematically and aurally as well. Digital rhetorical performance is becoming increasingly multimodal and increasingly synchronous.

Although it might seem that these virtual environments exist mostly for the sake of game-playing, entertainment, and, yes, virtual sex, that is only the first-generation version and popular representation of such environments. These virtual worlds are already becoming spaces for business transactions, for legal consultations, for political activity, for community support groups, and for training and education.[3] Game-playing worlds and "second life worlds" are environments supporting a wide variety of human interactions. We need a robust rhetoric of digital delivery to understand how to be an effective rhetorical participant within these environments.

2.2. Distribution/Circulation

In the offline world, when you arrange a lunch appointment with a colleague, you decide how you are going to contact her—by phone, by email, by dropping by her office and asking her face to face. Your decision is based on contextual factors, including proximity to her in time and space and the immediacy of the appointment (Is her office close to yours? Is she there now? Is the lunch for next week, or next hour?), as well as knowledge about user preferences (Is she OK with phone calls at home? Is she a regular email user?). If you know that your colleague only occasionally checks email, and it is thirty minutes before lunchtime, then email is probably a poor choice for distributing your message. If you want to effect a felicitous outcome—one that results in you and your colleague actually meeting for lunch—then you reflect on this question of message delivery. Your reflection might take eight seconds—i.e., it is a brief, nearly instantaneous decision—but the choice of distribution matters to the success of the communication.

Digital distribution refers to rhetorical decisions about the mode of presenting discourse in online situations: What is the most effective way to distribute a message to its intended audiences, in a timely manner, and in a way that is likely to achieve the desired outcome? Circulation is a related term that pertains to how that message might be recycled in digital space (should you want that to happen).[4] When you add a phrase like "Please feel free to re-post this call for proposals" to an email announcement, you are signaling to readers that you want broad circulation of your message. Distribution refers then to the initial decision about how you package a message in order to send it to its intended audience. Circulation refers to the potential for that message to have a document life of its own and be re-distributed without your direct intervention. You can design your discourse to achieve a high degree of circulation, or you can design it to limit circulation, depending on your wishes.

When I decide whether to submit an article manuscript to the print journal *College Composition and Communication* or to the online journal *Kairos*, I am making a *techne* decision regarding delivery, distribution, timing, and audience impact. If the article is accepted for publication in *CCC*, then I will wait probably two years for that article to appear (that's bad), but it will be read by a broad cross-section of rhetoric/composition scholars and teachers (that's good). If the article appears in *Kairos*, it will come out sooner (perhaps six months), but its audience will be different (more technorhetoricians, scholars and teachers already invested in teaching in online environments). Making this distribution decision requires understanding the relationship between my article and possible audiences, and knowing which publication venue is more suitable given the focus of the article and what kind of impact I want it to have and *when* I want to have it. Timing is a particularly important consideration—the *when* of rhetorical performance (see Ridolfo & DeVoss, 2009). The rhetorical term *kairos* refers to timing, to the appropriate time to deliver a discourse but also to the appropriateness of the discourse for its occasion (its audience, its immediate context, its historical and cultural context). It is a key concept for rhetoric in general, and for the canon of delivery in particular.

When I first distribute a digital document, I usually send it to a single designated location, or perhaps a few locations, for "publication." However, to what extent do I want that document to circulate, to be recycled, reused, and reshipped? If I want a high degree of circulation, then it is important to understand the technological and rhetorical procedures for helping that document cycle in digital space. If I send that document as a Word file or PDF, I have already limited its circulation potential on the Internet. However, if I want to encourage broad circulation, I would write the piece in HTML and make sure to include appropriate meta-tags (that is, keywords embedded in the HTML code, visible in the code but invisible in the rendering of that code on the Web) that will assist searchers in locating that article. If I want broad distribution of a video I have created, I load it on YouTube and make sure that it is tagged with keywords that will invite viewing. If I want an online article to be shipped easily across a variety of digital formats, then I make sure to divide the content from the format—i.e., I design the writing using CSS, an approach to web authoring that separates the format file from the content file. Why do that? Because that enables the content to be shipped easily to different formats—for example, for display on a PDA screen or for easier rendering by a screen reader that will translate textual information into audio format for users with sight or reading disabilities.

To further encourage distribution I can attach a Creative Commons license like an Attribution-Noncommercial-ShareAlike license[5] to my document that will clarify for users how they can use the work. I can license the work to encourage others to reuse and redistribute it but disallow commercial uses and insist that my authorship of the work be credited. How I design the work, license it, and tag it—and the location(s) I choose for its original distribution, and *when* I distribute it—all these matters play a part in determining the circulation potential for that digital document. In the print realm, such matters are typically handled by publishers and editors, along well-established axes of distribution (e.g., academic journals get shipped to libraries and individual subscribers). For a print journal article, I submit my typed, double-spaced manuscript and let the editors and publishers worry about distribution and circulation. In the digital realm, online writers need to become rhetorically smart *distributors* as much as *producers* of discourse.

2.3. Access/Accessibility

Numerous scholars in computers and composition have addressed the question of access (e.g., Banks, 2005; Grabill, 2003; Moran, 1999; Powell, 2007; Selfe & Hawisher, 2004; Slatin, 2006), but beyond identifying (and regretting) the problem of computer resource inequity, what can a writer or designer *do*? As Charles Moran (1999) said, "the rich have more, the poor less" (p. 215), but how does one approach the problem proactively? Moran advised university teachers to address the inequity problem locally by, for example, advocating "less-expensive equipment" (p. 218) and ensuring that computer-based writing curricula do not disadvantage the students with less or no access to computers. Such a strategy begins by challenging some of the technology policies and decisions that contribute to lack of access for many: teachers can be advocates for open-source software applications rather than costly proprietary applications; they can design writing assignments to make use of less expensive or free applications; they can teach students to be creative producers using less expensive tools (e.g., using Google docs, a free collaborative authoring tool, for team projects).

But this approach addresses the needs of a small and relatively privileged segment of society: those with the educational background and resources to attend universities. Outside the university, the problem of access is more severe: the absence and inadequacy of computer resources and the lack of an adequate network infrastructure in homes, schools, and public places mean that large segments of the population cannot access and benefit from digital information. That problem is a growing one in the United States where government documents, news media, health information, public archives, and even public debate have increasingly moved to online spaces, leaving people with limited access to those spaces cut off from information, public debate, and cultural knowledge vital to their health and well-being and necessary for their participation as citizens.

It is not enough to say that Internet usage is now "widespread," just because we have data that tells us that there are over 220 million Internet users in the United States and that "most" of the people in the United States have access to an Internet connection. Those grand generalities by themselves mislead. Although the United States is near the top of the list of nations in terms of percentage of citizens with Internet access, it is important to note the significant income and education disparities. For example, for those with household incomes of less than

$30,000 per year, the level of Internet usage is only 57%, compared to 94% for those with household incomes over $75,000 per year (Pew, 2008). Certain groups continue to lag in their Internet adoption, including Americans age 65 and older, black Americans, and those with less than a high school education (Fox, 2005; Pew, 2008).[6] A large number of US citizens have *no* Internet access, and a large number have uneven or irregular access. "One in five American adults say they have never used the Internet or email and do not live in an internet-connected household" (Fox, 2005).[7]

It is important to distinguish between "access" and "accessibility," overlapping terms that nonetheless refer to distinct spheres of concern. "Access" is the more general term related to whether a person has the necessary hardware, software, and network connectivity in order to use the Internet—and to whether certain groups of persons have a disadvantaged level of access due to their race, ethnicity, socioeconomic status, gender, age, or other factors.

"Accessibility" refers to the level of connectedness of one particular group of persons—those with disabilities.[8] When you take into account the wide variety of disabilities, it is not hard to imagine that at some point in their lives practically everyone has a disability of some kind, at least a minor one, and probably knows someone, or many someones, with a major and/or permanent disability of some kind. As John Slatin (2006) argued, the goal should not be "simply to make online information and services accessible" but rather "to ensure that the world has access to the ideas and information that are generated by individuals who have disabilities, individuals whose sensibility and consciousness may be radically different from those whose voices are most commonly heard—people who may have valuable solutions to problems that face all of us" (p. 161). In other words, the reason to write/design for accessibility is not only to enable people with disabilities to *consume* information but to help them *produce* it.[9]

From the standpoint of digital production, putting the concept of access into action means designing information so as to help audiences with limited access to digital resources engage that information via alternate media and formats. This could mean strategies such as promoting the installation of computer resources in publicly accessible places such as libraries, government buildings, and kiosks; maintaining information in both print and digital formats; and designing information for access via mobile phones and other handheld devices.

For instance, while a health clinic might move much of its patient information into web-based delivery systems, it should consider maintaining that information in print forms (and in robust forms of print distribution) so that lower income users can still access it.

Designing information for ready and usable access by mobile phones is perhaps the most important way to support access by a broader socioeconomic range of users—and also by users across the globe. From a broader global perspective, computers and Internet access simply don't exist for much of the world. (Africa has a population of 975 million, 14.5% of the world's population, but only 5.6% of the African population are Internet users. India has a population of over 1 billion people, of whom only 7.1% are Internet users [Internet World Stats, 2009; US Aid, 2003].) The penetration rate for cell phone usage is much greater than for computers, particularly in countries like India and China. (As of 2007, China had 487.4 million cell phone subscribers—or about 38% of the population (Data Group News Service, 2007; see also Associated Press, 2006; Lemon, 2007). Europe is approaching 90% saturation [Reardon, 2007].) The emerging area of "mobile web design" (Gohring, 2006; Jones, 2004; Moll, 2005) focuses on strategies for writing web-based information in ways that will make it readable via handheld devices, because for many users that will be the principle mode of access to web-based information.

Designing for accessibility requires a certain kind of *techne* knowledge related to delivery. If I am given the technical writing assignment to "write a manual that helps people set up their DVD player," the first thing I should understand is that the assignment is flawed. The instruction to "write a manual" confuses ends with means. It is confusing the formal aspect of *techne* (make an object, a manual) with the final goals of *techne* (help people use their DVD players). In Aristotelian terms, the assignment confuses formal cause and final cause.

Focusing on delivery—and, particularly, emphasizing access and accessibility—means starting the writing process with audience and working backwards to made object. We might then rearticulate the writing task along these lines: "People need to set up their DVD players—and some of these people do not have access to the Internet, some are seeing-impaired, some cannot read, etc. How do we help these people install their DVD players? What types of help do we offer?" Approaching the problem from the perspective of audience access/accessibility means starting with audience need—and with the diversity of audiences—and then developing a rhetorical approach (or, more likely, a variety of approaches) to address that need.

Levels of interactivity

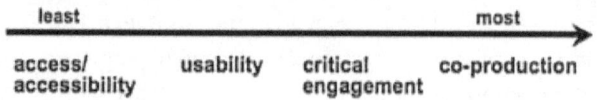

Fig. 1. Interactivity continuum.

2.4. Interaction/Interactivity

Interaction, or interactivity, refers to how users engage interfaces and each other in digital environments. When I access my bank account using an ATM machine for the purpose of withdrawing cash, the interface of the machine takes me through a series of steps aimed at, first, determining what I want to do and then assisting me in accomplishing the transaction. The first step of the process is verification—determining that I am indeed a valid account holder by asking me to swipe my bankcard and then enter the appropriate PIN number. The second step might be determining whether the interaction should be conducted in English or Spanish. The ATM transaction is a standard kind of human-computer interaction.

I consider the term "interaction" as a rhetorical topic pertaining (a) to how humans engage computer interfaces in order to perform various actions (e.g., withdraw cash from an ATM, post an entry to a blog), and (b) to how humans engage other humans through computer-mediated spaces. The fundamental principle of interaction is that different types of computer interfaces and spaces enable different forms of engagement—and the digital writer has a wide range of interaction options. Thus, rhetorically, the writer needs to consider what kinds of designs will enable and encourage the kinds of audience interactions desired.[10]

Defining interactivity in terms of potential for audience involvement can help us imagine a broader range of human interactions with machines, systems, interfaces, and with other humans. The continuum in Fig. 1 identifies four levels of interactivity—Access, Usability, Critical Engagement, Co-Production—that refer not to technical features of a digital product but rather to "interaction potential," or the range of possible human uses and responses to that product.

Most digital information actually falls into the narrow range of access and usability—ideally (when the information is well designed) people can access the information, read it and understand it, and perform tasks successfully. Although access and usability are certainly important design criteria, they do not represent the full range of interactivity, and they are not a particularly robust measure of interactivity. At the left end of the interactivity continuum the digital audience is positioned as passive consumers of digital content: at this level interactivity means pointing and clicking, through a range of limited and highly channeled choices—e.g., using an ATM machine to get cash or using Travelocity to purchase airline tickets. At this level, interactivity means viewing, maybe reading and viewing, maybe inserting information into forms. Even well-intentioned educational programs and web style guides often tend toward this passive consumption model.

Much of what was advertised as "interactivity" on the Web—at least for Web 1.0—was technical bells and whistles—video animation, creative art, multimedia extravaganza, and fancy features designed to dazzle, impress, or wow users, to persuade them to consume or to collect rote information, but not to enable them to do very much, at least not do in the sense of contribute, participate, or co-create (see Shedroff, n.d.; Anderson, 2003). The Web 1.0 user could choose, search, find, read, scan—and, most importantly, buy. Much new media work allows the user to gaze in awe. But in many cases the user isn't allowed to advise, create, or collaborate. Merely providing hyperlink choices or blank forms for users to fill out should not be regarded as interactivity, and yet a lot of discussions (particularly in advertising and business contexts) define interactivity in precisely those terms. Merely giving readers options is nothing special. (The old print newspaper does that. So does a shopping mall.) Like choices on a multiple-choice exam, such choices are highly constrained, predetermined by the producer. Consumers are given the myth of choice rather than being allowed to generate their own options (Manovich, 2001, p. 61).

Defining interactivity in terms of human interaction potential, rather than by reference to technical features, helps us imagine a broader range of human interactions with machines, systems, interfaces, and designs. And indeed this is what the phenomenon of Web 2.0 is all about. On the right side of the continuum we have more emphasis on the highly interactive forms of design, forms that critically engage the user and that even invite the audience to co-produce knowledge (when appropriate of course—when I'm ordering airline tickets I don't need to be a co-producer). The true revolution of the Internet lies at the right end of the interactivity spectrum—when users can critically engage what they read (e.g., by commenting on a published editorial posted on a blog) or further to the right, when they co-produce and become writers, when the distinction between audience and writer blurs. At this level, a site actively invites the audience to become a co-producer of content. What social networking sites, video games, wikis, and simulated worlds are demonstrating is that audiences participate enthusiastically when they are invited to become co-producers of content, when the activity is meaningful, when the content is engaging and compelling.

In a study published in Technical Communication Quarterly, Carl Whithaus and Joyce Neff (2006) examined the quality of interactivity in a hybrid writing course (for another important study of online interaction, see Wysocki, 2001). Their study involved students taking the same course, but from three different locations with three different types of interaction: "those physically present with [the instructor, Joyce Neff] in the classroom, those participating in small groups at distant sites, and those at isolated computer terminals without direct voice access" (p. 433). One of the key findings of their study is that the quality they call "liveliness" is a critical component of learning, and living, in online spaces. They define "liveliness" as "a moment in which discussion emerges in an unpredictable, but not necessarily unplanned for, form" (p. 451). It could be a moment when the students are engaged in genuine problem solving (and there is no one right expected answer); it could be a moment of frustration or tension (e.g., when students are negotiating assignment requirements with the teacher). Whithaus and Neff concluded that teachers should script in "spaces or activities that encourage open-ended student discussion about their writing projects" (2006, p. 451) in order to encourage liveliness to emerge in a hybrid course.

The Whithaus and Neff study affirms that a key feature for effective interaction is liveliness, or what Nathan Shedroff (n.d.) called "interesting and compelling experiences." Yes, access and usability are critical measures of audience interactivity, but they represent only the minimal criteria for interactivity. Digital information that is designed in ways that interest and engage audiences and that calls upon them to actively participate in co-production seem to be more effective than those designs that position the audience as passive consumers of information.

2.5. Economics

When rhetoric asks questions about audience and purpose—What is my purpose for writing? Who is my audience?—it is also implicitly asking questions about the economics of delivery. What motivates someone to produce and distribute a piece of writing? What motivates someone else to access it, read it, interact with it? What drives the interaction and makes it productive for both parties? These are basic questions of rhetorical production that are also basic questions of economics. These are questions that need to be included in a robust canon of digital delivery.

Writing—all writing, I would say—resides in economic systems of value, exchange, and capital. These systems are not necessarily monetary or commercial systems (think about Pierre Bourdieu's [1983] notions of cultural capital and social capital), but they are economic systems nonetheless. The kind of economics I am talking about has to do with value more broadly defined: yes, it might involve the exchange of currency—but the motivation could be based on desire, participation, sharing, emotional connectedness. This is the secret of the Web 2.0 dynamic.

I use the phrase "the economics of rhetoric"[11] as shorthand for a number of different delivery concerns, including questions about motivation (what prompts somebody to write?); questions regarding intellectual property, ownership, and rights to writing; and matters related to credit, payment, and the labor of writing. The economics of rhetoric is dramatically changed in the realm of digital discourse.

This dramatic economic shift has occurred because of technological developments involving "the internetworked computer" (Porter, 1998; Porter, 2003) and because of the social networks that the technology has helped to promote.

The computer plus the Internet and the World Wide Web provide publishing capacity to the individual writer. With a networked computer with a copy-paste function, the writer has the capacity to download and upload files and, if she has broadband Internet access, "the means to distribute and access a wide variety of information (text, graphics, audio, video) globally, quickly, and relatively easily" (DeVoss & Porter, 2006, p. 195). Such a capacity threatens the traditional print-based and analog models of publishing and media distribution because it puts publishing capacities in the hands of a much broader cross-section of society. Not everybody has this capacity, to be sure, as we have seen in our consideration of Access/Accessibility, but a much broader range of ordinary users now has the economic means to "compete" (in some sense) with traditional publishers and media conglomerates—in the same way that the printing press opened new avenues for print distribution in the 16th century, threatening the Church's control over the distribution of knowledge.

The first major crisis of the new digital economy was "the Napster crisis" (DeVoss & Porter, 2006). This Internet-based service enabled thousands of users to upload and share their music files in a comprehensive way that was not possible with analog audiotapes. What Napster labeled as "filesharing" the recording industry signified with a different term: "piracy." The Napster case is just one example of how, in creating new mechanisms for distribution and circulation, Internet technology has created the cyberinfrastructure allowing for new digital economies to emerge—economies that can create significant challenges for industries built on nondigital economies.

Traditionally, rhetoric/composition has typically conceptualized writing from the standpoint of "composing" (creating the isolated text) and "reading" it. But when writing enters digital spaces, we need to reconceptualize writing from the point of view of production, consumption, and exchange (see Marx, 1970; Trimbur, 2000). This shift in vocabulary is not innocent or neutral. It forces us to think about writing as involving labor, as being involved in an economic system of exchange, as having status as a commodity with value (both use value to the reader, but also exchange value).

What are the motivations for distributing information online? What motivates someone to maintain and post to a political blog, or to help strangers solve their technical problems in a user help forum, or to contribute an encyclopedia entry to Wikipedia—all instances of unpaid writing? As Clay Shirky has said, from an economic standpoint "it sure is weird that the Wikipedia works" (Aigrain, 2003). It is not weird if you accept that people write because they want to interact, to share, to learn, to play, to feel valued, and to help others. And that drive of people to interact socially is a key feature of the new digital era. It explains the popularity of blogs and of social networking spaces like Facebook, MySpace, and YouTube.

Yochai Benkler has been investigating this phenomenon of social sharing in the digital realm, framing such sharing in terms of a gift exchange economy (Benkler, 2003; Benkler, 2004; Benkler, 2006). His first point was that conventional monetary notions of economics are inadequate for explaining the phenomenon of social networking. Like carpooling, social networking does not usually generate dollars directly—but, like carpooling, it does generate economic value, value that is not easily captured by standard economic models. The term that Benkler employed to describe this phenomenon is "commons-based peer production," which refers to a mode of economic production in which the creative energy of large numbers of people is coordinated into meaningful projects, mostly without traditional hierarchical organization or financial compensation. Most scholars are involved in commons-based peer production, or at least they are if they are participants in email discussion groups (i.e., listservs). Most professional discussion groups—like H-RHETOR (for scholars working in the history of rhetoric), AoIR-L (listserv for the Association of Internet Researchers), and CHI-WEB (discussion group for web designers)—are based on a gift-exchange economy. Scholars and practitioners participate on these lists not to make money directly but rather to share information and resources of value to the community.[12]

The other crisis involving digital economics is the plagiarism crisis—the perception (backed by some evidence) that the academic problem of plagiarism has become much worse in the digital era, thanks to easier access to available texts (through the Internet) and thanks to the growth of the online term paper industry. In the realm of the Internet and World Wide Web, plagiarism makes a lot of sense from an economic standpoint—that is, if we are willing to suspend the ethical standpoint. In the world of digital filesharing, it makes much more sense to find available material and to recycle it than to create new material. From the standpoint of efficiency, recycling makes a lot of sense. The issue for digital writers is distinguishing between licit and illicit recycling—with the understanding that the guidelines for determining that distinction rely on a rhetorical understanding of the contexts of use. In academic contexts, the rules for crediting others' work differ from those in professional workplace contexts or social networking contexts. In a digital economy, the role of the professional writer/designer shifts from production of original content to managing information: that is, overseeing the design, development, and testing of information products. What we have in digital writing is a different economic exchange system than in print culture. Capital resides not so much in the original texts you produce as (a) in your ability to deliver and circulate texts in ways that make them accessible and useful to others and (b) in your ability to collaborate with others, to share files, to co-create meaning in social spaces. In other words, in the digital economy, what we think of as "writing ability" is shifting toward a collaborative notion of networked writing.

The production, distribution, use, and circulation of digital materials always involve issues of intellectual property—sometimes trademark issues, but almost always copyright issues. I see the issue of copyright, and the related issues of ownership, licensing, and control of digital material, as a key subtopic of digital delivery. Take the example of the screen shot, a common technique for capturing or copying online images. Almost every screen shot involves the capturing of copyrighted material. The question is, Who owns the copyright? For a screen capture, there are likely to be multiple copyright holders involved. For example, if I capture a Facebook page, I am likely picking up three types of copyrighted material: (a) original work created and uploaded by the account holder, the "user" (e.g., photos, comments and captions, messages); (b) potentially, work copyrighted by others that the user has "borrowed" for use on her/his site; and (c) most likely, pieces of the Facebook interface copyrighted or trademarked by Facebook. Negotiating questions about the rights of users (writers) vis-à-vis the rights of copyright holders (authors, publishers) is one of the key economic questions for digital rhetoric: deciding what is usable and what isn't, who needs to be credited and who doesn't, and who has the right to control these decisions involves both legal and ethical considerations. Such questions are important for individual writers, but they are also large social and political questions involving copyright laws and information policy. To be an effective digital writer and designer, one who has sufficient understanding of the techne involved here, requires extensive and current knowledge of the status of law and policy.

Thus, as pertains to delivery, the topos of economics includes issues of rhetorical economics—that is, motivation and exchange value: determining what information content, strategies, designs, architecture, etc. will likely encourage the participation of desired audiences. It includes questions of payment or credit for labor. It includes ethical questions of economic rights as well, questions that the field of computers and composition has long been raising in regards to digital copyright, plagiarism, and filesharing.

3. Delivery in Action

Technical knowledge is integral to digital rhetoric, but that knowledge is not merely mechanical, routinized procedure. Yes, it can certainly be reduced to that (and often is), but when practiced as art (techne) technical knowledge intersects with rhetorical and critical questions in order to assist discursive production and action.

The *techne* of digital rhetoric required here must be of two types: (1) productive how-to knowledge—i.e., the art of knowing various technological options and knowing how to use them to achieve various rhetorical effects; and (2) practical judgment, ethical *phronesis*—i.e., the ability to ask and answer critical questions about one's choices, such as what serves the common good, what are the human implications of various options, who is in/excluded, who is helped/hurt, who is empowered/disempowered by various technology designs? *Productive* knowledge about making and *practical* knowledge about doing (and the ethics of doing) should work in conjunction to guide writing/communication practice. Here is where humanistic thinking has much to contribute to HCI.

By themselves, as static topics, these *koinoi topoi* of delivery—Body/Identity, Distribution/Circulation, Access/Accessibility, Interaction, Economics—do not do very much. To maximize their generative or productive power you must put them into dynamic interaction with one another and with other rhetorical topics. In other words, you connect up questions of delivery with rhetorical invention, with audience, with design of online information, and so on. Sort of like the relationship between Kenneth Burke's (1969) pentad and the ratios.[13]

Here is one example of what I mean: A real-world communication problem for emergency room healthcare is how to locate relevant patient records quickly and how to render those records textually, aurally, and/or visually—sometimes on an extremely small handheld screen—so that healthcare providers can quickly determine the proper course of medical care. In an emergency room, getting the right information quickly to the right medical personnel can mean the difference between life and death. Studying this process and designing information systems to meet the needs of multiple healthcare users are concerns of designers in HCI and researchers in usability studies (see, for example, Mirel, 2003).

This is not a merely mechanical task but rather one of *techne*: a task involving critical decisions about audiences and their disciplinary orientations (e.g., given their differing roles in healthcare, nurses, doctors, hospital administrators, and lab technicians need different kinds of information and at different levels of granularity); questions of information selection and arrangement; ethical issues regarding patient privacy and who should have access to what information; and deep understanding about the workplace context and the rapid information dynamics of that context (What happens in emergency rooms? How do healthcare providers do their work, how do they access information while providing patient care?).

The distributed information is not just digital, of course. The communication dynamic involves print, oral, and digital forms of information intersecting (and, at times, conflicting)—and of course the patient's body is right there as the key focal point of the entire scene. The canon of memory plays a key role in this setting: i.e., retrieving a patient's medical history, lab test results, and so on. Memory here is not only a mechanical question of information storage but a *techne* question involving the process for generating information content and considering audience (*inventio*), design of information (*dispositio*), and mechanisms for technological delivery (*actio*).

Solving this problem for healthcare requires a *rhetorical* approach, and it requires putting the topics of the rhetorical canon into dynamic tension: we must understand how to store patient information (*memoria*) so that it can be quickly retrieved by different users who are accessing that information for different purposes at different stages of patient care. The information has to be arranged (*dispositio*) in a way that is easily comprehensible. It has to be delivered (*actio*) via different media. The persons responsible for entering that data have to understand what data is needed by what audiences for what purposes (*inventio*) and design the information (*dispositio*) in a style that is clear and concise (*elocutio*).

The question of delivery of information is similarly complex: How do I ensure that different audiences, accessing the information via different media and browsers and devices, "see" the same information? What mechanisms do I install to enable certain designated users to change or update patient information—and who has the right to change the patient's record? What policies and technological constraints need to be built in to ensure that patient information is distributed quickly to those who need it while simultaneously protecting the information, screening it from those who do not have a right to see it? Treating the problem as a strictly mechanical question or as a matter of information storage and retrieval misses the complexity of the rhetorical setting, particularly the complexity of the use of this information by and for humans. This situation needs smart technological thinking for sure, but it also requires smart rhetorical thinking (and legal and ethical thinking) that is sensitive to audience needs and the context of the information's use, a context that includes legal and political considerations as well as health-related and disciplinary ones.

The point of reviving delivery is not to demonstrate the enduring truth of classical categories. What matters is developing useful rhetoric theory. A useful rhetoric theory should raise significant questions and encourage productive thinking about how to communicate with others. The real value in developing a robust rhetorical theory for digital delivery lies in production: How can this theory aid productive action? How can it prompt the critical thinking of writers/designers and help them produce better (more valuable, usable, and useful) online communications and thereby help people with their lives? As always, the ultimate point of rhetoric is to help writers/speakers/designers do a better job of helping people live their lives—or, even, save lives. Developing a robust rhetorical canon for digital delivery is necessary to achieve that end.

James E. Porter is Professor of English and Interactive Media Studies at Miami University where he directs the program in College Composition.

NOTES

1 Recently, several important discussions on the canon of delivery have appeared in print, including significant efforts to remediate the canon of delivery for the digital age: Kathleen Blake Yancey's (2006) edited collection *Delivering College Composition* focused on issues pertaining to the delivery of composition instruction in the digital age. Paul Prior et al. (2007) have recognized the critical importance of reviving delivery and have developed a framework for remediating the five classical canons for the digital age. They suggested that the term "delivery" be reconceived as mediation and distribution and have gone one step further by demonstrating their theory through

a multimodal digital text. Though I very much agree with their theoretical approach to mediation and distribution, my framework for delivery includes more elements and critical components and is geared more toward production. Jim Ridolfo and Dànielle Nicole DeVoss's (2009) discussion of delivery focused on "rhetorical velocity," which is I see as a concern for what I am calling circulation, but with an eye particularly toward timing (*kairos*) and "recomposition"—or the deliberate strategy of designing a piece of writing not only for circulation but also for re-use or remixing. This, too, I see as an important feature of the canon for digital delivery—but, again, not the entirety of the canon.

2 As Reynolds (1993) pointed out, "In composition studies, the first three canons—invention, arrangement, and style—are used to organize the materials presented in the vast majority of the textbooks, but the last two—memory and delivery—are typically ignored or, worse, deleted without a word of explanation" (p. 3).

3 For example, the "Serious Game Design" (n.d.) Master's program at Michigan State University was founded in 2007 to teach game design "with a purpose beyond entertainment, including but not limited to games for learning, games for health, and games for policy and social change."

4 I am indebted to Doug Eyman (2007) for helping me appreciate the relevance of the distinction between "distribution" and "circulation"—a distinction noted by Karl Marx (1970) but remediated here for application in the realm of Internet communication. Although Eyman's framework for understanding circulation is different from my own, his 2007 dissertation provided a detailed and valuable analysis of this concept and analyzed techniques for tracking circulation in digital spaces.

5 Such a license signals to others than they can "remix, tweak, and build upon your work non-commercially, as long as they credit you and license their new creations under the identical terms" (About: Licenses, n.d.). In short, this license encourages remixing and promotes sharing of remixed products.

6 Data reported by the Pew Internet and American Life Project (2008) show that, as of December 2008: only 41% of Americans over age 65 use the Internet; only 64% of black Americans use the Internet (compared with 77% for whites); and only 35% of those who have not graduated from high school use the Internet (compared with 67% of high school graduates and 95% of college graduates). For purposes of this survey Pew defines "use" as an instance of someone using the Internet or sending/receiving email "at least occasionally" (Pew, 2008).

7 As Internet information design becomes increasingly multimodal (i.e., incorporating audio and video), the question of level of access becomes more important. Even if a poorer household has modem access, without broadband access that household is not able, practically speaking, to access

certain forms of information that are presented only or mainly in multimedia formats. The groups that perhaps have the lowest levels of Internet access in the United States are Native Americans (particularly those on rural reservations) (Tristani, 2001; Twist, 2002) and disabled persons, a group that includes a wide variety of types of physical disability (Rainie et al., 2003; Slatin, 2006).

8 Mary Frances Theofanos and Janice Redish (2005) stressed the importance of designing online information for blind and "low-vision users"—a category that includes a large number of people (about 7.7 million people in the United States alone), and a category that will include almost every person at some point or other in their lives. Many users cannot fully access multimedia or animation on the Web: people with hearing disabilities need captioning or transcripts for audio content; people with vision disabilities need descriptions of video content.

9 Annette Harris Powell (2007) argued that it is important to approach access on the level of "actual practices" (p. 17). As Powell pointed out, the issue of access for many is not so much access to physical technology (hardware, software) as literacy and social access—i.e., understanding about online rhetorical conventions and dynamics and how to negotiate them. See also Porter, 1998, pp. 102-105.

10 Lucy Suchman (1997) argued that "the term 'interaction' might best be reserved to describe what goes on between persons, rather than extended to encompass relations between people and machines" (see also Winograd, 1997). Shedroff (n.d.) defined interaction as "the art of effectively creating interesting and compelling experiences for others."

11 Economics has always been an important component of rhetoric, as DeVoss and Porter (2006) have argued, but historically the relationship has only occasionally been articulated, appreciated, or examined within the field of rhetoric—most notably by Deirdre McCloskey (1998) and Richard Lanham (2006) (see also Carter, 2005). It is important to note the distinction, however, between McCloskey's focus on the rhetoric of economics, versus my focus on the economics of rhetoric.

12 Writing well before the digital age, Pierre Bourdieu (1983) told us two things of importance to digital distribution: (1) the importance of symbolic capital (or cultural capital) in a society should never be underestimated; and (2) the relationship between symbolic and material capital matters; they have an effect on one another. (Symbolic capital is tied to the potential and actual development of economic capital.) Figuring out how this works is not just the job of economics. It is the job of rhetoric as well.

13 Burke's pentad forms the basis for his dramatistic method. The five perspectives of the pentad—scene, act, agency, actor, purpose—represent five viewpoints one can take toward human situations. However, it is through forming the ratios—i.e., putting the five elements of the pentad into

dyadic relationships (scene-act, scene-agent, etc.)—that the writer/producer can achieve critical understanding about human action and motives. Similarly with the koinoi topoi of delivery: it is by making connections among and across the topics that the writer/producer can achieve productive, creative thinking.

REFERENCES

About: Licenses. (n.d.). *Creative Commons.* Retrieved from http://creativecommons.org/about/licenses/ Aigrain, Philippe. (2003). The individual and the collective in open information communities. *Free/Open source research community.* Retrieved from http://opensource.mit.edu/papers/aigrain3.pdf

Alexander, Jonathan, & Banks, William (Eds.). (2004). *Sexualities, technologies, and the teaching of writing* (Special issue). Computers and Composition, 21.

Alexander, Jonathan. (1997). Hypertext and queer theory. *Kairos: A Journal of Rhetoric, Technology, and Pedagogy,* 2(2). Retrieved from http://english.ttu.edu/KAIROS/2.2/features/reflections/jon.htm

Alexander, Phill. (2007, March 22). Gaming literacies and character generation in City of Heroes. In *Presented at the Conference on College Composition and Communication.* New York, NY.

Anderson, Daniel. (2003). Prosumer approaches to new media composition: Consumption and production in continuum. *Kairos: A Journal of Rhetoric, Technology, and Pedagogy,* 8(1). Retrieved from http://kairos.technorhetoric.net/8.1/binder2.html?coverweb/anderson/index.html

Aristotle (1991). *On rhetoric: A theory of civic discourse.* (George A. Kennedy, Trans.). New York: Oxford University Press.

Armstrong, Rhiannon. (2005, February). Performing identity in the digital age. Proquest-CSA. Retrieved from http://www.csa.com/discoveryguides/perform/overview.php

Associated Press. (2006, February 23). China claims 400M mobile phone users. MSNBC. Retrieved May 25, 2009, from http://www.msnbc.msn.com/id/15519322/

Austin, Gilbert. (1644/1966). In Mary Margaret Robb, & Lester Thomssen (Eds.), *Chironomia; or a treatise on rhetorical delivery* [1806]. Southern Illinois University Press. Carbondale.

Bailie, Brian. (2007, March 22). Dystopia online: The (re)productive rhetoric of EverQuest. In *Presented at the Conference on College Composition and Communication* New York, NY.

Banks, Adam J. (2005). *Race, rhetoric and technology: Searching for higher ground*. Mahwah, NJ: Erlbaum.

Benkler, Yochai. (2003). The political economy of commons. *Upgrade*, 4(3), 6–9.

Benkler, Yochai. (2004). Sharing nicely: On shareable goods and the emergence of sharing as a modality of economic production. *The Yale Law Journal*, 114, 273–358.

Benkler, Yochai. (2006). *The wealth of networks: How social production transforms markets and freedom*. New Haven, CT: Yale University Press.

Blair, Kristine, & Takayoshi, Pamela. (1997). Navigating the image of woman online. *Kairos: A Journal of Rhetoric, Technology, and Pedagogy*, 2(2). Retrieved from http://kairos.technorhetoric.net/2.2/binder2.html?coverweb/invited/kb.html

Blair, Kristine, & Takayoshi, Pamela. (1999). Mapping the terrain of feminist cyberscapes. In Kristine Blair, & Pamela Takayoshi (Eds.), *Feminist cyberscapes: Mapping gendered academic spaces* (pp. 1–18). Stamford, CT: Ablex.

Bourdieu, Pierre. (1983). The forms of capital (Richard Nice, Trans.). In Reinhard Kreckel (Ed.), Ökonomisches Kapital, kulturelles Kapital, soziales Kapitaln Soziale Ungleichheiten (pp. 183-198). Goettingen, Germany: Otto Schartz. Retrieved from http://www.marxists.org/reference/subject/philosophy/works/fr/bourdieu-forms-capital.htm

Burke, Kenneth. (1969). *A grammar of motives*. Berkeley: University of California Press.

Carter, Locke. (2005). Rhetoric, markets and value creation: An introduction and argument for a productive rhetoric. In Locke Carter (Ed.), *Market matters: Applied rhetoric studies and free market competition* (pp. 1–52). Cresskill, NJ: Hampton Press.

Cicero (1981). *Ad C. Herennium de ratione dicendi (Rhetorica ad Herennium)*. (Harry Caplan, Trans.). Cambridge, MA: Loeb Classical Library, Harvard University Press.

Cicero (1988). *De oratore*. (H. Rackham, Trans.). Cambridge: Harvard University Press.

Connors, Robert J. (1983). Actio: A rhetoric of manuscripts. *Rhetoric Review*, 2(1), 64–73.

de Pisan, Christine (1405/1985). *The treasure of the city of ladies; or the book of three virtues*. (Sarah Lawson, Trans.). New York: Penguin.

DeVoss, Dànielle Nicole, & Porter, James E. (2006). Why Napster matters to writing: Filesharing as a new ethic of digital delivery. *Computers and Composition*, 23(2), 178–210.

Eisenstein, Elizabeth L. (1979). *The printing press as an agent of change (Complete in one volume)*. Cambridge, UK: Cambridge University Press.

Eyman, Douglas Andrew. (2007). *Digital rhetoric: Ecologies and economies of digital circulation.* (Doctoral dissertation, Michigan State University, United States). Retrieved from Dissertations & Theses @ CIC Institutions database. (Publication No. AAT 3282094).

Fox, Susannah. (2005). Digital divisions. *Pew Internet & American life project.* Retrieved from http://www.pewinternet.org/Reports/2005/Digital-Divisions.aspx

Gerrard, Lisa. (1997). Computers, gender, and the body electric. *Kairos: A Journal of Rhetoric, Technology, and Pedagogy,* 2(2). Retrieved from http://kairos.technorhetoric.net/2.2/binder2.html?coverweb/invited/lg.html

Gohring, Nancy. (2006, June 28). W3C sets best practices for mobile web design. *ComputerWorld.* Retrieved May 26, 2009, from http://www.computerworld.com/action/article.do?command=viewArticleBasic&articleId=9001503

Grabill, Jeff. (2003). On divides and interfaces: Access, class, and computers. *Computers and Composition,* 20(4), 455–472.

Halbritter, Scott A. (2004). *Sound arguments: Aural rhetoric in multimedia composition.* (Doctoral Dissertation. University of North Carolina, Chapel Hill, NC). Retrieved from http://sunzi1.lib.hku.hk/ER/detail/hkul/3839533

Haraway, Donna. (1991). A cyborg manifesto: Science, technology, and socialist-feminism in the late twentieth century. In *Simians, cyborgs and women: The reinvention of nature.* pp. 149–181. New York: Routledge.

Haraway, Donna. (n.d.). *Donna Haraway – Links.* Retrieved from http://www.egs.edu/faculty/haraway-links.html

Hawisher, Gail E., & Sullivan, Patricia A. (1999). Fleeting images: Women visually writing the web. In Gail E. Hawisher, & Cynthia L. Selfe (Eds.), *Passions, pedagogies, and 21st-century technologies* (pp. 268–291). Logan, UT: Utah State UP.

Hayles, N. Katherine. (1999). *How we became posthuman: Virtual bodies in cybernetics, literature and informatics.* Chicago: The University of Chicago Press.

Herring, Susan C. (2001). Gender and power in online communications. CSI Working Paper WP-01-05. Retrieved May 24, 2009, from http://rkcsi.indiana.edu/archive/CSI/WP/WP01-05B.html Internet World Stats. (2009, May 22). Internet usage statistics: The big picture. Retrieved from http://www.internetworldstats.com/stats.htm

Jacobi, Martin. (2006). The canon of rhetoric in rhetorical delivery: Selections, commentary and advice. In Kathleen Blake Yancey (Ed.), *Delivering college composition: The fifth canon* (pp. 17–29). Portsmouth, NH: Boynton/Cook.

Jones, Robert. (2004, February 6). Creating web content for mobile phone browsers, part 1. *O'Reilly Media*. Retrieved from http://www.oreillynet.com/pub/a/wireless/2004/02/06/mobile browsing.html

Lanham, Richard A. (1991). *A handlist of rhetorical terms* (2nd ed.). Berkeley: University of California Press.

Lanham, Richard A. (2006). *The economics of {attention}: Style and substance in the age of information*. Chicago: The University of Chicago Press.

Lauer, Janice M. (2004). *Invention in rhetoric and composition*. West Lafayette, IN: Parlor Press.

Lemon, Summer. (2007, May 29). China heads toward 500 million cell phone subscribers. *ComputerWorld*. Retrieved May 25, 2009, from http://www.computerworld.com/action/article.do?command=viewArticleBasic&articleId=9021578&intsrc=news ts head

Lessig, Lawrence. (n.d.). *Lessig 2.0*. Retrieved from http://www.lessig.org/

Lunsford, Andrea A. (2006). Writing, technologies, and the fifth canon. *Computers and Composition*, 23(2), 169–177.

Manovich, Lev. (2001). *The language of new media*. Cambridge: MIT Press.

Marx, Karl. (1970). Production, consumption, distribution exchange (circulation). In Maurice Dobb (Ed.), *A contribution to the critique of political economy* (pp. 188–217). New York: International.

McCloskey, Deirdre N. (1998). *The rhetoric of economics* (2nd ed.). Madison: The University of Wisconsin Press.

McKee, Heidi. (2006). Sound matters: Notes toward the analysis and design of sound in multimodal webtexts. *Computers and Composition*, 23(3), 335–354.

Mirel, Barbara. (2003). General hospital: Modeling complex problem solving in complex work system. In *Proceedings of the 21st Annual International Conference on Documentation* (SIGDOC'03)(pp. 60-67). New York: ACM. Retrieved from http://doi.acm.org/10.1145/944868.944882

Moll, Cameron. (2005, October 27). Mobile web design: Tips and techniques. *CameronMoll*. Retrieved from http://www.cameronmoll.com/archives/000577.html

Moran, Charles. (1999). Access: The A-word in technology studies. In Gail E. Hawisher, & Cynthia L. Selfe (Eds.), *Passions, pedagogies, and 21st-century technologies* (pp. 205–220). Logan, UT: NCTE.

Nadeau, Ray. (1964). Delivery in ancient times: Homer to Quintilian. *Quarterly Journal of Speech*, 50, 53–60.

Pew Internet & American Life Project. (2008, December) *Demographics of Internet users*. Retrieved from http://www.pewinternet.org/Data-Tools/Download-Data/⊠/media/Infographics/Trend Data/January 2009updates/DemographicsofInternetUsers1609.jpg

Porter, James E. (1998). *Rhetorical ethics and internetworked writing*. Greenwich, CT: Ablex.

Porter, James E. (2003). Why technology matters to writing: A cyberwriter's tale. *Computers and Composition*, 20(4), 375–394.

Powell, Annette Harris. (2007). Access(ing), habits, attitudes, and engagements: Re-thinking access as practice. *Computers and Composition*, 24(1),16–35.

Prior, Paul; Solberg, Janine; Berry, Patrick W.; Bellwoar, Hannah; Chewning, Bill; Lunsford, Karen; Rohan, Liz; Roozen, Kevin; Sheridan-Rabideau, Mary; Shipka, Jody; Van Ittersum, Derek; & Walker, Joyce. (2007). Re-situating and re-mediating the canons: A cultural-historical remapping of rhetorical activity. *Kairos: A Journal of Rhetoric, Technology, and Pedagogy*, 11(3). Retrieved from http://kairos.technorhetoric.net/11.3/binder.html?topoi/prior-et-al/mapping/index.html

Quintilian. (1922). *Institutio oratoria* (H.E. Butler, Trans.). Cambridge: Loeb Classical Library, Harvard University Press. Retrieved from http://penelope.uchicago.edu/Thayer/E/Roman/Texts/Quintilian/Institutio Oratoria/home.html

Rainie, Lee; Madden, Mary; Boyce, Angie; Lenhart, Amanda; Horrigan, John; Allen, Katherine; & O'Grady, Erin. (2003, April 16). The ever-shifting Internet population: A new look at Internet access and the digital divide. *The Pew Internet & American life project*. Retrieved from http://www.pewinternet.org/Reports/2003/The-EverShifting-Internet-Population-A-new-look-at-Internet-access-and-the-digital-divide.aspx

Reardon, Marguerite. (2007, February 14). Emerging markets fuel cell phone growth. CNet News. Retrieved May 25, 2009, from http://news.com.com/2100-1039 3-6159491.html

Reynolds, John Frederick (Ed.). (1993). *Rhetorical memory and delivery*: Classical concepts for contemporary composition and communication. Hillsdale, NJ: Erlbaum.

Reynolds, John Frederick. (1996). Delivery. In Theresa Enos (Ed.), *Encyclopedia of rhetoric and composition: Communication from ancient times to the information age* (pp. 172–173). New York: Garland.

Rhodes, Jacqueline (Ed.), (2004). Sexualities, technologies, and literacies: Metonymy and material online (Special issue). *Computers and Composition Online*. Retrieved from http://www.bgsu.edu/cconline/rhodes/CCOintro.htm

Rice, Jeff. (2006). The making of ka-knowledge: Digital aurality. *Computers and Composition*, 23(3), 266–279.

Ridolfo, Jim, & DeVoss, Dànielle Nicole. (2009). Composing for recomposition: Rhetorical velocity and delivery. *Kairos: A Journal of Rhetoric, Technology, and Pedagogy*, 13(2). Retrieved from http://www.technorhetoric.net/13.2/topoi/ridolfo devoss/index.html

Selfe, Cynthia L., & Hawisher, Gail E. (2004). *Literate lives in the information age: Narratives of literacy from the United States*. Mahwah, NJ: Erlbaum.

Selfe, Richard J., & Selfe, Cynthia L. (1994). The politics of the interface: Power and its exercise in electronic contact zones. *College Composition and Communication*, 45(4), 480–504.

Serious game design. (n.d.). Michigan State University. Retrieved from http://seriousgames.msu.edu/

Shankar, Tara Rosenberger. (2006). Speaking on the record: A theory of composition. *Computers and Composition*, 23(3), 374–393.

Shedroff, Nathan. (n.d.). What is interactivity anyway? *Nathan Shedroff's world*. Retrieved May 24, 2009, from http://www.nathan.com/thoughts/interpres/

Slatin, John M. (2006). Becoming an accessibility researcher: A memoir. In James A. Inman, & Beth L. Hewett (Eds.), *Technology and English Studies: Innovative professional paths* (pp. 143–162). Mahwah, NJ: Erlbaum.

Suchman, Lucy. (1997, July). Interactions to integrations: A reflection on the future of HCI. Keynote address of *Interact 97: Discovering new worlds of HCI*. Retrieved from http://www.acs.org.au/president/1997/intrct97/suchman.htm

Sunkowsky, Robert P. (1959). An aspect of delivery in ancient rhetorical theory. *Transactions and Proceedings of the American Philological Association*, 90, 256–274.

Theofanos, Mary Frances, & Redish, Janice. (2005). Helping low-vision and other users with web sites that meet their needs: Is one site for all feasible? *Technical Communication*, 52(1), 9–20.

Trimbur, John. (2000). Composition and the circulation of writing. *College Composition and Communication*, 52(2), 188–219.

Tristani, Gloria. (2001, February 21). Connecting Indian Country to the information age. Remarks before the National Congress of American Indians.Washington, DC. Retrieved from http://www.fcc.gov/Speeches/Tristani/2001/spgt103.html

Twist, Kade. (2002, March 4). A nation online, but where are the Native Americans? *Digital Divide Network*. Retrieved from http://www.digitaldivide.net/articles/view.php?ArticleID=153

US Aid. (2003). Increasing computer access in Africa. Retrieved May 25, 2009, from http://africastories.usaid.gov/searchdetails.cfm?storyID=19&countryID=4&sectorID=0&yearID=3

Welch, Kathleen E. (1990). Electrifying classical rhetoric: Ancient media, modern technology, and contemporary composition. *Journal of Advanced Composition*, 10(1), 22–38.

Welch, Kathleen E. (1994). Interpreting the silent "Aryan Model" of classical histories: Martin Bernal, Terry Eagleton, and the politics of rhetoric and

"Western Civilization". In V. Victor (Ed.), *Writing histories of rhetoric* (pp. 38–48). Carbondale, IL: Southern Illinois University Press.

Welch, Kathleen E. (1999). *Electric rhetoric: Classical rhetoric, oralism and a new literacy*. Cambridge: The MIT Press.

Whithaus, Carl, & Neff, Joyce Magnotto. (2006). Contact and interactivity: Social constructionist pedagogy in a video-based, management writing course. *Technical Communication Quarterly*, 15(4), 431–456.

Wild, John. (1941). Plato's theory of techne: A phenomenological interpretation. *Philosophy and Phenomenological Research*, 1, 255–293.

Winograd, Terry. (1997). From computing machinery to interaction design. *Stanford University Program in Human-Computer Interaction*. Retrieved from http://hci.stanford.edu/winograd/acm97.html

Wysocki, Anne Frances. (2001). Impossibly distinct: On form-content and word/image in two pieces of computer-based interactive multimedia. *Computers and Composition*, 18(3), 209–234.

Yancey, Kathleen Blake (Ed.). (2006). *Delivering college composition: The fifth canon*. Portsmouth, NH: Boynton/Cook.

JAC

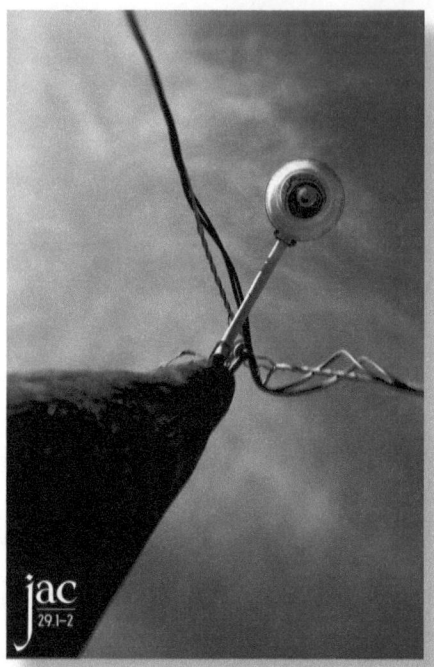

In 1980 *JAC* was created as the *Journal of Advanced Composition* to publish theoretical scholarship on written discourse and advanced writing (beyond the first-year sequence). Today, *JAC* continues to publish cutting-edge theoretical scholarship, but it is no longer the *Journal of Advanced Composition*. It has broadened its scope to include articles on a variety of topics related to rhetoric (broadly conceived), culture, discourse, and politics, with a view toward examining the power of language and discourse to produce social change. Therefore, the journal is known only as *JAC*, an acronym without a referent.

"Pass It On: Revising the Plagiarism is Theft Metaphor" by Amy Robillard

Amy Robillard's "Pass It On: Revising the Plagiarism Is Theft Metaphor" is an example of scholarship at its best, not only within the field of rhetoric and composition but also in the broader domain of the humanities. What makes it exemplary is the scope of its ambition: it operates at several critical levels simultaneously. It examines what is for most scholars and teachers a self-evident truth—plagiarism is theft—and shows that this truism is a conceptual metaphor that uncritically authorizes thought and practice. It seeks to revise how we conceptualize plagiarism and how we talk to students about the ethics and practice of drawing on the work of others. In so doing, it operates at an ethical level in its effort to transform the social relations between teachers and students, relations that are supported and sustained by the theft metaphor. In drawing on a wide variety of scholars both in rhetoric and composition and in the humanities, the article enacts the very model of citational practice that it forwards and thereby passes on a rich conversation about our lives with texts.

Pass It On: Revising the *Plagiarism Is Theft* Metaphor

Amy Robillard

In *Words for the Taking: The Hunt for a Plagiarist,* Neal Bowers' account of his years-long search for the thief who stole his poems and published them under another name, the author recalls the plagiarism lectures he used to give to students in his writing courses. Bowers writes,

> Everyone who teaches basic courses in writing has a standard admonition for plagiarism. When I taught freshman composition in the early 1980s, I referred to it as my thou-shalt-not-steal spiel. It was serious business, but I had presented the warning so many times I had begun to mock myself, the way a weary actor sometimes does in a bad role. One whole class period early in the term would be given over to a definition of plagiarism and a stern lecture on why it is the academic world's equivalent of a capital offense. Invariably at least one student would express concern that true originality is impossible, and I would jokingly refer him to the philosophy department while reminding him that any thief knows when he puts something in his pocket that doesn't belong to him. It seemed that simple. (28)

Bowers continues his reflection by noting that it never really was all that simple, that he came to understand that "most instances of student plagiarism resulted from ignorance rather than willful theft" (29). The established poet of course no longer teaches first-year composition, but as his book repeatedly makes clear, the theft metaphor still shapes both his conception of and his actions with regard to plagiarism. Plagiarism for Bowers is stealing. But of course, even in the midst of a complicated "hunt" for the plagiarist David Jones, aka David Sumner, the theft metaphor sometimes falls short. "How," Bowers imagines his attorney wondering, "could I be so upset over an action which deprived me of nothing?" (61). He lost nothing financially. But what Bowers' story makes clear is the extent to which an author whose work is plagiarized feels the sting of a lack of proper acknowledgment.

Consider what happens when we understand Bowers' loss as one of *credit* rather than of words or remuneration. How might we move from Bowers' representation of loss to a more nuanced representation of the psychic functions of credit for writers? I'm thinking here of Dustin Hoffman's performance in Barry Levinson's *Wag the Dog*. Hoffman plays Stanley Motts, a Hollywood producer hired by the president's spin doctor, Conrad Brean, to stage a television war in order to direct attention away from a presidential sex scandal. Connie promises Stan an ambassadorship in exchange for his efforts, the understanding being that Stan can never publicly take credit for this work. In one of the final scenes, once the "war" has been successfully pulled off and the presidential sex scandal quieted, Stan and Connie watch news reports of the president's 89% approval rating implicitly attributed to a hokey commercial cautioning against changing horses midstream. When the reporters announce that they'll be taking telephone calls, Stan goes to the phone. He's going to call and set them straight about who deserves the credit for that 89% approval rating. When Connie tries to stop him by reminding Stan that he can have an ambassadorship, a secret account for extra expenses, guards who will "salute you all the time," Stan replies, "No. It's tempting. But I gotta answer to a higher calling."

"Money? Okay."

"Money. You think I did this for money? I did this for credit. For credit."

"You always knew you couldn't take the credit."

"That's one thing," Stan replies, "but I'm not gonna stand here and let two dickheads from film school take it."

My concern in this essay is not, of course, with poets whose work has been plagiarized or with the work of spin doctors. Rather, my concern lies at the intersection of Bowers' mocking of his own "thou-shalt-not-steal" spiels to students and his observation that what is stolen when a plagiarist steals the work of another cannot be accounted for financially. I want to consider what happens when we revise the ubiquitous *plagiarism is theft* metaphor by calling attention to the *credit* that is lost. This instead of the commonplace understanding that what is stolen in acts of plagiarism is words or ideas. Such a reconception is dependent upon a more nuanced understanding of the metaphors that underwrite the *plagiarism is theft* metaphor—namely, what George Lakoff and Mark Johnson call the Moral Accounting metaphor and its entailment, a *right is an I.O.U.* I will demonstrate the ways in which such a nuanced understanding can help us shift pedagogical attention away from currently unarticulated assumptions about the relationship between plagiarism and morality to similarly unarticulated beliefs we all hold about the morality of social norms of attribution. The *plagiarism is theft* metaphor erodes social relations because it operates from beliefs about the morality of attribution that until this point have gone without saying in rhetoric and composition. The most basic of my goals in this essay, then, is to make the moral content of the metaphor explicit.

My work in this essay depends upon the fact that our talk about plagiarism is a rhetorical event with implications that we have not yet fully considered. Further, our reliance on the theft metaphor for explaining plagiarism often results in obscuring the social relationships that are established by responsible citation practices. Let me be clear up front. I do not believe nor do I wish to claim that all writing teachers themselves believe in or subscribe to the *plagiarism is theft* metaphor; rather, I wish to analyze the implications of a collective reliance on the metaphor to *explain* plagiarism to students. Indeed, we as scholars involved in disciplinary conversations understand our own work and the work of others as *contributions* rather than as objects to be stolen; we *want* others to use our work. We might say that in our work as scholars, we emphasize the *passing on* of new knowledge—a socially and morally responsible act—while in our work as teachers, we endorse conceptions of citation as *passing off*—a socially and morally reprehensible act.

In what follows, I suggest that a careful examination of the *plagiarism is theft* metaphor offers new opportunities for both explaining and understanding what it means to draw on the work of others. I draw on George Lakoff and Mark Johnson's classic *Metaphors We Live By* and on their more recent *Philosophy in the Flesh* to demonstrate the ways in which our uncritical dependence on the theft metaphor sabotages our professed commitment to valuing student writing. I focus much of my analysis on what is perhaps the most unexamined part of the metaphor: the object of theft. For a fresh perspective on this question, I turn to the work of Stuart P. Green, a legal scholar whose work on plagiarism and theft law I believe has the potential to radically alter the way we think about theft, ownership, and morality, thereby affecting the ways we talk about plagiarism with students.

OUR TALK ABOUT PLAGIARISM IS A RHETORICAL EVENT

Plagiarism is a hot-button issue for mass media and academics alike. The proliferation of scholarship on plagiarism in composition studies alone over the past decade and a half attests to both the complexity of the problem and the commitment we have made to understanding the problem in ways that have allowed us to enact theoretically sound pedagogical responses. Much of the early work in composition studies on plagiarism was definitional; scholars sought—and still seek—to distinguish between intentional and unintentional plagiarism (Howard, "Plagiarisms," "Ethics"; Kroll), between fraud and patch writing (Howard, *Standing*), between plagiarism as a purely textual issue and plagiarism as a relational issue, a phenomenon dependent on both writer and reader (Hutcheon; Randall; Valentine; Robillard and Fortune), and between cut-and-paste plagiarism and whole-text plagiarism (Ritter, "Economics," "Buying"). Is plagiarism an ethical issue? A textual issue? A criminal issue? Scholars have examined the links between our conceptions of plagiarism and the autonomous authorial genius (Howard, *Standing*; Woodmansee), between plagiarism and copyright law (Woodmansee and Jaszi; Butler; Stearns; Murray), between plagiarism and intellectual property (Zebroski; Rose; Lunsford; Lunsford and West). Pedagogies designed to prevent plagiarism have cropped up in our journals (Howard, *Standing*, "Forget"; Price; Ritter) and conference presentations (Fitzgerald), on blogs too numerous to name, and in the form of an officially sanctioned statement by the Council of Writing Program Administrators. Scholars have suggested revisions to university plagiarism policies (Howard, "Plagiarisms"; Price; Anson). We have recently begun to consider what happens when such pedagogies fail to prevent plagiarism; teachers' responses to suspected plagiarism show us that plagiarism is not the purely textual issue we would sometimes like to make it out to be (Robillard).

Finally, the impact of internet technology on plagiarism has not gone unnoticed; the internet has affected students' access to texts (Howard, "Understanding"), teachers' access to software designed to detect plagiarism (Marsh; Gibaldi), and even the ubiquity of published reports decrying an increase in internet plagiarism (Zwagerman).

DEFINE. ASSIGN. PREVENT. SUSPECT. DETECT.

Contributors to Howard and Robillard's recent collection, *Pluralizing Plagiarism: Identities, Contexts, Pedagogies*, argue that plagiarism is not a universal issue but rather an issue dependent on institutional and local contexts. And most recently, Sean Zwagerman's rhetorical analysis of the outraged discourse of plagiarism detection rightly demonstrates the ways in which a culture of distrust functions only to fuel more of the behavior we're allegedly trying to root out. To Howard and Robillard's emphasis on rhetorical context and to Zwagerman's analysis of discourse aimed at teachers and administrators, I add in this essay a consideration of the ways in which our lectures and our policies and our pedagogies of prevention are composed for and received by student audiences with particular needs, desires, agendas, and conceptions of what it means to write from sources. We are the rhetors, our students the audience, and our conceptions of them both reflect and shape the ways we talk about plagiarism.

As we see with Neal Bowers' book, the theft metaphor is the central means of understanding plagiarism in the world of journalism and professional writing. Thomas Mallon's popular book on plagiarism is called, after all, *Stolen Words*. Popular accounts of Doris Kearns Goodwin's alleged plagiarism unapologetically refer to her actions as "theft," as "steal[ing] someone else's sentences" (Noah). That plagiarism is theft goes without saying in professional publications; it is this conception of plagiarism that students likely carry with them when they enter our writing classrooms. They've heard the news, too, about the historians and the journalists plagiarizing. And they've been schooled for years in the notion that the primary purpose of citation is to demonstrate that you haven't plagiarized. Plagiarism is a constant danger; one must cite in order to *prevent* it.

In *Ethics in the 21st Century*, Mary Alice Trent relies on this commonsense notion of plagiarism when she explains to a student audience that "when students take information without acknowledging the source, they are not borrowing but stealing! The efforts of universities to teach accurate documentation and bibliography in the academy are being challenged by Web sites that encourage plagiarism" (195). In *The Little Penguin Handbook*, Lester Faigley begins Chapter 13, "Using Sources Ethically and Effectively" with the heading "Avoid Plagiarism." The section on source use in Jane E. Aaron's *Little, Brown Essential Handbook* is titled "Avoiding Plagiarism and Documenting Sources" (136) and includes a checklist for avoiding plagiarism (137). Andrea Lunsford's section on source use in *The St. Martin's Handbook* is called "Acknowledging Sources and Avoiding Plagiarism" (393). In *The Curious Writer*, Bruce Ballenger explains that "Modern authors get testy when someone uses their work without giving them credit" in his chapter subsection called "Avoiding Plagiarism" (372). Lynn Quitman Troyka and Douglas Hesse title their chapter on source use "Using Sources and Avoiding Plagiarism" (538). Explanations of source use and the admonition to avoid plagiarism seem to be inseparable.

In his rhetorical analysis of the discourse of plagiarism detection, Sean Zwagerman notes that when "enacted as policy, words such as *stealing, tracking,* and *catching* fuel the self-fulfilling cycle of suspicion: if we put more energy into rooting out plagiarism we are likely to find more plagiarism, become further convinced of a rising tide, become increasingly alarmed and reactive, and thus continue to put more energy into the solution—rooting out plagiarism" (679–80). But what happens when this language of suspicion is used to explain the very thing we're asking students to do when we invite them into the academic conversation? Before you even think of a topic to write about, we tell students, keep in mind that we already suspect you of plagiarism, so here are some tips on how to avoid it.

The rhetorical situation: teachers talking to their students about plagiarism. Rhetor understands audience members to be generally selfish and lazy, out to get the most benefit from the least amount of work. Students know that the teacher believes this about them. But we don't believe this, do we? Do we really believe, as Jonathan Malesic, a professor of theology at King's College and a regular columnist for *The Chronicle of Higher Education* does, that students "believe that any means to a good grade are legitimate"? When we caution students against plagiarizing before they even begin and when we explain plagiarism to them in terms of theft, we send the message that we believe they are selfish and lazy. If we don't trust them, why would they ever trust us?

The Many Metaphors for Plagiarism

Plagiarism has been explained by use of a number of metaphors that have been the subject of important composition scholarship. While I will argue that the theft metaphor is the dominant and thus invisible metaphor, the one that shapes our understanding and thus our actions with reference to plagiarism, I believe it is important to recognize these other metaphors for what they reveal about plagiarism as a concept. So dependent on metaphor, plagiarism cannot be comprehended without it.

It has become standard practice in all academic discussions of plagiarism to note that the word *plagiarism* derives from the Latin word *plagiarius,* meaning the kidnapping of a child or a slave—people who could, in Lise Buranen and Alice M. Roy's words, "in some sense be owned" (xvi). This fact is generally called upon to support the commonplace definition of plagiarism as theft. In her recent article for *Slate Magazine,* Meghan O'Rourke explains that

> Roman satirist Martial gave us its modern sense when he wrote an epigram complaining that another man (whom he labeled a "plagiarius") had kidnapped his writings (which he metaphorically labeled his slaves) and was passing them off as his own. What had been a metaphor for a slave-stealer—someone who got labor for free—became a symbolic expression for the theft of words. (2)

In composition studies, David Leight's 1999 "Plagiarism as Metaphor" notes that "it is not surprising, then, that many definitions talk about plagiarism as a form of stealing or 'kidnapping' of another's words" (222). Leight publishes the results of his study of nearly seventy writing textbooks published in the 1980s and 90s. Leight observes that the textbooks compare plagiarism to (1) stealing; (2) an ethical violation; (3) borrowing; and 4) intellectual laziness (221–27). Leight's essay is valuable for its focus on the ways plagiarism is explained to *students.*

In scholarly discussions of plagiarism aimed at other scholars, plagiarism has been compared to disease (Howard, *Standing*), to lying, to academic fraud (Howard, "Abolitionism"), to conquest (Randall), to collaboration (Wilson), and, more recently, to false alchemy (Marsh). Each of these metaphors has the potential to shape the ways we understand our experiences with plagiarism and thus to shape the ways we respond to students whose work we suspect may have been plagiarized. To understand plagiarism as a disease, for instance, is to understand the student writer as a diseased body, one who must be "cured" of the disease with the proper "medicine." To understand plagiarism as conquest is to understand "discursive borrowing as colonization," as Marilyn Randall explains:

> It is no longer foreign riches that are to be imported into the indigenous culture for its own benefit, but savage territories which the colonizer, Crusoe-like, makes his own by the appropriative labor of improvement and civilization. (134)

Imitation becomes pillage, plagiarism conquest, when understood in terms of "the colonial logic of possession by improvement" (134). These metaphors certainly have the potential to shape our understanding of and our explanations of plagiarism to others. It is my sense, though, that these metaphors for plagiarism apply only in our discussions with one another as teachers and scholars; we don't often address students directly as or speak to them as though they are colonizers or disease carriers. Rather, when addressing our students about plagiarism and citation, about writing from sources, we most often rely upon the theft metaphor, and our uncritical reliance on this metaphor has important consequences for the ways we perceive what students are doing and the ways students perceive what they are doing when writing from sources.

LAKOFF AND JOHNSON ON CONCEPTUAL METAPHOR

In *Metaphors We Live By*, Lakoff and Johnson suggest that the source of many of the metaphors we live by can be found in our everyday lived experience. Our understanding of the concept of *argument*, for example, is dependent upon our everyday understanding of the concept of *war*. Thus, *argument is war* (2–6). We *win* and *lose* arguments, we *attack* our opponents' positions, we *strategize*, and some arguers *take no prisoners*. This seems so simple. Of course arguments have winners and losers. But Lakoff and Johnson want us to understand that the metaphor *argument is war* is not a rhetorical flourish; instead, it is a concept we live by. "We talk about arguments that way because we conceive of them that way—and we act according to the way we conceive of things" (5). Metaphors we live by both shape and reflect our ordinary ways of understanding, so much so that many of these metaphors have become invisible to us. Crucial to their early work on metaphor were the tenets that metaphors are "rooted in physical and cultural experience" (18), that they "can never be comprehended or even adequately represented independently of [their] experiential basis" (19), and that the primary purpose of metaphor is understanding (36). Thus, not only do our cultural experiences with war shape our conceptualizations of argument, but such conceptualizations cannot be understood or represented independently of our physical and cultural experiences of war. We do not know how to talk about argument except to invoke war.

Since the publication of *Metaphors We Live By*, Lakoff and Johnson have amplified their claim about the experiential basis of primary metaphors by focusing in more depth on the degree to which such metaphors are dependent upon an understanding of knowledge as fundamentally embodied. Embodied not in the simple sense that we think with our brains and we need bodies to have brains. Rather, knowledge is fundamentally embodied in two important ways. First, reason is "shaped crucially by the peculiarities of our human bodies, by the remarkable details of the neural structure of our brains, and by the specifics of our everyday functioning in the world" (*Philosophy* 4). Because we have the bodies we have, we understand the world in very particular ways and our primary metaphors reflect this understanding. For instance, our primary experience of feeling warm when being held close to another body affectionately induces us to understand and live by the metaphor *affection is warmth*. Thus, we know what it means to say that he is a cold person. We are not referring to his literal body temperature but to his tendency to withhold affection (*Philosophy* 50). Second, knowledge is fundamentally embodied via neural connections in our brains. Lakoff and Johnson explain that

> whenever a domain of subjective experience or judgment is coactivated regularly with a sensorimotor domain [e.g., the subjective experience of affection is coactivated regularly with the physical experience of being held closely to another person] permanent neural connections are established via syn-

> aptic weight changes. Those connections, which you have unconsciously formed by the thousands, provide inferential structure and qualitative experience activated in the sensorimotor system to the subjective domains they are associated with. (*Philosophy* 57)

Neural connections established repeatedly between the abstract concept *affection* and the subjective experience *warmth* allow us not just to understand affection metaphorically in terms of temperature but to *reason* about affection based on our understanding of warmth. How do we talk about a person who seems to slowly be letting down his guard and opening up to another? We reason about affection by reasoning about temperature. If affection is warmth and a person is slowly becoming more affectionate, we say he is "warming up to us." It is worth noting here that my moving away from the warmth metaphor led me to talk about affection in terms of enclosures that are guarded. Like the concept plagiarism, affection is practically impossible to talk about or refer to without recourse to metaphor.

Lakoff and Johnson repeatedly make the point that the metaphors we live by are most often neither voluntary nor conscious. We cannot simply change metaphors at will. "Our system of primary and complex metaphors is part of the cognitive unconscious," Lakoff and Johnson explain, "and most of the time we have no direct access to it or control over its use" (*Philosophy* 73). This is not to say, though, that we shouldn't try to change the metaphors, just that it will take persistence and time. As Lakoff explains in *The Political Mind*,

> Language gets its power because it is defined relative to frames, prototypes, metaphors, narratives, images, and emotions. Part of its power comes from its unconscious aspects: we are not consciously aware of all that it evokes in us, but it is there, hidden, always at work. If we hear the same language over and over, we will think more and more in terms of the frames and metaphors activated by that language. (15)

We have all heard again and again, repeatedly and forcefully, that plagiarism is theft. It is a metaphor we live by, one that has become all-but-invisible to us and, as such, has gone unanalyzed in the rhetorical context of our talk about plagiarism to student audiences.

Reasoning about Plagiarism

Theft is a relatively concrete concept that seems to provide the right kind of structure with which to understand the abstract concept *plagiarism*. We can and we have, therefore, used our experiential understanding of *theft* to reason about and to draw inferences about *plagiarism*. First we consider the structure of the concept *theft*:

A thief intentionally steals an object from its rightful owner with the express goal of getting away with it.

It is the police's job to prevent and detect crime.

A thief, once caught, deserves to be punished.

A thief will be punished by an entity more powerful than the police, usually the court system.

The metaphor maps the following structure:

The student is a thief.

The teacher is the police.

Punishment is the consequence.

Plagiarism policies spell out appropriate punishment.

Punishment is carried out by university administrators.

Therefore, when we use the structure of the concept *theft* to reason and draw inferences about *plagiarism*, we get the following commonplaces:

A student intentionally steals an object from its rightful owner with the express goal of getting away with it.

It is a teacher's job to prevent and detect plagiarism.

A student, once caught, deserves to be punished.

A student will be punished by an entity more powerful than the teacher, usually an organization housed in Student Affairs or Community Rights and Responsibilities.

This all seems straightforward enough. We reason about plagiarism by reasoning about theft. There are very specific rhetorical effects that follow from reasoning about plagiarism by reasoning about theft. Until very recently, I would have stopped my analysis at this point because it seems as though there's nothing more to say. Yet, something nags. Two things, actually. First, Lakoff and Johnson's profound observation that knowledge is embodied and that any understanding of metaphor must take this embodiment into account seems to be missing in this mapping of theft onto plagiarism. Second, stopping at this point in the analysis allows the *moral content* of our everyday understanding of theft to remain unarticulated and thus unchallenged. These two points are not unrelated. As I will demonstrate below, the embodied knowledge we have of theft derives from a combination of a conception of property as a *right* and of a conception of a *right* as a moral I.O.U. Both of these metaphors are dependent on the morality of ownership.

The morality of ownership can be demonstrated by parsing out the fine distinctions between theft as a violation of law and theft as a violation of a moral norm. In his book, *Lying, Cheating, and Stealing: A Moral Theory of White-Collar Crime*, legal scholar Stuart P. Green notes that the concept of stealing carries a moral significance independent of its legal significance (*Lying* 88) by providing examples of instances in which stealing would be illegal but not immoral—as in the paradigmatic case of the poor man stealing from a millionaire to feed his family—and instances in which stealing would be technically illegal but not considered by most members of a society to be immoral, as in the case of downloading music illegally (92). Our understanding of ownership, while often conflated with legal definitions, is, Green suggests, "in some fundamental sense pre-legal. Small children and primitive man both have a sense of what it means to own things. And they undoubtedly have a sense that having such things involuntarily taken from them in some way constitutes a 'wrong'" (89–90). One need not understand or even be aware of the legal definition of theft in order to understand that one has been wronged when one's property is taken without permission. When we reason about plagiarism by reasoning about theft, we assert the wrongfulness of plagiarism without ever being required to assert the moral wrongfulness of theft. It simply goes without saying that stealing is wrong because we understand ownership as a right. Green explains that "it is a commonplace that property rights are really bundles of rights, organized around the idea of securing, for the right of the holder, exclusive use of or access to, a thing" (90). Green's approach to moral wrongfulness, as we will see in more detail below, emphasizes the morality of the social norms that we live with and abide by every day. Such an approach, he argues,

> is more suggestive of the richly nuanced way people actually think about the content of their moral lives. Even people who have never had occasion to read a single page of moral philosophy are capable of making fine-grained distinctions about, say, what properly constitutes cheating or stealing. (*Lying* 45)

Lakoff and Johnson would likely suggest that part of the reason for the resonance of Green's approach to understanding stealing by articulating the morality of its social norms is that we understand morality itself in terms of metaphor.

Perhaps nothing more frequently goes without saying in contemporary social theory than the rhetorical effects of morality metaphors on our conceptions of right and wrong and thus on our reasoning about everyday acts with a presumed moral content. Morality, Lakoff and Johnson show us, stems from "our fundamental human concern with what is best for us and how we ought to live" (*Philosophy* 290). Like all metaphors we live by, the metaphors we have for morality are grounded in our bodily experiences of well-being. Our well-being is dependent on, for instance, health, connection, nurturance, protection, wealth, and the more of each we have, the better off we are. "Morality is fundamentally seen as the enhancing of well-being, especially of others," Lakoff and Johnson write. The primary metaphor *well-being is wealth* is rooted in the fact that "most people find it better to have enough wealth to live comfortably than to be impoverished," and we therefore understand that an "increase in well being is a *gain*; a decrease, a *loss*" (291). *Well-being is wealth* is the basis for what Lakoff and Johnson call the Moral Accounting metaphor wherein "increasing others' well-being is metaphorically increasing their wealth. Decreasing others' well-being is metaphorically decreasing their wealth. In other words, doing something good for someone is metaphorically giving that person something of value, for example, money" (292). The Moral Accounting metaphor conceptualizes moral action in terms of financial transactions (292) and thus provides a number of reasoning structures for understanding right and wrong, such as reciprocation, retribution, revenge, and restitution (see 293–97). Reasoning about morality is, in many cases, dependent upon our reasoning about finances or wealth. Lakoff and Johnson point out, too, that the source of the metaphor, "the domain of financial transaction, itself has a morality: It is moral to pay your debts and immoral not to" (293).

Green's suggestion that theft is a concept whose moral content is in some sense "pre-legal," his use of the example of small children understanding what it means to own things, is reflected in Lakoff and Johnson's explanation of the bodily basis of our conception of rights and our understanding of rights in terms of the Moral Accounting metaphor wherein giving is increasing and taking is subtracting. "Very early on, infants and toddlers acquire the idea that something (such as a toy or pacifier) belongs to them—they *possess* it, and it is *theirs* to do with as they wish. Taking away a possession they see as fundamentally theirs leads them to protest loudly" (*Philosophy* 329). We might imagine that toddler's protest to be voiced as something like, "Give that back," a confirmation of the toddler's understanding, at the most basic level, of the right and wrong of give and take. To take something from someone without permission is morally wrong, a violation of that person's right of ownership. To give that object back to the original owner is morally right, a confirmation of that person's right of ownership. When we reason about rights (unconsciously) using the Moral Accounting metaphor, Lakoff and Johnson explain,

> Rights are conceived as rights to one's property. If the bank is keeping your money, you have a right to get it back upon request. If someone has borrowed money from you, you have a right to be paid back. Combining this notion of financial property rights with the Well-Being is Wealth metaphor yields a notion of a broader right—a right to one's well-being, special cases of which are life, liberty, and the pursuit of happiness. Having a specific right is equivalent to holding an I.O.U. redeemable for various specific forms of human well-being, such as the freedom to vote, equal access to public offices, and equal opportunities for employment. (298)

Ownership of a thing grants us exclusive rights to the possession, use, and access to that thing. Lakoff and Johnson explain that "a right is a form of metaphorical social capital that allows you to claim certain debts from others" (298). Ownership of a thing, then, grants us the exclusive right to claim debts from others should we decide to let others access or use that thing.

When we reason about plagiarism by reasoning about theft, and when we encourage students to engage in this reasoning with us, we reactivate neural connections between not just the logical structure of one and the logical structure of the other but also between the moral content of one and the moral content of the other. We suggest that plagiarism is wrong because theft is wrong and plagiarism is just like theft in that it involves the unauthorized taking of another person's property. But we rarely take the next step and explain *why* theft is wrong because to do so would require an articulation of the moral basis of ownership and the metaphor of a right as an I.O.U. that entitles an author to *credit* for his or her work. Giving credit to the cited author enacts recognition, a specific form of human well-being without which social life would be virtually meaningless. Explaining why theft is wrong and thus why plagiarism is wrong thus requires an examination of precisely what is stolen when someone plagiarizes. The object of theft, the thing for which the author holds exclusive rights, is not the words or the language or even the ideas, but the *credit*.

PLAGIARISM AS A VIOLATION OF THE SOCIAL NORM OF ATTRIBUTION

The fact that so many writers on plagiarism have used the language of theft is revealing; it is more than just a metaphor. To its victims, plagiarism is no less harmful than fraud or embezzlement.

—Stuart P. Green

According to SUNY Albany's online library tutorial, plagiarism is "theft of another's intellectual property." Robert DiYanni and Pat C. Hoy II tell students in *The Scribner Handbook for Writers* that "to plagiarize is to steal, to take from someone else (from a source other than yourself) what is not yours to take *unless you acknowledge the taking*" (633). In *The Essentials of Academic Writing*, Derek Soles tells students that plagiarism is "the theft of one writer's knowledge or direct written text by another writer, an attempt by one writer to imply to readers that work he has stolen from another is actually his own" (50). Parks, Levernier, and Hollowell speak of plagiarists in the third person when they tell students that if writers in college "'borrow' words or information from other writers without giving those writers credit, then they are guilty of plagiarism" (247). And in *Universal Keys for Writers*, Ann Raimes provides the origin of the word in her explanation of plagiarism as theft: "The word *plagiarize* is derived from a Latin verb meaning 'to kidnap,' and kidnapping or stealing someone else's ideas and presenting them as your own is regarded as a serious offense in Western academic culture and public life" (740). So the object of theft is variously defined as another's intellectual property, what is not yours to take, a writer's knowledge or direct written text, words or information, and someone else's ideas. As good scholars, we know that there is an important difference—a legal difference, in fact—between taking an idea and taking direct written text. It is the difference between plagiarism and copyright infringement. By not distinguishing between ideas and expression, we're conflating plagiarism, a college and university policy, with the laws of intellectual property based in copyright law.

Green's article, "Plagiarism, Norms, and the Limits of Theft Law: Some Observations on the Use of Criminal Sanctions in Enforcing Intellectual Property Rights," appeared in *Hastings Law Journal* in 2002[1]. Green's purpose in this article is to determine the extent to which plagiarism can be prosecuted under the auspices of criminal law, his exigence for doing so twofold. First, Green notes that the language of criminal law permeates discussions of plagiarism despite the fact that "no plagiarist has ever been prosecuted for theft" (170). If our understanding of plagiarism is predicated on the workings of theft law, might we, and should we, prosecute plagiarists under criminal law? Second, as his title suggests, Green is interested in understanding better why "people whose internal moral codes would never allow them to walk into a store and steal a piece of merchandise apparently think there is nothing wrong with making an unauthorized copy of a videotape or downloading a bootlegged computer program" (238). Why, in other words, is the rule against plagiarism—which is not law—enforced socially in ways that intellectual property laws—which are, indeed, laws—are not? In his working through these two questions,

Green provides insights into the relationship between theft and plagiarism that can help us rethink what it means to say that a plagiarist is a thief. More specifically, Green's work can help us articulate the moral content of the plagiarist's transgression by making explicit the thing that is stolen when a student plagiarizes.

Green takes the metaphor quite literally, considering in great detail what it means, legally, to refer to plagiarism as theft. He defines plagiarism as involving two separate actions: the copying of another's words without attribution and passing them off as one's own. This is an important point to consider, for my purposes, in determining what we mean when we say that a plagiarist steals. But more important is Green's explanation of the social norms that underwrite the rule against plagiarism both in the wider culture and in academia. The rule against plagiarism "is regarded as having something very much like the force of law" (173) in large part because of the social norms in which the rule is embedded. Most pertinent is what Green calls the "norm of attribution," produced by what he describes as a desire for the esteem of others:

> We begin with the proposition that people generally value the esteem of others, particularly their peers. Among the ways one can earn the esteem of one's peers is by being recognized for one's originality, creativity, insight, knowledge, and technical skill. This is particularly so among writers, artists, and scholars, who, in addition to achieving satisfaction through the creative act itself, usually wish to see those acts recognized by others. (174)

This desire for recognition for one's achievements produces the norm of attribution, which Green characterizes as being, for those who have internalized the norm, "a moral obligation, rather like showing respect to one's elders. People who have internalized the norm of attribution would regard credit earned for someone else's work as illegitimate" (175). According to the norm of attribution,

> words and ideas may be copied if and only if the copier attributes them to their originator or author. This norm leads to a form of social cooperation with obvious social benefits. It maximizes the author's chances of achieving esteem by providing, at relatively low cost to the author, copier, and society generally, opportunities for both wide dissemination of, and

> credit for, the author's words and ideas, without which there would be fewer incentives to create new work. (174)

Credit, then, becomes an incentive for creating work. While copyright law protects an author's *economic* interests for a period of years, the social norm of attribution that underwrites the rule of plagiarism protects what Green calls "a personal, or moral, interest" (202). It is the right thing to do to give credit to the original author. The rule against plagiarism carries a perceived legitimacy that laws protecting intellectual property do not, Green suggests, because the laws protecting intellectual property are not underwritten by the force of the social norm of attribution. As Green explains, "the primary factor in shaping law-related behavior is morality. People avoid engaging in conduct they might otherwise engage in because they believe it is morally wrong to do so. A second important factor is the perceived legitimacy of a given law. People need to respect the institutions that create and enforce the laws by which they are bound; they need to feel that such institutions are fair and can be trusted" (237–38). Green's purpose in this article, keep in mind, is to understand how the laws protecting intellectual property might be better enforced, but his explanation of the difference between the rule against plagiarism and laws protecting intellectual property demonstrates the significant role the social function of acknowledgment plays in our moral decision-making:

> One of the reasons the attribution norm is so powerful is that people can relate to the potential victims of plagiarism. If I plagiarize your work today, you may turn around and plagiarize my work tomorrow. If people were convinced that the unauthorized downloading of MP3 files over Napster and similar websites was likely to hurt the artists who created the music, rather than simply the multi-national media conglomerates that own the rights to that music, they might be less likely to persist in violating those copyrights. (239–40)

We do not feel a moral obligation to repay a debt to multinational media conglomerates because we do not conceptualize their ownership of the music as morally legitimate; we do, however, conceptualize the *artists'* rights to credit for their work as legitimate and therefore feel a moral obligation to give them credit for their work. How many times have we heard the argument that if we could pay the artists directly, we wouldn't illegally download songs?

To what extent, Green wants to know, is credit a thing of value that can be stolen? To answer this question is to come closer to understanding the consequences of referring to plagiarism in the language of criminal law. Green claims that "a thing is not subject to theft unless it is the sort of thing that can be bought or sold" (217), which then leads him to the question of whether "plagiarism involves the taking of something that is commodifiable" (218). While a physical book or article is something that can be bought or sold, it is not the physical work but the intangible credit that the plagiarist steals. While plagiarism is most often understood as the theft of words or ideas or intellectual property, Green argues that "the better view is that what is stolen is not the author's words or ideas (since they are essentially there for the taking), but rather the 'credit' to which the author is entitled" (219). Green's next question then becomes, for the purposes of theft law, whether credit is something that can be bought or sold.

A "thing of value" for the purposes of theft law is something that can be bought and sold. What kind of value does credit hold for authors, and can it be bought and sold? There is no question that credit is a thing of value; as Green writes, "for many literary and academic writers, garnering recognition is at least as, if not more, important than receiving financial compensation" (219–20). Credit carries a psychic value for academic writers, but it also carries an exchange value that most of us recognize but rarely talk about:

> Recognition of one's work and the development of a reputation as a creative scholar or artist in a given field often do result, even if indirectly, in significant tangible rewards, such as tenure and promotion, bonuses, pay increases, grants and scholarships, publishing contracts, job offers, invitations to conferences, client referrals, appointment to political or judicial office, and other forms of career advancement and compensation. Indeed, the number and prestige of citations is regarded by some academics as a means of "keeping score." In the absence of universally accepted criteria for determining academic and scholarly achievement, faculties and individual professors are often ranked by the frequency with which their work is cited. Such rankings, in turn, may be relevant to important judgments about status and reputation. (220)

The norm of attribution protects our interest in receiving both recognition for our work *and* compensation in the form of promotion, raises, and so on. In the context of the Moral Accounting metaphor, each time our work is recognized or cited by others, our moral rights to such credit are reaffirmed and we experience a *gain* in our intellectual well-being. We could even argue that credit is a financial term itself, a metaphor for the acknowledgment that is our due when we've written something that we offer to the world. To make use of my work, you give me an I.O.U. for credit. When you cite my work, you make good on your I.O.U. You hold up your end of the bargain struck by the norm of attribution, and we both benefit.

While the question of whether credit can be bought and sold is a tricky one, which Green readily admits (220), the question of whether it can be stolen seems more straightforward. Because of this, Green writes that there "is a reasonable argument that 'credit' for authorship should be regarded as 'property' for purposes of theft law" (221). This claim makes it possible for Green to solidify his argument that credit is the thing stolen in the case of plagiarism; for even if a plagiarist claims to be merely "borrowing" words or ideas from a source—and we've all used this entailment of the economic metaphor—"the deprivation of credit is permanent and ongoing" (222). To fail to cite is to steal credit, to violate the social norm of attribution.

Green's explanation of the relationship between plagiarism and the social norm of attribution is dependent upon our acceptance of the norm as moral. And morality, we know, is concerned primarily with increasing the well-being of ourselves and others. When we acknowledge the work of others by giving them credit for their work, we are increasing their well-being and we are affirming the social relationships that are necessary to any intellectual endeavor. After all, we *want* people to cite our work:

> An author offers her work to the world by publishing it in a book or magazine. Under the widely accepted academic, literary, and journalistic norms and practices described above, the author's presentation of her ideas constitutes a conditional offer to the effect that anyone may read the work and quote it or take ideas from it, *provided that such person makes attribution to their originator.* (218)

It is this conditional offer than an author makes each time he or she publishes a work that the plagiarist refuses. A plagiarist does not simply steal the work of another; a plagiarist violates the property rights of the author when he or she refuses to make good on the metaphorical I.O.U. that the author has issued when he or she offered his or her work to the world.[2]

Passing off Versus Passing on

In "The Ecstasy of Influence: A Plagiarism," Jonathan Lethem copies Lawrence Lessig's idea that "A time is marked not so much by ideas that are argued about as by ideas that are taken for granted. The character of an era hangs upon what needs no defense" (63). Though he labels his work a plagiarism, he names all of his sources at the end of the piece, encouraging readers to pursue the ideas in the essay by reading further. This is one of the functions of a Works Cited list or a bibliography: to assist readers in their pursuit of the ideas drawn upon in the work. One of the ideas that is taken for granted in our time is that plagiarism is theft. But might we also say that another idea that is taken for granted in our time is what Green calls the social norm of attribution? *Because* this social norm is taken for granted, it is not articulated. And because it is not articulated, and because we live in a capitalist society in which buying and selling have become moral imperatives, it seems only natural that we understand plagiarism as theft of another's ideas or words. But if we reconceive of the object of theft as *credit*, new ways of doing things become possible. Indeed, we don't have to talk about theft at all if we begin discussions of citation from the positive, from an explanation of how the norm of attribution works and what it does.

First, we can begin to shift the terms with which we define plagiarism from simple comparisons to stealing a book or a CD to taking credit for someone else's work. Even better, we can begin the discussion from the concept of citation rather than plagiarism, beginning by talking with students about why we cite the work of others. We cite to acknowledge their work, and we cite to pass on their ideas to new groups of readers. Jonathan Lethem's article in *Harper's* calls attention to itself for being a plagiarism, but the larger function of that work is to pass on to readers not necessarily steeped in the discourse of copyright law or composition studies the work of Lewis Hyde, Eric

Lott, Siva Vaidhyanathan, Lawrence Lessig, and many, many others. Understanding and explaining the object of theft as credit allows us to explain the work of writing from sources in terms of *passing off* and *passing on*. Both require a third party. To pass *off* an idea is to say something along the lines of, "I've found this great idea and I want you to think it's mine." To pass *on* an idea is to say something along the lines of, "I've found this great idea, and look what it can do to help us rethink x, y, and z. Have you heard about it?" Passing on is the very definition of collaboration, and it is the primary intellectual reason we cite the work of others. Moreover, passing on assumes the existence of an interested audience. Passing on enacts a different kind of social relation than passing off. Passing on highlights the relationships among readers and renders visible the kind of sharing that is necessary for the construction of knowledge.

Green suggests that one of the positive effects of the norm of attribution is that it provides opportunities for the "wide dissemination of" the cited author's words and ideas." That is, in addition to providing credit to the cited author, the norm of attribution gives writers a relatively simple way of sharing information, of passing on ideas and knowledge that might otherwise remain hidden from readers' view. And this line of thinking leads rather seamlessly into discussions of the non-textual ways in which citation figures in our everyday conversations. When we "cite the source of a joke or anecdote or notable fact" (Murray 178), we usually do not do so out of obligation but because we want to give credit. Laura J. Murray, drawing on the work of Janet Giltrow, notes that in everyday conversation, "it is normal to cite: it is part of the social fabric and habitual modes of speech. . . . Sometimes it bolsters social status to declare a prestigious source. Or . . . it helps your listener to evaluate your information: if you don't say where you got it, they may ask" (178). Murray suggests that explaining academic citation systems with reference to other citation systems can help students understand better the motivation behind academic citation. She notes that "Internet links are one endless chain of footnotes, only handier. Blogs invite their readers to trace back through their sources like any good academic historian" (177–78). Students do grant credit to others all the time in everyday situations like these, and we might take advantage of their familiarity with such relatively informal citation economies to highlight the social aspect of citation rather than the obligatory.

Recently I explained this line of reasoning to a group of English majors in a rhetorical theory course, and one student, an English Education major named Mary Rose Volkman, made an analogy that is worth noting here. I asked Volkman if she'd be willing to write her idea down so that I could cite it in my work, and she responded that she'd be honored to do so. Here is what she wrote:

> As an aspiring teacher, I have begun to toy with the idea of how I will talk to my students about the issue of plagiarism. In my past experiences, especially in high school, my teachers viewed my fellow classmates and myself as criminals. We were already assumed to have plagiarized even before we began to script our first drafts. Knowing how I felt as a student in this situation, being accused of stealing someone else's work and writing it off as my own, I have decided not to take the same approach with my students. . . . I will try to explain to the students that citing someone in their paper is just giving the original author 'props.' An example that I could offer my class would be describing a situation where someone compliments the shirt they are wearing and the appropriate response would be name dropping the brand of the shirt or the store they bought it at. It is in fact their shirt, and they are wearing the shirt as a reflection of their identity. However, they did not design the shirt themselves, so this case calls for recognition of the creator of the shirt. "I got it at Macy's" or "It is from the Marc Jacobs collection." Citation should not be looked down at as a chore. I feel students should be encouraged to research other authors and other words to better their writing. By citing the author's work, students are just giving kudos to the original author while at the same time making the chosen entry benefit their own writing. (1)

Murray notes that the "essential distinction between citation and copyright is that proper citation practice turns on acknowledgment, whereas proper copyright practice turns on permission" (176). Volkman might note here that we rarely, if ever, feel the need to ask permission of a clothing designer to drop their name in conversation. This is because we conceive of this kind of citation as a means of giving credit; it seems preposterous to understand this exchange as a kind of theft, an attempt to pass off the work of others as our own.

Second, we open up space for disciplinary discussions of *why*, exactly, we draw on the theft metaphor in the first place. Or *who* among us draws on the theft metaphor to explain plagiarism to students? Might the norm of attribution be a more readily available topic of discussion for teachers who have written something that they believe is worthy of attribution? Green suggests that the norm of attribution works in large part because we can imagine others plagiarizing from us; perhaps students plagiarize because they cannot identify with the victim of plagiarism because they haven't written anything they—or others—believe to be worthy of attribution. I must admit that the idea that *graduate teaching assistants* and *adjunct writing instructors* might be disinclined to talk with students about the norm of attribution because *they* haven't written anything they believe deserves attribution hadn't occurred to me until a reviewer suggested it to me in response to an earlier version of this essay. That this hadn't occurred to me as a reason some teachers of writing—certainly not all—use the theft metaphor to explain plagiarism to students suggests something significant about the effects of having written and published something worthy of attribution. You see, recently an article appeared in *CCC* that probably should have, but didn't, cite my earlier work on plagiarism. I felt like I had the right to credit for already having written about "the anger aroused, even in informal [faculty] conversations, when the subject turns to plagiarism" (Zwagerman 679). I felt *wronged*, and while it is certainly not disciplinarily correct to acknowledge such a feeling, doing so is as socially necessary as acknowledging that public recognition of my work contributes to my well-being. Most students, I imagine, can understand what it feels like to have an idea they shared with others go unrecognized or claimed by another. So, while students may not yet feel that they have a right to ownership of anything they've written because they have a hard time conceiving of themselves as authors (see Ritter, "Economics"), they do have an unconscious conception of the Moral Accounting metaphor wherein refusing to do something to contribute to another's well-being is understood to be incurring a debt. When we make explicit the norm of attribution with students, we also make explicit the moral basis of that norm: to abide by the norm of attribution is to contribute to a framing of knowledge as that which is produced socially and collaboratively, and to a conception of credit, or recognition, as crucial to our individual and social well-being.

Bruce Ballenger's stern warning to students that "Modern authors get testy when someone uses their work without giving them credit" (392) leaves the reasons for such testiness unsaid, but is clearly dependent on what Green calls the social norm of attribution. Ballenger's reliance on unstated moral beliefs about ownership, authorship, and the social relations of intellectual work is anything but unusual. It is the norm. I am suggesting that using the language of *passing off* and *passing on* can go a long way toward a cognitive reframing of what it means to draw on the work of others. Each makes explicit the function of the social in the creation of knowledge, and each provides opportunity for open discussions of the Moral Accounting metaphor upon which so much of our intellectual work depends. Citation is passing on. We need to say this again and again. Lakoff and Johnson explain that "certain neural connections between the activated source- and target-domain networks are randomly established at first and then have their synaptic weights increased through their recurrent firing. The more times those connections are activated, the more the weights are increased, until permanent connections are forged" (*Philosophy* 57). The neural connections between plagiarism and theft have been forged and forged again since the days we first learned what it meant to draw on the work of another. It's time now for us to begin the work of reshaping those connections for ourselves and for our students.

Psst. Pass this on.[3]

Illinois State University
Normal, Illinois

Notes

1. I first learned of Green's work when I read Stefan Senders' "Academic Plagiarism and the Limits of Theft," a chapter in Vicinus and Eisner's *Originality, Imitation, and Plagiarism: Teaching Writing in the Digital Age*. Acknowledging the source of my source seems to me to be an extension of the argument I'm making here about the social effects of *passing it on*. Works Cited lists are more than just a compilation of sources; they represent a writer's network of sources, each item on the list bearing its own often concealed histories of social relations.

2. If credit is the thing of value that is stolen when a student plagiarizes, what are we to make of whole-text plagiarism, in which a student purchases a paper from one of the many online paper mills and turns that work in to her teacher as though it were her own work? Kelly Ritter points to this

problem in her essay, "The Economics of Authorship." Because students have been persuaded to understand authorship in consumerist terms, they may approach the prospect of purchasing a paper in a way no different than purchasing a pair of shoes. Ritter writes,

> *If a student logs on to an online paper mill and buys a paper that was put there by another student or paid contributor, thereby entering into a business transaction agreed upon by both parties, the consumer-minded student, unable to distinguish authorship from ownership, might wonder where the "stealing" is in this transaction. (615)*

Green would acknowledge that in the case of whole-text plagiarism, the norm of attribution does not apply because the original author of the text has willingly given up any right to credit for the piece, whether in exchange for money or for other services. Thus, the student is not stealing credit. But the student *is* passing off another's work as her own (190). Recall that plagiarism involves the copying of another's words without attribution *and* passing them off to another as one's own. To copy the words of another with no intentions of passing them off—as I do every time I take notes on a text—does not constitute plagiarism. It is important to remember that the norm of attribution is a *social* norm and so involves the acknowledgment of one's intellectual debts *to others*, to a third party. This is why simply purchasing a term paper from a paper mill does not in itself constitute plagiarism. Once a student turns that paper in to a teacher, passing it off as her own, it becomes plagiarism.

3. Sincere thanks to both Lynn Worsham and the anonymous reviewer for their generous and transformative suggestions for revision. To you I owe much of this argument's heft.

Works Cited

Aaron, Jane E. *The Little, Brown Essential Handbook,* 5th ed. New York: Pearson, 2006.

Anson, Chris M. "We Never Wanted to Be Cops: Plagiarism, Institutional Paranoia, and Shared Responsibility." *Pluralizing Plagiarism: Identities, Contexts, Pedagogies.* Ed. Rebecca Moore Howard and Amy E. Robillard. Portsmouth: Boynton, 2008.

Ballenger, Bruce. *The Curious Writer, Concise Edition.* New York: Pearson, 2007.

Bowers, Neal. *Words for the Taking: The Hunt for a Plagiarist.* Carbondale: Southern Illinois UP, 2007.

Butler, Paul. "Copyright, Plagiarism, and the Law." *Authorship in Composition Studies*. Ed. Tracy Hamler Carrick and Rebecca Moore Howard. Boston: Wadsworth, 2006. 13–26.

Buranen, Lise, and Alice M. Roy. "Introduction." *Perspectives on Plagiarism and Intellectual Property in a Postmodern World*. Ed. Lise Buranen and Alice M. Roy. Albany: State U of New York P, 1999.

DiYanni, Robert, and Pat C. Hoy II. *The Scribner Handbook for Writers*, 4th ed. New York: Pearson, 2004.

Faigley, Lester. *The Little Penguin Handbook*. New York: Pearson, 2007.

Fitzgerald, Lauren. "The Plagiarism 'Crisis' as Opportunity for Community Building." Conference on College Composition and Communication. Chicago. 21 Mar. 2006.

Gibaldi, Joseph. *MLA Handbook for Writers of Research Papers*. 6 ed. New York: Modern Language Association, 2003.

Green, Stuart P. *Lying, Cheating, and Stealing: A Moral Theory of White-Collar Crime*. Oxford: Oxford UP, 2006.

———. "Plagiarism, Norms, and the Limits of Theft Law: Some Observations on the Use of Criminal Sanctions in Enforcing Intellectual Property Rights." *Hastings Law Journal* 54 (2002): 167–242.

Howard, Rebecca Moore. "The Ethics of Plagiarism." *The Ethics of Writing Instruction: Issues in Theory and Practice*. Ed. Michael A. Pemberton. Stamford, CT: Ablex, 2000.

———. "Forget About Policing Plagiarism. Just *Teach*." *Chronicle of Higher Education* (16 Nov. 2001): B24.

———. "The New Abolition Comes to Plagiarism." *Perspectives on Plagiarism and Intellectual Property in a Postmodern World*. Ed. Lise Buranen and Alice M. Roy. Albany: State U of New York P, 1999.

———. "Plagiarism, Authorships, and the Academic Death Penalty." *College English* 57 (1995): 787–806.

———. *Standing in the Shadow of Giants: Plagiarists, Authors, Collaborators*. Stamford, CT: Ablex, 1999.

——. "Understanding 'Internet Plagiarism.'" *Computers and Composition* 24 (2007): 3–15.

Howard, Rebecca Moore, and Amy E. Robillard, eds. *Pluralizing Plagiarism: Identities, Contexts, Pedagogies*. Portsmouth: Boynton, 2008.

Hutcheon, Linda. "Literary Borrowing . . . and Stealing: Plagiarism, Sources, Influences, and Intertexts." *English Studies in Canada* 12 (1986): 229–39.

Kennedy, X. J., Dorothy M. Kennedy, and Sylvia A. Holladay. *The Bedford Guide for College Writers*. 6th ed. Boston: Bedford, 2002.

Kroll, Barry M. "How College Freshmen View Plagiarism." *Written Communication* 5 (1988): 203–21.

Lakoff, George. *The Political Mind*. New York: Penguin, 2009.

Lakoff, George, and Mark Johnson. *Metaphors We Live By*. Chicago: U of Chicago P, 1980.

——. *Philosophy in the Flesh*. New York: Basic, 1999.

Leight, David. "Plagiarism as Metaphor." *Perspectives on Plagiarism and Intellectual Property in a Postmodern World*. Ed. Lise Buranen and Alice M. Roy. Albany: State U of New York P, 1999.

Lethem, Jonathan. "The Ecstasy of Influence: A Plagiarism." *Harper's* Feb. 2007: 59–71.

Levinson, Barry, dir. *Wag the Dog*. Baltimore, 1998.

Lunsford, Andrea A. "Intellectual Property in an Age of Information: What is at Stake for Composition Studies?" *Composition in the Twenty-first Century: Crisis and Change*. Ed. Lynn Z. Bloom, Donald A. Daiker, and Edward M. White. Carbondale: Southern Illinois UP, 1996.

——. *The St. Martin's Handbook*. 5th ed. Boston: Bedford, 2003.

Lunsford, Andrea A., and Susan West. "Intellectual Property and Composition Studies." *College Composition and Communication* 47 (1996): 383–411.

Malesic, Jonathan. "How Dumb Do They Think We Are?" *Chronicle of Higher Education* 11 Dec. 2006.

Mallon, Thomas. *Stolen Words*. New York: Ticknor, 1989.

Marsh, Bill. *Plagiarism: Alchemy and Remedy in Higher Education*. Albany: State U of New York P, 2007.

Murray, Laura J. "Plagiarism and Copyright Infringement: The Costs of Confusion." *Originality, Imitation, and Plagiarism: Teaching Writing in the Digital Age*. Ed. Caroline Eisner and Martha Vicinus. Ann Arbor: U of Michigan P, 2008.

Noah, Timothy. "Doris Kearns Goodwin, Liar." *Slate Magazine*. 22 Jan. 2002.

O'Rourke, Meghan. "The Copycat Syndrome: Plagiarists at Work." *Slate Magazine*. 11 Jan. 2007.

Parks, A. Franklin, James A. Levernier, and Ida Masters Hollowell. *Structuring Paragraphs and Essays: A Guide to Effective Writing*. Boston: Bedford, 2001.

Price, Margaret. "Beyond 'Gotcha!': Situating Plagiarism in Policy and Pedagogy." *College Composition and Communication* 54 (2002): 88–115.

Raimes, Ann. *Universal Keys for Writers*. Boston: Houghton, 2004.

Randall, Marilyn. "Imperial Plagiarism." *Perspectives on Plagiarism and Intellectual Property in a Postmodern World*. Ed. Lise Buranen and Alice M. Roy. Albany: State U of New York P, 1999.

Ritter, Kelly. "Buying In, Selling Short: A Pedagogy Against the Rhetoric of Online Paper Mills." *Pedagogy* 6 (2006): 25–51.

———. "The Economics of Authorship: Online Paper Mills, Student Writers, and First-Year Composition." *College Composition and Communication* 56 (2005): 601–31.

Robillard, Amy E. "We Won't Get Fooled Again: On the Absence of Angry Responses to Plagiarism in Composition Studies." *College English* 70 (2007): 10–31.

Robillard, Amy E., and Ron Fortune. "Toward a New Content for Writing Courses: Literary Forgery, Plagiarism, and the Production of Belief." *JAC* 27 (2007): 183–210.

Rose, Mark. *Authors and Owners: The Invention of Copyright*. Cambridge:

Harvard UP, 1993.

Sender, Stefan. "Academic Plagiarism and the Limits of Theft." *Originality, Imitation, and Plagiarism: Teaching Writing in the Digital Age.* Ed. Caroline Eisner and Martha Vicinus. Ann Arbor: U of Michigan P, 2008.

Soles, Derek. *The Essentials of Academic Writing.* New York: Houghton, 2005.

Stearns, Laurie. "Copy Wrong: Plagiarism, Property, and the Law." *Perspectives on Plagiarism and Intellectual Property in a Postmodern World.* Ed. Lise Buranen and Alice M. Roy. Albany: State U of New York P, 1999.

Trent, Mary Alice. *Ethics in the 21st Century.* New York: Longman, 2004.

Troyka, Lynn Quitman, and Douglas Hesse. *Simon and Schuster Handbook for Writers.* New York: Simon, 2007.

Valentine, Kathryn. "Plagiarism as Literacy Practice: Recognizing and Rethinking Ethical Binaries." *College Composition and Communication* 58 (2006): 89–109.

Volkman, Mary Rose. Untitled. Unpub. Manuscript. Normal, IL: Illinois State University, 2008.

Wilson, Henry. L. "When Collaboration Becomes Plagiarism: The Administrative Perspective." *Perspectives on Plagiarism and Intellectual Property in a Postmodern World.* Ed. Lise Buranen and Alice M. Roy. Albany: State U of New York P, 1999.

Woodmansee, Martha. "The Genius and the Copyright: Economic and Legal Conditions of the Emergence of the 'Author.'" *Eighteenth-Century Studies* 17 (1984).

Woodmansee, Martha, and Peter Jaszi, eds. *The Construction of Authorship: Textual Appropriation in Law and Literature.* Durham: Duke UP, 1994.

Zebroski, James Thomas. "Intellectual Property, Authority, and Social Formation: Sociohistorical Perspectives on the Author Function." *Perspectives on Plagiarism and Intellectual Property in a Postmodern World.* Ed. Lise Buranen and Alice M. Roy. Albany: State U of New York P, 1999.

Zwagerman, Sean. "The Scarlet *P*: Plagiarism, Panopticism, and the Rhetoric of Academic Integrity." *College Composition and Communication* 59 (2008): 676–710.

THE JOURNAL OF TEACHING WRITING

The *Journal of Teaching Writing* is on the Web at http://www.iupui.edu/~jtw/

The *Journal of Teaching Writing* (*JTW*), in its thirtieth year, is a journal devoted to the teaching of writing at all academic levels and in any subject area. Our mission is to publish refereed articles that address the practices and theories that bear on our knowledge of how people learn and communicate through writing. An important part of our mission is demystifying the editorial review process for our contributors and modeling the teaching of writing as a process of reflection and revision. Owned by the Indiana Teachers of Writing, *JTW* is edited and published at Indiana University-Purdue University Indianapolis (IUPUI).

"Freewriting and Free Speech: A Pragmatic Perspective" by Janet Bean and Peter Elbow

Janet Bean and Peter Elbow's "Freewriting and Free Speech: A Pragmatic Perspective" takes a familiar subject—freewriting as a classroom practice in writing classrooms—and examines it in relation to free speech, responding to the critique of postmodernist thinking by asserting the need for a pragmatic view that answers the "problem of universals in a postmodern age." The result is an informative, engaging, and provocative essay, one that leaves readers with a renewed awareness of freewriting's political implications. This essay was selected because it reinvigorates our thinking about a widely accepted teaching practice.

Freewriting and Free Speech: A Pragmatic Perspective

Janet Bean and Peter Elbow

> *This book is dedicated to those people who actually use it— not just read it.*
>
> —Epigraph to Writing Teachers

Freewriting seems to have lost its political edge. When Ken Macrorie brought it to the attention of writing teachers, it was controversial (his first mention in print was in 1951), and it remained radical for a while after Peter started celebrating it in 1973. Gradually it became orthodox—widely used (or at least tried out) in composition classrooms, and widely described in textbooks as an effective invention strategy. Then in the 1990s, it came under sharp criticism as part of the critique of expressivist pedagogy. Now it's scarcely talked about: freewriting seems to have become commonplace, depoliticized, simply a classroom activity—ignored as often as used, and seldom used for its political force. In almost an aside, Bizzell and Herzberg call it "part of every writing teacher's repetoire" (8).

Why has freewriting, which seemed so strongly countercultural when Peter wrote about it in the 1970s, become disconnected from its political roots? This question has been the driving force behind our research, and it has taken us in some unexpected directions—specifically, to the First Amendment and legal scholarship on free speech. It was Janet who came up with the idea of comparing freewriting with free speech, in fact through a piece of extended freewriting. Here is a passage from it:

> I have the feeling that free speech actually WORKS as a widely held concept, but people really don't believe in free writing

.... It's ironic that we might view free speech as a political act but freewriting as an asocial, politically naive practice. Of course, the first thing someone might say is, of course they're different—free speech is rhetorical and public, freewriting is expressive and private. (I've just sat here for five minutes, thinking—by god, that's right.) .... But maybe we need to free writing (like those posters, FREE MANDELA, FREE THE WHALES)—free writing from the racist and classist practices of educational institutions. ha. no small order, there.

Janet's comparison of free speech and free writing began as a simple, even playful, association. But soon we realized that putting these two concepts in conversation with one another was a rich and fruitful approach: it pushed our thinking, challenged our theoretical frameworks, and helped us look at freewriting in a new way.

At first glance, free speech and freewriting may seem to be very different, but both are attempts to foster freedom of thought, inquiry, and expression. And both have come under criticism for their universalist, modernist foundations. Although freewriting is generally accepted as an effective classroom exercise, its theoretical underpinnings remain suspect. How can there be a neutral space where writing is "free"? Isn't language always part of a social and ideological context? Doesn't an emphasis on "one's own" personal voice and individual autonomy blind students to the ways in which language itself is caught up in an oppressive structure of society? Legal scholars have critiqued free speech in strikingly similar ways: feminist and critical race theorists have raised strong objections to the idea of a utopian space for free expression, and postmodern theorists have discounted the possibility that free speech can even exist.

Yet as we looked at legal scholarship, we were struck by a flexibility and robustness in free speech as a live functioning part of our culture—even in the face of strong critique. Free speech is vulnerable because it is commonly understood in modernist terms as giving an absolute freedom. As such, it runs into a buzz saw of criticism from postmodernist thinking that undermines the validity of absolutes like freedom. But First Amendment legal thinking and court rulings are grounded not only in modernism, but also in pragmatic philosophy. Pragmatism frames free speech in terms of effects rather than absolutes, opening up a "third way" around the epistemological dead end argument about whether there is such a thing as freedom. This pragmatic perspective has helped us to see freewriting in a new light. Instead of viewing it as an absolute open space for absolutely free personal expression, we've come to think of it as a social contract—an agreement to treat language in a particular way because of the good effects this has. (Here are a few: when used regularly and thoughtfully, freewriting acts as a site of negotiation between the individual and institutions; it helps students draw on the languages of their communities for academic work and invites them to explore the relationship of those languages to the language of the academy; and it allows writers to work in the liminal space between their public and private lives, between speech and writing.)

In the first part of this essay we'll explore how modernist habits of thought shape our understandings of free speech and freewriting. This will lead us to address the problem of universals in a postmodern age. We'll end by exploring the political implications of freewriting from a pragmatic perspective.

FREEDOM, AUTHORITY, AND HABITS OF THOUGHT

Free speech and freewriting both draw on the rhetoric of rights: individuals have a right to express themselves, free from undue restraints. This rhetoric is particularly powerful because freedom of expression is linked closely to how we define our national identity. We tend to understand free speech in terms of individual rights, and we locate the source of these rights in our founding documents. Perhaps no other part of the Constitution is more familiar to Americans than the First Amendment:

> Congress shall make no law respecting an establishment of religion, or prohibiting the free exercise thereof; or abridging the freedom of speech, or of the press; or the right of the people peaceably to assemble, and to petition the Government for a redress of grievances.

The text seems to provide a clear mandate, simple and elegant. Yet First Amendment legal doctrine has proven to be highly complex, and scholars have found it difficult—if not impossible— to develop a unified theory that justifies free speech or explains how it should be applied (Alexander; Bunker).

According to David Strauss, there are two basic competing models that explain the authority of law: command theory and common law theory. In command theory, law has power because it is mandated or commanded by a sovereign entity—whether it be a king or a legislature or even a hallowed document. But in common law theory, law is more a matter of custom; legal rules evolve through judicial practice, case by case. Our U. S. Constitutional law finds its somewhat slippery footing somewhere between these two theories and sets of assumptions, with the question of authority in continual dialogue: does authority lie in the Constitution (in effect mandated by the sovereign text), or does it lie with a "custom" that consists of how judges interpret precedent and apply it to new contexts? Command theory, with its general-to-specific approach, encourages us to think in universals. Common law theory, on the other hand, works from specific interpretations and rulings to generalizations—and this makes it impossible to think of legal concepts in terms of universals. These two broad interpretative approaches fuel not only legal arguments but also larger debates within the political culture (Strauss 34-35).

What's most significant for this essay is Strauss's claim that most people—including many lawyers—tend to frame freedom of speech issues in terms of command theory. We assume that free speech derives deductively from a universal principle mandated by a sovereign body ("We the People") in an authoritative text (the Constitution). But there is a catch, says Strauss:

> [C]ommand theory simply cannot account for the constitutional law of freedom of speech today. Neither the text nor the original understandings provide much support for the principles of free expression that we today take for granted (36).

Freedom of speech is not a "given" derived from the First Amendment. Rather, it developed largely through a common law process, evolving through time as justices made rulings case by case. For example, the original framers were comfortable with government restrictions that we today would see as violations to our right of free expression.

It is habit of thought, Strauss argues, not our legal history, that leads us to locate the authority of free speech in the Constitution. These habits of thinking are rooted in eighteenth-century Enlightenment ideals and the works of John Milton, John Locke, and John Stuart Mill. Liberal political theory infuses our basic conceptions of democracy; Americans are well schooled in the idea of "inalienable rights" and the necessity for citizens in a democracy to have freedom of press and freedom of expression. These ideals are expressed in our Constitution, but they also grow from our sense of natural rights—and our habit of thinking in generalizations. It's important, though, to remember that these are modernist concepts that developed in a modern context. They seem timeless because they are framed as universals.

Yet free speech as we know it is far from timeless. It is a relatively recent development in Constitutional doctrine, beginning as a response to the silencing of dissent after World War I. Our current understanding of free speech is "largely a creation of the twentieth century" (Bollinger 1). As the protection of free speech expanded through a trio of landmark Supreme Court cases in 1919, justices drew on modernist ideas of individual liberty, faith in progress, and autonomy (White).

Ironically, the evolution of First Amendment legal doctrine represents the classic working out through time of common law theory, yet the Supreme Court decisions themselves drew on the universals invoked by command theory—tracing the law's authority back to the Constitution. In 1927 Supreme Court Justice Louis Brandeis defended free speech in these absolutist terms:

> Those who won our independence believed that the final end of the State was to make men free to develop their faculties . . . . They valued liberty both as an end and as a means. They believed liberty to be the secret of happiness and courage to be the secret of liberty.

Justice Hugo Black called the language of the First Amendment "absolute," reinforcing the command theory assumption that the power of the law flows from a sovereign mandate (Strauss 35). And so freedom of expression becomes a truth that is "selfevident": a universal right set in a modernist framework.

Our habits of thinking about freewriting take a similar form, leading us to frame it in terms of universals. Freewriting taps into deeply held cultural ideals of individualism and freedom. It sees the threat of coercion coming not from the government but from the teacher and even from an imperious internal editor. As Peter wrote in 1973, "The editor is, as it were, constantly looking over the shoulder of the producer and constantly fiddling with what he's doing while he's in the middle of trying to do it" (5). The power of freewriting lies in the opportunity it gives individuals to develop their ideas with little or no editorial interference, toward the same goal that Brandeis articulated: to "make men free to develop their faculties." Like free speech, freewriting seeks an open space for expression to occur without intervention or restriction, so that we might explore without fear and find out what we think.

And like the modernist concept of free speech, freewriting makes even broader universal claims. It configures the writer as a universal subject in a newly democratic classroom. *Writing Without Teachers*, which popularized the concept of freewriting, makes the claim that everyone can write and everyone's voice should be heard. The locus of authority is decentered in the teacher-less writing classroom, democratizing writing instruction and giving power to the people. In the introduction to Writing Without Teachers, Peter explicitly addresses the way writing can create agency: "Many people are now trying to become less helpless, both personally and politically: trying to claim more control over their own lives. One of the ways people most lack control over their own lives is through lacking control over words. Especially written words" (vii). Freewriting, then, becomes attached to the ideals of autonomy, liberty, and democracy.

This deep current of modernist thinking that runs through so many people's conversations about free speech and freewriting has left both concepts open to criticism. Most readers of this essay will be quick to acknowledge that all speech takes place within cultural contexts where power and authority are always in play. Before anyone opens her mouth to speak, whether or not there are any listeners, she has been "socially constructed," her language infused by larger cultural forces. Rita Felski critiques the "ideal of a free discursive space that equalizes all participants . . . but is achieved only by obscuring actual material inequalities and political antagonisms among its participants" (168, quoted in Slaughter 1408). The idea of free speech can serve to obscure real inequities and thereby heightens them. The First Amendment right of free speech can be used to protect the interests of powerful corporations, economic and political elites, and even those who instill hatred. The Supreme Court has ruled that money is free speech when it comes to campaign financing, so huge corporations or other groups can spend all they want to try to influence elections. When the "universal right" of free speech is granted to some, it is likely to conflict with the rights of other individuals or groups—for example, ethnic or sexual minorities or majority groups like women. Even in the small worlds of our individual classrooms, we suspect that most of our readers have struggled with the question of limiting free speech in order to stop racist, sexist, and homophobic comments.

So too, freewriting (insofar as it means writing that is truly free) is open to the same powerful critique. Writing can never be free of social contexts and constraints. To believe otherwise, argue Min-zhan Lu and Bruce Horner, is to participate in "the politics of linguistic innocence: that is, a politics which preempts teachers' attention from the political dimensions of the linguistic choices students make in their writing" (57). In his widely read exchange with Peter (*CCC*, 1995), David Bartholomae argues that the notion of

> a free writing . . . is an expression of a desire for an institutional space free from institutional pressures, a cultural process free from the influence of culture, an historical moment outside of history, an academic setting free from academic writing (64).

Bartholomae's critique reflected a growing concern in the field about the dangers of understanding students and writing processes in universalist terms. The social turn in Composition Studies, exemplified by books like Lester Faigley's *Fragments of Rationality* and Kurt Spellmeyer's *Common Ground*, rejected the modernist ideals of individualism, the autonomous self, and progress. Freewriting's emphasis on voice—with its implications of a coherent self and individual autonomy—made it suspect, as did its reliance on a psychological model of the writing process at a time when universal cognitive processes were being called into question.

Critics of modernism have made powerful and persuasive arguments, shaking the very concept of freedom. "There is no such thing as free speech," declares Stanley Fish in an essay with that title, and he goes on: "'Free Speech' is just the name we give to verbal behavior we wish to advance. . . . Free speech, in short, is not an independent value but a political prize" (102). Fish, who has been highly influential in the field of Composition and Rhetoric as well as literary and legal studies, argues that there is never a neutral ground for language, written or spoken. From an epistemological perspective, freedom is not possible.

This is one way to tell the story of free speech and freewriting: through the lens of modernism and the subsequent challenge of postmodernism. But we'd like to call attention to the limitations of this approach. We grant that the social turn in both legal theory and Composition theory has done important work. Since modernist habits of thought have dominated and still strongly influence the way we see the world, postmodernism has called much needed attention to the problems that come from absolute faith in progress and individual agency. But this story— modernism trumped by postmodernism—leaves us at an impasse. The concept of freedom is left so tenuous as to be unusable.

Yet there remains a resilience in the notion of free speech— not just among the (sentimental) general public but also among hard headed and scholarly lawyers. Although there are good reasons to believe free speech and freewriting participate in a vulnerable modernist tradition, there are also good reasons to question whether modernism provides a sufficient framework for understanding and critiquing the concept of freedom. The rhetoric of free expression may be individualistic and universal, but free speech also has foundations that are deeply grounded in the social and contextual. In short, there is another way of telling the story—one that is framed not in absolutes but in experience.

Pragmatism and the Law: More Freedom Rather than Less

Free speech would not have had its long history even into the present if it were seen only as a universal absolute or metaphysical right. The soil that has nourished it in our country is the long tradition of American pragmatism. In an important book for our field (*Reason to Believe: Romanticism, Pragmatism and the Teaching of Writing*), Roskelly and Ronald explore how this tradition goes back to the earliest days of English settlement in this country.

Cornel West celebrates the American roots of pragmatism in a striking phrase, "the American evasion of philosophy." He insists that pragmatism involves "a kind of inseparable link between thought and action, theory and practice" (West 10, quoted by Roskelly and Ronald 56). The colonists, for understandable reasons, developed a tradition of crude, everyday, see-what-works pragmatism. But Peirce and James and others developed pragmatism as a philosophical theory. Pragmatism assumes that truth, values, and what we think of as "reality" are not eternal, universal givens but relative and contextual. As Roskelly and Ronald put it, there is a "strong emphasis on experience as opposed to a priori assumptions" and pure theory (86).

The goal of pragmatism is to avoid the swamps and dead-ends that come from debating absolutes (for example, does freedom exist or not exist?). "Grant an idea to be true," pragmatism says, then ask "what concrete difference will its being true make in anyone's actual life" (James, qtd. in Roskelly and Ronald 87). The questions—what works? How does it matter to lived experience?—these are central to pragmatic methodology. And they radically change the nature of philosophical inquiry. As James puts it: "It is astonishing to see how many philosophical disputes collapse into insignificance the moment you subject them to this simple test of tracing a concrete consequence" (qtd. in Roskelly and Ronald 21). (Compositionists should not forget how much Ann Berthoff was indebted to Peirce).

Once we understand the pragmatist frame of thinking, it's worth looking again at the First Amendment. As the framers wrote about freedom of speech, press, assembly, and so on, they were working out a pragmatic response to the specific conditions of their lives. The founders didn't pretend they were protecting the speech of women and slaves. What gave meaning and urgency to the first amendment were the historical and contingent circumstances they were living through. The force of the First Amendment had to do with consequences and effects—the essential pragmatic criteria. People were put in American and English jails for what they wrote and said in public, and even for gathering in groups on street corners to criticize or even just discuss government policy. The framers took concrete action to prevent the creation of explicit laws that would underwrite the use of police or troops to stop people who dared speak.

Some people may fall into the trap of thinking that the First Amendment creates a perfect space for pure freedom, and others into the trap of thinking that "freedom" is nothing but a naïve illusion. But the genuine traction that free speech manages to retain in our society comes from an awareness that we continue to live in historical conditions where free speech is so easily abridged—where we are continually confronted with a choice between more freedom and less. Free speech seems all the more precious in light of the Patriot Act and other contemporary government activities. (On discouraging days, a cynical thought recurs: free speech survives as a concept but not as a practice; freewriting survives as a practice, but not as a concept.)[1]

First Amendment legal practice is notably complex and context-dependent. Free speech cases have always necessitated a pragmatic approach. Even though justices like Brandeis might sometimes frame free speech as human universal, Supreme Court decisions are always about particular, contingent, historical judgments. Lawyers for one side argue that the particular case should be seen as an instance of one statute or precedent, while lawyers for the other side say that a different statute or precedent should decide the case (or at least that the first rule should not apply). Pragmatism, perhaps even more than Enlightenment ideals, has shaped how the First Amendment actually operates in our society through the legal system. When legal scholars and lay people evoke the metaphor of free speech as a "marketplace of ideas" or the concept of "clear and present danger," they are indebted to the Supreme Court Justice Oliver Wendell Holmes (who, as a young man, was a member of the Metaphysical Club with William James and C.S. Pierce). In classic pragmatist fashion, he argued that truth is contingent and must be tested by experience. The Constitution itself, he argues, is grounded in pragmatic theory:

> . . . the best test of truth is the power of the thought to get itself accepted in the competition of the market, and that truth is the only ground upon which their wishes safely can be carried out. That at any rate is the theory of our Constitution.

Freedom, argues Holmes, is valuable because of its usefulness. Even bad ideas need to be heard (just as Peter has argued that "bad" writing needs to be committed to paper). Society—and individual writers—need an arena for uncensored expression, not only to discover the (contingent) truth but to serve the ultimate good.

Reclaiming the Universal: Pragmatism and Possibility

In recent decades, a number of scholars who accept the postmodern critique of universals nevertheless find themselves trying to rescue the notion of universals. In Paris in 1948, a special U.N. committee adopted the Universal Declaration of Human Rights, calling for "a world in which human beings shall enjoy freedom of speech and belief and freedom from fear and want" (1406). Joseph Slaughter calls the idea of universal human rights an "enabling fiction" (1407). It is a piece of "naïve," "commonsense," "liberal-democratic ideology," he acknowledges, that can be used against marginalized groups. But he points out how it has also been used politically and effectively by marginalized groups themselves in fighting for human rights. He shows how the principle of human rights can be critiqued as mere tautology and paradox—an "enabling fiction which presupposes that the person is a person in order to effect the person as a person." But instead of critiquing this tautology, he insists that "we can attend to its productive possibilities" (1412-13).

Stephen Mailloux, in an important recent book, develops a theory that universal concepts like "human rights" can be meaningful and useful, and yet not be based on a metaphysical absolute or preestablished notion of human nature. He draws on work by Fish, Richard Rorty, Edward Said, Alain Badiou, and Etienne Balibar, but he works out his own "way to salvage a rhetorical pragmatist use for the notion of universality" (119):

Universals, in my sense, are not philosophical notions at all. They are actual or perceived commonalities, empirically not metaphysically established as rhetorical resources for supporting specific beliefs and practices at specific times and places. . . . [for example the] promotion of peace, say, or prevention of injustice . . . . (119) Mailloux points us to the ultimate pragmatic question: what does the universal do? (For another scholar in our field who is working in this same pragmatist direction, see Spellmeyer.)

We concede that absolute freedom may be a fiction, a delusional impossibility, even a philosophical mistake. But if there are only two possible human conditions, free and unfree, we are cut off from thinking about whether some conditions are less free than others, whether some spaces are more free than others—free from institutional pressures and the influence of culture and the past. Under certain conditions we are more likely to be forcibly silenced than in other conditions. We are in trouble if we cut ourselves off from the kind of careful analysis and observation that distinguishes between differences of degree and talks only about absolute yes and no.

If we look at freewriting through this pragmatic lens, we see that it has striking political effects. Neither free speech nor freewriting are formulated in terms of universals (despite that word "free"): both are about institutional power. They don't pretend to legislate absolute freedom; they rest on formulations that are pragmatically negative.

The entire multi-pronged First Amendment is powered by a single negative clause: "Congress shall make no law . . . respecting . . . prohibiting . . . abridging . . . ." So too, freewriting (despite the positive name) is characteristically conceived and explained in negative terms: don't stop writing, don't try for good or correct language, don't worry about making sense, and most of all, don't worry about being evaluated, because no one will grade this or even read it. To conceive things negatively in this way is to acknowledge the impossibility of pure freedom—but the possibility nevertheless of fighting against restrictions on freedom.

In both cases, the negativity reflects a sturdy, political pragmatism. Politically, the First Amendment is all about the power of the state to lock people up and freewriting is all about the power of teachers to collect and grade writing. We can't create a country where everyone can speak with absolute freedom, but a pragmatic lens emphasizes that we can at least stop Congress from making a law abridging freedom of speech. We cannot create a classroom or even a ten minute period where people can write with complete freedom, but we can refrain—at least temporarily—from treating writing the way it is normally treated in a classroom, as something that will be collected and graded. Indeed, we can refrain from treating writing as it's usually treated in the world: in most people's minds, the medium itself of writing implies being careful and doing things right. Freewriting invites us to be careless and wrong.

If we stay stuck in the postmodern frame of thinking that declares "There's no such thing as freedom," we have a poverty of language for talking about the difference between whether a teacher collects writing or not, grades it or not, marks errors or not, insists on care and standard language or not. The postmodern critique of freedom is essentially totalistic and blots out distinctions between degrees. In contrast, the pragmatic emphasis on negative formulations (at least we can restrict restrictions), serves pragmatically as a way to work towards future possibility and action. By creating ways to limit restriction, it insists that in certain contexts of teaching and writing, we can struggle to move towards more freedom. We act differently and think differently when we adopt the pragmatic principle that it is possible to make progress toward goals that are nevertheless impossible to reach.

POLITICAL VIRTUES OF FREEWRITING

No one doubts the political dimension of free speech. It's always been about helping individuals and small groups speak out and indeed speak back—not be silenced by governments or powerful organizations. The political roots of freewriting are also widely acknowledged. It was introduced in the 1960s and 70s and associated with anti-war and anti-establishment thinking. But those politics have often come to be felt as fossilized "sixties thinking." We sense that many teachers now see freewriting not as a mode of political action but rather primarily as a technique or exercise for helping students feel more comfortably fluent and generative in writing and to find more ideas about a topic. In this essay we're insisting that freewriting carries an inherent political effect—an effect that is blunted if teachers use it only as an occasional exercise for fluency or invention. Here are five ways that freewriting can powerfully help students resist institutional and cultural pressures and thereby to achieve more freedom of thought and inquiry.[2]

(1) Where free speech is a way to open up more thinking in society, freewriting is a way to open up more thinking inside the individual. Freewritten words may have no public political impact since they are private, but it's this very privacy that helps open up an internal "town meeting." That is, people need a safe space for "dangerous" thoughts and feelings—and also, just as important, for writing out their confusion. Frequent practice in freewriting helps create a space where students can articulate thoughts and feelings they might not otherwise write or even say to teachers— or even to classmates.

(2) Freewriting helps students glimpse ways in which their identities are shaped by social forces—at least it does if the freewriting is paired with a chance for reflection. For one thing, freewriting leads to blurted, unplanned thinking that sometimes startles the writer: "Am I really that angry? Maybe I need so-andso more than I realized. Do I really hate those people?" In our own teaching, we try to exploit this benefit of freewriting when we are treating issues of race, gender, sexual orientation, or class.

As we are discussing the issue (whether or not in response to a reading), we specifically invite fast uncensored freewriting about the issue at hand. We invite students to use private writing for feelings they don't want to say out loud.

Of course we're not arguing that a piece of freewriting gives a perfect picture of the writer's mind. Even in freewriting, we often censor our words and thoughts—consciously or unconsciously—especially with loaded issues like these. But we learn from students that they feel much freer and safer here to let words tumble out than when speaking in class or writing for the teacher. So we like to invite our students to look back over what they've written as a snapshot (however imperfect) of their thoughts and feelings. Then we ask for more private writing—but this time slower and more conscious and reflective. We suggest they address questions like these:

- Which elements in your freewriting most reflect what you have inherited or breathed in from growing up with family, friends, or society? Can you remember particular experiences or people that played a big role in leading to any of these thoughts or feelings?
- Of these "inherited" thoughts and feelings, which are you most willing to "own" or stand behind or affirm as your own? Which do you now question or reject?
- Which thoughts and feelings seem least inherited—most derived from your own experience or worked out from your own thinking?
- Discussions of issues like race, class, and sexual orientation become much more thoughtful and productive after using freewriting in this way. If teachers use freewriting with political and ideological awareness, they can help students explore the ways in which they are often shaped by or "written by" larger forces of authority and society—family, friends, and the wider culture. In this way, a very abstract theoretical concept ("social construction") turns into something students can investigate concretely.

(3) Frequent freewriting helps students develop a metaawareness of the complex forces of authority and convention in the classroom and in the culture. When students experience a teacher using institutional authority to get them to write—yet with no explicit mechanism to require it . . . and promising not to collect it . . . and pushing them to write without stopping and without worrying about whether it even makes sense or is any good—this feels very strange. But strangeness is

the point. Students get a chance to glimpse how their own ideas and goals for a piece of writing—even a graded piece—might be more important than those of their teachers.

Many students don't quite notice that when they start to write for a teacher, they unthinkingly use a linguistic and mental gear that's different from what they normally use for writing outside the classroom. But the discipline of not stopping almost forces them to produce unplanned language, which almost invariably forces them to use speech for writing. Even the "standard" speech of "mainstream" speakers is wrong for "correct writing" or the grapholect. Yet freewriting can help students discover that "inappropriate" "talking onto the page" sometimes yields language that's better for writing than their careful "writing language."

As teachers continue taking time for freewrites but not even collecting it, students gradually begin to notice, bit by bit, what it's like to feel less of the teacher's presence in their "school" writing. They get a politically salutary chance to notice their habitual fear of writing wrong. This effect of freewriting can be particularly powerful for students who speak stigmatized varieties of English (whether or not they try to freewrite in standardized English).

But often it's skilled, diligent students who benefit most from the political (and linguistic) benefits of unplanned language and thinking. They are so skilled at planning thought and language that they don't know how to not plan; so good at giving teachers what teachers want that they don't have the experience of writing what they know teachers would criticize. Through freewriting, these students get a better view of how they function and how institutional contexts have led to these habits of functioning.

(4) Freewriting fosters equality. The practice of freewriting helps communicate a crucial assumption: that students walk into our classrooms already possessing the core linguistic resources they need to develop as writers. Their experience with speech can be the foundation of their written literacy. This notion of student competence is a profoundly political one, for it asserts the basic equality of all languages and dialects. Not all dialects have the same cultural capital, but all are equal from a linguistic perspective: intricate, complex, and rule-governed language systems. Freewriting invites students to notice how they draw on their

spoken language competencies to develop their literacy skills (see Bean et al.).

In this claim about the politics of language, we connect freewriting with what is perhaps the most radical document in our field, Students' Right to their Own Language (STROL—see Conference). Freewriting helps students see that even the most stigmatized versions of English are rich and intricate and work fine for writing. In removing the pressure to write "correctly," freewriting helps students focus on clarifying and developing their ideas. This is especially important for students with diverse linguistic backgrounds: "Perhaps the most serious difficulty facing 'non-standard' dialect speakers in developing writing ability derives from their exaggerated concern for the least serious aspects of writing" (*CCC*, Students' Right 8).

Teachers who use freewriting when they actually care about a student's right to his or her own language are likely to assign some respected published literature or nonfiction that's not written in standardized English—and also invite students to share some public freewriting that's not in "correct revised edited 'standard' English"—and also revise and copy-edit some pieces without trying to get them into that orthodox dialect. Freewriting and these other practices invite students to question the idea that written language works best for readers only if it conforms to standardized written English. Which readers? The students themselves are readers, and they often have a different experience. And many of them will know audiences who would appreciate writing entirely in other versions of English. Ultimately, freewriting moves us toward a hybrid discourse— home and academy, personal and public, rational and emotional— with profound political and social implications (see Canagarajah). It helps us reject simplistic either/or arguments that try to force us to choose between standardized edited English and other versions of English.

(5) Freewriting often brings pleasure. There's an unexpectedly subversive dimension here. First, there is the pleasure in breaking rules. As Bordieu points out, literacy is continual training in having to do things "the right way." In response to this pressure, we see a widespread human pull to do things the wrong way. De Certeau explores the myriad ways people resist the authority of propriety, many of them seemingly trivial—like wearing baseball caps "backwards" or using "bad" "vulgar" language. People cannot seem to resist flaunting "wrong" writing

in the public space— whether it's special spelling for text-messaging or graffiti or neon signs that say Kwik Kleeners, E-Z Car Wash, 7Eleven, or Toys Us).

No less important from a political point of view is the pleasure of spontaneous generativity. The free play of unplanned language issuing from moving fingers tends to give a kind of pleasurable release. It's not uncommon for freewriting students to find themselves pulled forward when words pour forth on their own.

T.R. Johnson speaks of

> that strange, highly positive surge of energy that can possess students when they enter the zone and their pens begin to wiggle across the page more quickly than a moment before, their heads lower a notch, and they emanate a whole new kind of intensity (624).

Spariosu, in an ambitious study of "Play, Poetry, and Power in Hellenic Thought," explores the pleasure of emotional release that comes from experiencing words and feelings that well up. He explores how this kind of carnival play resists power when power is based in rational control. (See also Bakhtin on "carnival" in Rabelais.) Our schools are largely dedicated to rational control or even obedience, and have developed a culture characterized by domination and apathy. Freewriting offers a space for a counterculture of pleasure, one that decouples writing from punishment.

Conclusion

There's no way to freewrite wrong. (If the only way you can get yourself to write without stopping for ten minutes is to write the same word over and over—or even to quickly plan every word first in your head—that's fine. Repeated freewriting will lead somewhere.) But is there a wrong way for teachers to use freewriting? In earlier drafts, we wrote that freewriting needed to be used with thoughtful awareness of its political implications. But the more we reflect on how freewriting works—theoretically and in our teaching—the more we toy with a more ambitious claim: if freewriting is used frequently, it will do some of its political work even if the teacher and students are not conscious of it.

But, as politicians often remind us, freedom isn't free. One of the most important things we have learned from free speech scholarship is that society will not maintain it without intervention. The strong tend to out-shout the weak: governments and large corporations tend to move toward a monopoly of power unless there is a mechanism of restraint. The First Amendment depends on the exercise of power by people with institutional authority, and the courts have the explicit job of using their authority to help protect and preserve individual expression from undue restriction. So too with writing: unless we use our authority as teachers to intervene and create spaces of relatively more freedom of expression through practices like freewriting, teaching will tend to push in the direction of conformity and the restriction of discourse.

Notes

1. Domna Stanton, speaking as president of MLA, underscores the importance of a particular form of free speech: the tradition of academic freedom that goes with tenure in most colleges and universities. She points to a threat in the "Academic Bill of Rights" that has been introduced in fifteen state legislatures that "claims [in her words] to protect the rights of students by empowering those who feel uncomfortable in class because of something a teacher says or does to institute grievance procedures against that teacher" (4). She concludes: "As crucial as conceptual clarity may be, and as difficult—perhaps impossible—as it may be to realize this idea(l) in any society, academic freedom nonetheless needs to be defended wherever it is under attack." (3) Even as we recognize the impossibility of absolute freedom, most academics hold to the idea that freedom of expression is crucial to our work as academics.

2. The term freewriting is used rather freely. (It's remarkable how many teachers collect students' freewriting.) It's worth spelling out the main points of definition. Regular default freewriting is private and doesn't specify a topic. It's an exercise; the goal is not a product. There are two variations on freewriting that result from reimposing two constraints. Focused freewriting says, "Try to stay on one topic; when you wander off, pull yourself back." Public freewriting says, "Write with the understanding that you'll share what you write." (Focused freewriting can be private or public; public freewriting can be focused or unfocused.) For a volume of essays about freewriting, see Belanoff, Elbow, Fontaine.

WORKS CITED

Alexander, Larry. *Is There a Right of Freedom of Expression?* New York: Cambridge UP, 2005.
Bakhtin, Mikhail. *Rabelais and His World.* Trans. Helene Iswolsky. Bloomington IN: Indiana UP, 1984.
Bartholomae, David. "Writing with Teachers: A Conversation with Peter Elbow. *College Composition and Communication* 46.1 (Feb 1995): 62-71.
Bean et al. "Should We Invite Students to Write in Home Languages? Complicating the Yes/No Debate." *Composition Studies* 31.1 (Spring 2003): 25-42.
Belanoff, Pat, Peter Elbow, and Sheryl I. Fontaine. *Nothing Begins with N: New Explorations of Freewriting.* Southern Illinois UP, 1990.
Bizzell, Patricia and Bruce Herzberg. *The Bedord Bibliography for Teachers of Writing.* Boston: Bedford/St Martins, 2000.
Bollinger, Lee C. "Dialogue." *Eternally Vigilant.* Eds. Lee. C. Bollinger and Geoffrey R. Stone. Chicago, U Chicago P, 2002. 1-31.
Brandeis, Louis. "Whitney v. California." Basic Readings in U.S. Democracy. Info USA. U.S.Department of State. <http://usinfo.state.gov/usa/infousa/facts/democrac/44.htm>.
Bunker, Matthew. *Critiquing Free Speech: First Amendment Theory and the Challenge of Interdisciplinarity.* Mahwah, NJ: Lawrence Erlbaum, 2001.
College Composition and Communication (CCC). Students' Right to Their Own Language. CCC 25.3 (Fall 1974): 1-32.
Canagarajah, A Suresh. "The Place of World Englishes in Composition: Pluralization Continued." *CCC* 57.4 (June 2006): 586-619.
De Certeau, Michel. *The Practice of Everyday Life.* Tr. Steven Rendall. Berkeley: U Cal Press, 1988.
Elbow, Peter. *Writing Without Teachers.* New York: Oxford UP, 1973.
Felski, Rita. *Beyond Feminist Aesthetics: Feminist Literature and Social Change.* Cambridge, MA: Harvard UP, 1989.
Fish, Stanley. *There's No Such Thing as Free Speech...and It's a Good Thing, Too.* New York: Oxford UP, 1994.
James, William. *Pragmatism, A New Name for Some Old Ways of Thinking: Popular Lectures on Philosophy.* New York: Longmans, 1914.
Johnson, T.R. "School Sucks." *College Composition and Communication* 52.4 (June 2001): 620-650.
Laclau, Ernesto, and Chantal Mouffe. *Hegemony and Socialist Strategy: Toward a Radical Democratic Politics.* London: Verso, 1985.
Lu, Min-Zhan, and Bruce Horner. *Representing the "Other": Basic Writers and the Teaching of Basic Writing.* Urbana, IL: NCTE, 1998.
Macrorie, Ken. *Writing to be Read.* NY: Hayden Book Co, 1968.

Mailloux, Stephen. *Disciplinary Identities: Rhetorical Paths of English, Speech, and Composition.* New York: MLA, 2007.

Roskelly, Hephzibah, and Kate Ronald. *Reason to Believe: Romanticism, Pragmatism and the Teaching of Writing.* Albany NY: SUNY P, 1998.

Slaughter, Joseph R. "Enabling Fictions and Novel Subjects: The Bildungsroman and International Human Rights Law." *PMLA* 121.5 (October 2006): 1405-23.

Spariosu, Mihai I. *God of Many Names: Play, Poetry, and Power in Hellenic Thought from Homer to Aristotle.* Durham, NC: Duke UP, 1991.

Spellmeyer, Kurt. *Common Ground: Dialogue, Understanding, and the Teaching of Composition.* Englewood Cliffs, NJ: Prentice Hall, 1993.

---. *Arts of Living: Reinventing the Humanities for the Twenty-first Century.* Albany NY: SUNY P, 2003.

Strauss, David A. "Freedom of Speech and the Common-Law Constitution." *Eternally Vigilant.* Eds. Les C. Bollinger and Geoffrey R. Stone. Chicago, U Chicago P, 2002. 32-59.

West, Cornel. *The American Evasion of Philosophy: A Genealogy of Pragmatism.* Madison, WI: University of Wisconsin Press, 1989.

White, Edward G. "The First Amendment Comes of Age: The Emergence of Free Speech in Twentieth-Century America." *Michigan Law Review* 95.2 (Nov 1996): 299-392.

KAIROS

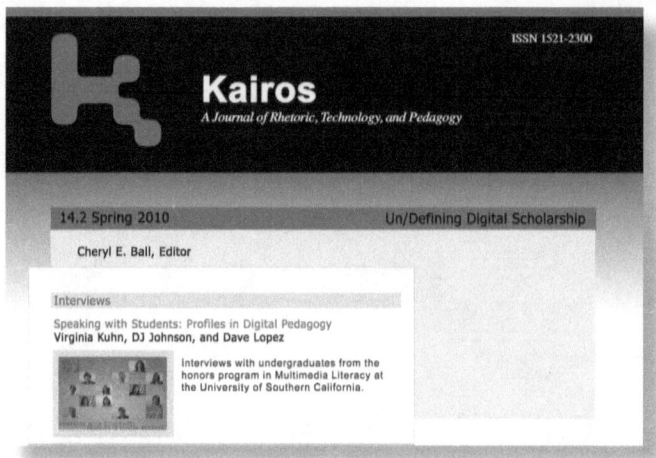

Published in *Kairos: A Journal of Rhetoric, Technology, and Pedagogy* 14.2 Spring, 2010 http://kairos.technorhetoric.net/14.2/interviews/kuhn/index.html

Kairos is an independent, refereed, open-access journal exploring the intersections of rhetoric, technology, and pedagogy. The journal reaches a wide, international audience, with over 45,000 readers per month. Since its first issue in January of 1996, the mission of *Kairos* has been to publish scholarship that examines digital and multimodal composing practices, promoting "webtexts" that enact their scholarly argument through rhetorical and innovative uses of new media. *Kairos* is the longest, continuously running online journal in digital writing studies, thanks to its volunteer staff's dedication to rigorous, collaborative peer-review and editorial production processes. The acceptance rate is 10%.

"Speaking with Students: Profiles in Digital Pedagogy" by Virginia Kuhn, with DJ Johnson and David Lopez

Speaking with Students" crosses a lot of boundaries, exemplifying Kairos's ethos in digital writing studies. This webtext ran in the Interviews section, which primarily features well-known scholars of interest to *Kairos* readers. This text, however, features undergraduate students reflecting on their digital media projects and presents the assessment heuristic used by the Institute for Multimedia Literacy to grade the students' honors theses. As both a journal editor and a teacher invested in theoretically driven evaluative measures for multimodal scholarship, I appreciate how this webtext provides straightforward praxis with student reflection to show how this heuristic is useful in the classroom and in the kinds of texts *Kairos* publishes.

Speaking with Students: Profiles in Digital Pedagogy

Virginia Kuhn, with DJ Johnson and David Lopez

INTRODUCTION

The Honors in Multimedia Scholarship Program

Founded in 1998, the Institute for Multimedia Literacy (IML) is an organized research unit dedicated to developing educational programs and conducting research on the changing nature of literacy in a networked culture. Although its institutional home is the School of Cinematic Arts, the IML supports faculty research and curricula that seek to transform the nature of scholarship within the disciplines. The Honors in Multimedia Scholarship program is an university-wide undergraduate program located at the IML; it received official sanction and began enrolling its first cohort in Fall 2004, basing the curriculum on the previous six years of experience deploying multimedia scholarship in courses across the USC campus. The Honors program was the first of several academic programs launched by the IML.

In 2006, the IML, in collaboration with USC's College of Letters, Arts and Sciences, created the Multimedia in the Core Program which unites General Education courses with multimedia labs, offering all USC students the opportunity to explore new forms of scholarly expression. The following year, the Multimedia Across the College Program was created; here, upper division courses are paired with multimedia instruction, allowing students to investigate media-based forms of scholarly research and production. This year (2009), the IML's Minor in Digital Studies was approved which expanded the course offering further. IML courses now include everything from photo-essays to Web-based documentaries, from interactive videos to sophisticated Web sites, and from kinetic typography to 3-D visualizations. All IML courses include a hands-on lab component, in addition to a theoretical foundation borne of critical studies, semiotics, cinema studies, composition and rhetorical theory.

Like all IML academic programs, the Honors program is both reactive and proactive in relation to digital technologies for expression and communication. That is to say, while the idea is to identify and engage new media and the emerging practices they engender, the program is explicitly designed to be transformative in that it hopes to teach a new generation of scholars to enhance traditional academic practices through multimedia. The Honors program stands apart from other IML programs, however, in that its goal is advanced digital literacy. As such, the program culminates in the creation of a media-rich, digital thesis project. Honors cohorts are small (15-25 students per year) and they are well supported both technologically and conceptually. Students take IML440 and IML444 during their senior year, where they plan and execute these projects which are grounded in their disciplinary major. Each student has two faculty advisors, one from the IML, and one from their major and this ensures the type of student-faculty interaction that aids their scholarship, and allows us to be pedagogically responsive.

The Multimedia Thesis

The first Honors cohort completed their thesis projects in 2008 and the second in 2009; the planning and execution of these projects is the topic of these student profiles. The students featured here are mainly from the inaugural class, and graduated with the Honors designation in 2008 (they are filmed against a green background). There are also two students from the 2009 cohort (they are pictured against blue-gray draping). One of the greatest challenges of creating these projects is that there are few models for scholarly multimedia. Born-digital work requires us to consider the ability to explore issues with the sort of depth that comes from deploying the registers of text, image and interactivity, while it also has the potential to involve the reader/viewer in unprecedented ways. As scholars (both teachers and students), we must ask ourselves what we can do with digital media that we could not do otherwise, but we must also avoid uncritically adopting the conventions of commercial or entertainment media.

Since the goal of the Honors program is to be both academic and innovative, we did not want to impose generic conventions on the projects students might create, feeling that this might limit them. At the same time, we needed to be sure we retained the type of rigor appropriate to academic endeavors. Thus, the thesis parameters, conceived by the planning team, and updated by its program directors (Steve Anderson, from 2004 to 2006, and Virginia Kuhn from 2007 to the present), provide a way to ensure standards, while encouraging transformation and enhancement of scholarship in light of emergent technologies. These parameters are presented and discussed throughout the process of planning and executing their projects and, in this way, students gain the ability to articulate and defend the choices made in their work.

Speaking with Students: The Webtext

This webtext features students discussing their work. This reflective aspect is valuable on many levels, and documenting and sharing such reflection in this webext is equally vital. Here's why:

Media Variety

The digital archive able to house projects that cross numerous platforms does not exist. These projects run the gamut from 3D environments built in the virtual world of Second Life, to the weighty files of a Korsakow filmic database, to animated Flash-based webtexts, to sophisticated Sophie projects. Storing numerous file types in an online archive requires conversion into some uniform format which will limit functionality. Perhaps more profoundly though, the rise of social networking stimulates a sense of collaborative dynamism — we want reader feedback, user input, and viewer-generated content that extends and reinforces our efforts. And while this impulse may merely highlight the fact that academic work is always part of a larger conversation, the responsibility for maintaining the dynamic portion of digital work is problematic. Standards are difficult to establish since applications are perpetually evolving. Further, many digital objects will have several iterations depending on how a viewer might access them, particularly with new mobile content which requires a different sort of optimization than, say, a standard webtext.

Application Obsolescence

With no standards for maintenance, old applications will not run in just a few short years, making archiving whole projects increasingly untenable (even as algorithms that revert to earlier operating systems are gaining some ground). These videos offer insight into the process as much as the product. UCLA's Howard Besser suggests that archivists must shift their mindset from saving completed works to asset management. Given the demand for ancillary materials (outtakes, scripts, storyboards), Besser suggests archivists should focus on "saving a side body of materials that contextualize a work" (14). For our purposes, capturing a snapshot of student work while they contextualize it makes complete sense — the video format is fairly stable and selfcontained. Moreover, institutionalized curricula cannot hope to keep up with the rapidly evolving applications that arise in the Web 2.0 world and so we must teach students *how* to learn rather than *what* to learn. These pieces lend critical insight into students' processes while they give the IML a uniform repository that provides a model for students and faculty alike. For even as digital scholarship is on the rise, there remains a dearth of models on which to base such efforts. In cases where the student has opted to maintain their work online, urls are given.

Assessment

Although it is unpopular to discuss grading, at least at the faculty level, since that is the terrain of the "bean counters," we ignore our institutional constraints at our peril. Not only is it a disservice to students to fail to inform them of the criteria by which they will be judged — their financial aid, scholarships, or membership in certain student groups often depends upon maintaining a certain GPA — given its relative newness, digital work is subject to the charge of lack of academic rigor. Without the sustained analysis that comes from assessment criteria, digital work can be dismissed as bells and whistles. These criteria give us a lexicon with which to discuss digital work among ourselves and our students, even as explaining digital work in language that is familiar to traditional academics helps them appreciate its nuances and sophistication. And although institutional constraints can prove frustrating, this is something that academic institutions do well: they force a type of rigor that pushes us toward excellence. At the IML we feel our project parameters help to highlight aspects that may not be immediately apparent in the piece itself — they approach each project on its own terms. As such, there is far more freedom to be innovative with emerging platforms, while maintaining high quality work.

In creating the student profiles, we decided that a running time of roughly five minutes would be optimal. Much longer video profiles could have easily been created given the scholarly depth of the projects and their thickness in terms of the multitude of layers of visual, aural and textual elements contained in each. In addition, the student interviews covered a range of topics related to the production of their thesis projects, from initial inspiration, to design and implementation, to the students' subjective response to their completed work. We also asked them to discuss how their work in scholarly multimedia has impacted their undergraduate education and how it has shaped their future educational and professional goals. We had a wealth of materials from which to build these profiles, which heightened the challenge before us: how do we maintain the integrity of the students' projects and their unique voices within a five minute timeframe? We had to address key issues concerning the representation of students and their work in creating these profiles. In doing so, we are moved to consider best practices for documenting multimedia pedagogy, student experience and scholarly digital work. The *Notes on Process* section accompanying the student profiles illuminates key issues faced in creating these profiles and the strategies used to address them. Whereas many of these strategies are grounded in formal techniques of documentary production, they are deployed in deliberate and specific ways to highlight the scholarly and aesthetic nuances particular to each project.

In order to visually represent the depth of the issues involved in this Flash-based webtext, we created a type of layering effect by allowing traces of one page or screen to remain behind another. While reading one screen, a viewer might see the ghost of a video from the previous screen still playing. The color gradation was very deliberately adjusted in order to keep the text legible, even in the presence of these traces. We believe this feature of the webtext serves as a reminder of the type of depth that is emerging in digital technologies both in and out of the confines of the computer.

We feel that these students are pioneers in the area of digital scholarship and deserve to be documented in ways that are typically reserved for faculty. However, we do understand that no interview, no film, whether edited inside or outside of the camera, is ideologically neutral. We have framed students in a particular way and have created these five minutes, from the hour or so of interview footage each student gave, in order to tell a particular story. We hope the story is one the student sees as valid — and, indeed, all students have been quite pleased with their piece, often using them on job and graduate school applications — but we also understand the extent to which students tell us what we want to hear. Our only way to reconcile these issues is full disclosure: we have a vested interest in this program, these students and their work. To mitigate our bias however, we have adopted Norman Denizen's approach to the construct of the "interview" as a form. Throughout the process of filming, editing and writing about these interviews we have sought to make them "reflexive, dialogic [and] performative" (24) such that by creating them, we are "learning to use language in a way that brings people together" (24) rather than commodifying these students and their work for our own purposes. We hope you find these pieces as stimulating and productive as we do.

Virginia Kuhn is the Associate Director in charge of the Honors in Multimedia Scholarship program at the IML. Her work centers on the ways in which the affordances of digital technologies impact thought, discourse and expression in a highly mediated world. DJ Johnson has been the video documentarian for the IML since 2003. An award-winning filmmaker, Johnson has extensive experience producing and directing documentaries and promotional videos for educational institutions and social service organizations. David Lopez is an Interactivity Designer for the IML. For over five years, he has consistently worked to facilitate multimedia results from raw scholarly enquiry.

WORKS CITED

Besser, Howard. "Digital Preservation of the Moving Image Material?" *The Moving Image* (Fall, 2001). http://www.gseis.ucla.edu/~howard/Papers/amialongevity.html

Denizen, Norman. "The Reflexive Interview and a Performative Social Science." *Qualitative Research* 1.1 (2001): 23-46.

USC Institute for Multimedia Literacy Project Parameters

These are the parameters by which the thesis project is gauged. Students are given these criteria early on, and can therefore plan accordingly. These parameters are flexible enough to allow student innovation, but rigorous enough to ensure academic excellence. Each of the four areas is subdivided into three nuanced categories, and within the webtext you will find clips that demonstrate the ways students have met them.

Conceptual Core

The project's controlling idea must be apparent. The project must be productively aligned with one or more multimedia genres. The project must effectively engage with the primary issue/s of the subject area into which it is intervening.

Research Component

The project must display evidence of substantive research and thoughtful engagement with its subject matter. The project must use a variety of credible sources and cite them appropriately. The project ought to deploy more than one approach to an issue.

Form & Content

The project's structural or formal elements must serve the conceptual core. The project's design decisions must be deliberate, controlled, and defensible. The project's efficacy must be unencumbered by technical problems.

Creative Realization

The project must approach the subject in a creative or innovative manner. The project must use media and design principles effectively. The project must achieve significant goals that could not be realized on paper.

http://iml.usc.edu

PEDAGOGY

Pedagogy: Critical Approaches to Teaching Literature, Language, Composition, and Culture. Volume 9, Number 3 doi 10.1215/15314200-2009-005 © 2009 by Duke University Press

Pedagogy: Critical Approaches to Teaching Literature, Language, Composition and Culture (Duke University Press) is an independent journal, not affiliated with any association, conference or professional body. Indeed, Pedagogy was founded as a journal that would speak across the profession of English and unite us around our common work as teachers, building a new discourse around teaching in English studies. No other mainstream journal has devoted itself exclusively to pedagogical issues spanning the entire discipline. Fusing theoretical approaches and practical realities, the journal seeks to reverse the long history of the marginalization of teaching and of the scholarship produced around it.

"Remediating the Book Review: Toward Collaboration and Multimodality across the English Curriculum" by Christine Tulley and Kristine Blair

We have selected Christine Tulley and Kristine Blair's "Remediating the Book Review: Towards Collaboration and Multimodality across the English Curriculum" (*Pedagogy* 9.3) not only because of the quality of its scholarship--and in an emerging field--but also because of the collaborative model of scholarship that we try to promote at Pedagogy. In this essay, Tulley and Blair combine instructional and editorial perspectives to analyze how the process of digital composing reshapes often entrenched notions of authorship and composing practice within the English major by having students reenvision a traditional print genre, the book review, in digital space.

Remediating the Book Review: Toward Collaboration and Multimodality across the English Curriculum

Christine Tulley and Kristine Blair

Computer and writing specialists have devoted considerable attention to the complex processes students engage in to compose texts for the Web in technology-enhanced classrooms (see, for example, the collections of Harrington, Rickly, and Day 2000 and Galin, Haviland, and Johnson 2003). Yet, as Pam Takayoshi and Cindy Selfe (2007: 1) argue,

> although composition theories have evolved to acknowledge and study these new multimodal texts (texts that exceed the alphabetic and may include still and moving images, animations, color, words, music and sound), the formal assignments that many English composition teachers give to students remain alphabetic and primarily produced via some form of print media.

This continued privileging of print texts is pervasive throughout the English curriculum, as many programs struggle with balancing not only how to integrate multimodal texts but also how to evaluate such texts. For this reason, Craig Stroupe (2000: 607) suggests "those in English studies would benefit from revisiting the text/media dichotomy — particularly the dialogism between verbal and visual discourses on the single lexia."

Rather than deny the extent of digital writing practice that many students engage in outside of class by continuing to privilege print texts (and therefore reinforce this print versus screen dichotomy), a few programs have chosen to offer one course in digital composing practice for English majors as a way to balance existing traditional literature, rhetoric, linguistic, and writing courses.[1] Though a single course in multimodal composing appears to counteract the ideal of an integrated multimodality that examines texts in all forms across the English major, we argue it is a necessary first step to begin rethinking traditional genres while teaching critical thinking and critical composing skills. Additionally, a multimedia composing course has far-reaching implications as to how the English major itself will likely shift from an emphasis on analysis of texts to a more equitable mix of both analysis and production of texts. As we contend in this article, such a course helps to "remediate" (Bolter and Grusin 1999) familiar genres within English studies for both students and faculty. Focusing on two collaborative Web-based book reviews developed in class for eventual publication in an online journal allows us to revisit ongoing debates by rethinking productive similarities rather than focusing on the differences between alphabetic and multimodal texts.

Furthermore, offering a course in digital composing to English majors provides more effective integration of in-class and out-of-class literacies that Marshall Gregory (2001: 69) invites English faculty to keep in mind. He argues "that exposing students to a well-thought-out curriculum is not the same as educating them, if educating them means . . . helping them learn how to integrate the contents of the curriculum into their hearts, minds, and everyday lives." Teaching students multimodal composing practices (many of which they are already using in their everyday lives outside of classes) meets the end goal of most English programs: to teach students to communicate effectively. Takayoshi and Selfe (2007: 3) argue that multimodal instruction meets this need, as "the more channels students (and writers generally) have to select from when composing and exchanging meaning, the more resources they have at their disposal for being successful communicators."

Endorsing others' arguments supporting multimodal composing (Wysocki et al. 2004; Takayoshi and Selfe 2007), we combine our instructional and editorial perspectives to analyze how the process of digital composing reshapes often entrenched notions of authorship and composing practice of a representative English department using two sections of Tulley's advanced Web Writing for English Majors course.[2] We felt one such way to educate the students about the curricular connections between print and screen texts was to take a commonly taught assignment within the English curriculum, in this case the book review, and remediate it in a digital space. Jay Gordon (2005: 49) offers this justification for the importance of learning Web writing: "In learning to produce hypertext, students are introduced to an important form of written composition that encompasses not only text generation, but also visual communication and information architecture." In the following sections, we chronicle our own shift from print to digital and the resulting impact of that shift upon students' ability to collaborate and compose in multimodal environments.

ANALYZING A PRINT TEXT AND PRODUCING A SCREEN REVIEW

In the spring 2004 semester of this course,[3] students developed collaborative Web-based book reviews to submit to *Computers and Composition Online (C&CO)*. Based on our first experience, we repeated the project three years later with the spring 2007 class and noted how the two projects increased students' understanding of digital rhetoric and their evolving views of the author-text relationship. Because Web environments offer democratic spaces where anyone can publish and subject positions can change (Balsamo 2000; Dibbell 1999), it would make sense that a collaborative digital project such as a book review composed by teacher and students can break down traditional boundaries of the teacher as authority and primary writer/researcher in addition to the privileged perception of the existence of the solo author in this genre. In the case described here, the book review was authored by the senior Web writing class at the University of Findlay and instructor Christine Tulley, and revisions were discussed in class sessions with *C&CO* editor Kristine Blair. The context of actual publication encouraged students to look at the project as a mutually beneficial one where all parties (students, instructor, and editor) had a stake in the final version.

This concept of egalitarian access to publication and voice has been problematized by Grabill (2003: 462), who argues that a digital divide persists "between rich and poor, White and non-White, highly educated and not highly educated, [and] . . . because it continues to exist, it continues to describe situations of social hierarchy and inequality —

class divisions — that are harmful." Susan Romano (1993: 5) argues that with critical analysis students can be taught to be "rhetoricians, rhetors, and subjects under construction by others," combating some of these divisions. We argue here that such critical analysis of Web texts can be fostered especially well when students are positioned as coresearchers/coauthors of digital texts because multimodal texts push up against the solo-authored canonical texts studied within the English major's curriculum (Takayoshi and Selfe 2007: 1).

Situating a traditional project such as the book review within a nontraditional format such as an online journal critically engages students in the process of multimodal composing and has widespread pedagogical implications for how English majors are taught accepted discourse conventions of the discipline. Jeff Rice (2006: 130) argues that English studies already is familiar with the concept of "the space of the page" and its ties "to the single author, the individual who works in one fixed space . . . with a single identity tied to a singly motivated reading practice tied to a single idea expressed at a single moment." Yet, he notes that English studies has not addressed "the open space constructed out of connections where multiple writers engaging within multiple ideas in multiple media and multiple moments function" off the page (130).

As a result of both of these experiences, we ultimately conclude the collaborative research relationship of students, teachers, and editor in a digital environment subverts several traditional hierarchies in print composing, such as the notion of the solo-authoring researcher, while reestablishing others, despite claims of egalitarian access promised by digital composing. If the goal of increasing multimodal pedagogies is to happen across the English major, projects such as our collaborative book review offer the open spaces Rice describes to think about the pedagogies we use to foster collaboration within a digital composing context. We acknowledge that although the evolution of students' composing processes between the two projects does indicate that students are growing more aware of effective practices of digital rhetoric, the sustainability of such activities should be within the scope of the entire English major and not necessarily relegated to a single course or single genre.

INTRODUCTION TO THE WEB WRITING COURSE

As senior English majors, many of the nine students in the spring 2004 course were skilled at producing literary analysis, creative writing, and argumentative prose. Yet few students, beyond two in the creative writing emphasis who often submitted work for publication, had experience with honing their writing skills for an audience outside the English faculty or peers. Few also had experience writing in a multimedia environment, so initial projects included reading and developing a blog, completing a flash poetry/fiction text using Macromedia Flash, and composing a hypertext story modeled after Michael Joyce's oft-cited *afternoon, a story* (1990). With each new project, students practiced a range of multimodal writing tasks that used a variety of semiotic modes to design each text (Kress and Van Leeuwen 2001) but had yet to interact with a wider audience beyond friends, peers, and the instructor even though these texts were posted on the Web and theoretically accessible to anyone. Furthermore, most students took the course the last semester of their senior year, so they were well versed in discussing effective writing techniques of traditional prose and poetry but had little experience analyzing the extent to which such multimodal texts were rhetorically effective.

In one case, to bridge this gap, the class studied differences between a blog and a paper-based traditional diary and explored how the notion of "authorship" might change in a hypertext environment. Because these English majors were familiar with the concept of the solo author within the literary tradition, experiencing the collaborative nature of hypertext, which often allows readers to manipulate the initial author's text, complicated and broadened this traditional notion of authorship often entrenched in the English major's curriculum, not to mention within the larger field of literary studies (Brodkey 1987). Yet as research in both technical communication and English education suggests, the emphasis on technology is a vital part of business and industry and the language arts curriculum within the public schools (Gee 2003; Selber 2004; Rice 2006). As a result, the curricula for these subdisciplines of English studies include emphases on both teaching and learning in digital environments. Paradoxically, the traditional English major seldom includes such an emphasis, presuming that those students who will graduate and seek advanced degrees will not need such a digital skills set in either teaching or research, leading to a vicious cycle in which English majors and the professors who teach them privilege the print over the digital.

Yet scholars such as Jay David Bolter (2001) have long contended that the shift to electronic literacies does not signal the death of print, but rather that new media are what remediate print into the digital age, a point that suggests a need for more multimodal approaches than we currently see. More recently, Debra Journet (2007: 107) reaffirms that "alongside [a] commitment to alphabetic literacy . . . has been a professional reluctance to employ communication technologies for anything other than the production and the reception of written text." Significantly, Journet has recently collaborated with graduate students at the University of Louisville on the *C&CO* Web text "Digital Mirrors: Multimodal Reflection in the Composition Classroom" (2008), relying on video and audio to create a dialogue about how their own multimodal literacy acquisition will enhance their pedagogical practice in undergraduate writing courses. This discussion indicates faculty attitudes about the value of multimodal composing within the English curriculum may be shifting gradually. Our collaborative book review offers a look at one possible project that operates in the border space between print and digital by using an unconventional mode (Web writing) to deliver a conventional text (book review).

Remediating the Book Review

One of the ongoing struggles of teaching students multimodal writing is to balance pedagogical practice and critical examination of Web space with available technology choices. In fact, Melinda Turnley (2006: 133) argues, "Rather than letting hardware and software drive web-based learning activities, instruction should highlight contextualized technology use and articulate the cultural and rhetorical positionings of the Web." Up until the midterm point of the 2004 Web writing class, Tulley had been struggling with student enthusiasm over Web design projects where students were adding sound for sound's sake, rather than for considered rhetorical purposes. Kathleen Tyner (1998) discusses how this enthusiasm for technological prowess can be an inherent danger when using a media arts approach to technology use, an approach adopted here in the Web writing class, because students are taught media tools to "foster self-expression" rather than merely as a set of skills to learn. She notes "one danger of a media arts approach is that in the process of 'learning by doing,' students can inadvertently fall into a technist trap by marginalizing the analysis component in the quest for production" (156). Though our students can often use a variety of technological tools ranging from portable storage devices to social networking spaces such as Facebook, this does not mean the skills to effectively analyze digital texts from a rhetorical point of view are learned by association, though some savvy design choices by the 2007 class do indicate that by this time many students can distinguish between poorly designed and user-friendly digital texts (Selber 2004).

Regardless of the emphasis on our students as active users of technology (Prensky 2001; Gee 2003), very often Web design and rhetorical analysis of Web texts are as new to them as they are to their instructors. Although in theory scholars may advocate teaching digital writing (Wide Research Collective 2005), in practice digital writing curricula continue to be the exception rather than the rule, as most undergraduate English programs do not include courses on Web-based writing. Even with such curricula, the development of digital literacies — like the acquisition and development of any literacy — is a progressive acquisition process for teachers and students alike. From both an instructional and an editorial standpoint, Blair has experienced a range of digital dilemmas regarding electronic publishing, phenomena she has often referred to as the "Goldilocks syndrome": (1) because of limited Web-authoring and digital imaging skills, both students' and faculty's electronic texts often possess more substance than flash, or design savvy for digital audiences, or (2) some electronic texts may have design flash but be substandard in rhetorical purpose or argument, or finally (3) occasionally student or professional texts submitted for grade or publication have the appropriate ("just right") development of a design scheme that fits content to such an extent that both design and content work equally to contribute to overall rhetorical purpose. The second case was particularly true of early Web-based projects in the 2004 course, because few considered rhetorical purpose and often unintentionally constructed documents that incorporated several technologies (podcasts and video) but failed to engage the reader in a conversation. This weakness is noted by DigitRhet.org (2006: 236), which points out that such one-way reception interferes with "true activity and collaborative meaning making."

As a result of this privileging of design over content in early Web projects, Tulley hoped a "real-life" multimodal publication in *C&CO*

would provide a better opportunity to balance rhetorical and design concerns than previous course projects she had initially planned. Yet Jonathan Alexander (2002: 388) argues that merely publishing student texts to the Web "may be essentially equivalent to publishing class booklets" where visitors to the site would likely be restricted to students, proud parents and friends, and perhaps other writing teachers. Tulley preferred the review as a final project because it not only incorporated the technological skills but also rhetorical criticism of Web text and a research component exploring how the composing process for publication changes in a Web-based environment. Tulley also wanted to ensure that students were writing for an audience beyond their classmates and friends. Although students were aware when they signed up for the course that all texts produced would be "published" on the Web, at the point when the review was assigned students were not aware who would read this published work. This is important to note because as Steven Krause (2000: 119) argues, "students might not be as eager to publish their work on the web as might be assumed," a hesitancy we discuss later in the essay.

That same semester Tulley was invited by *C&CO*'s Blair to write a review of James Paul Gee's *What Video Games Have to Teach Us about Learning and Literacy* (2003), and Tulley thought a joint review with the Web writing class might provide a meaningful exit activity. Blair enthusiastically encouraged Tulley and her class to develop the collaborative review of James Gee's important connection between the gaming literacies of today's increasingly digital youth and learning processes valued within academic contexts but all too often presumed to not be a part of students' nonacademic literate lives. From Blair's perspective, the students' review fit with calls for multimodal literacies and digital rhetorical practice in the undergraduate curriculum (Digitrhet.org 2006), in addition to the potential for Web-based writing to expand students' understanding of audience and to invest more value in the classroom-based writing. Equally important, the review provided an opportunity for students to engage in multiple forms of technological literacy: the functional, students as users of technology; the critical, students as questioners of technology; and the rhetorical, students as producers of technology through the digital composing process (Selber 2004).

C&CO itself provides this established context and a built-in outside audience. In her own graduate seminars in computer-mediated writing, Blair had assigned collaborative hypertext reviews, first of Victor Vitanza's *Cyber- Reader* and later of Johndan Johnson-Eilola's *Nostalgic Angels: Rearticulating Hypertext Writing*. Her rationale was consistent with scholars both past and present who have stressed the potential of hypertext to break down hierarchies between readers and writers and to complicate understanding of authorship and ownership of texts. Such a process also provided Tulley's students with an opportunity to develop digital literacy skills in a team-development environment in which students could share expertise and workload, as well as rely on a technological buddy system designed to equalize the design and development skills (Tulley and Blair 2002).

To introduce the students to the process of constructing an academic book review, we first examined book reviews in paper-based journals such as *College Composition and Communication* and then contrasted these reviews with the electronic book reviews already featured on *C&CO*. After discussing common features of both the traditional and hypertext reviews, and the potential audiences for each, the students brainstormed as a class what features our review might have before we set out to read Gee's work.[4] The features the students deemed necessary for our hypertext review included the following:

Introduction to the work as a collaborative venture
Introduction to the text itself
Situation of the text among similar texts
Chapter synopsis reviews
Additional reading
Hyperlinks between elements of the reviews
Hyperlinks linking associative "words for thought" or provoking prose to texts outside the review

The students felt strongly about introducing the project as a collaborative class project because of their concerns about the potential cacophony of multiple voices. They were accustomed to the notion of a single author and felt that if the review did not have separately authored/attributed sections, it would look and read as a "student project" that did not have coherence. As graduating English majors, they were aware of the field's historical emphasis on single authorship. Though these students in previous English courses had been taught to "resist" being written by the academy and to cultivate "voice," particularly in creative writing courses, most struggled with this freedom in the face of having to write within the established academic context of a peerreviewed journal. This problem has been noted by Peter Elbow (1995). The issue of voice, as well as how students navigated this conflict, is described in more detail in the "Complications" section of this essay, as it was clearly our biggest stumbling block as we wrote the review as a class. Krause (2000: 120) notes that this real engagement with an authentic audience is sometimes potentially frightening for students, because an essay published on the Web can be read by a real, interested audience outside of the class. Although the students were excited to have the opportunity to publish work in a national journal, they were clearly apprehensive, even though as English majors they were confident in their writing abilities.

After students had established these features of the review, the class brainstormed how to "read" Gee's work. Because Blair and Tulley allowed students to design the review as they saw fit, students decided that the most practical way to work with Gee would be for each student to have responsibility for presenting a chapter and designing this segment in the review. One student offered to take a chapter of interest to her, and from there the rest of the students claimed chapters, with one student opting to explore further reading on Gee's topic. They unanimously assigned Tulley the first chapter and responsibility for introducing the project, another complication we also discuss later in this essay.

Questions of Authorship: Roles of Student, Teacher, and Editor in the Research and Writing Process

In 1998, Katherine Fischer and her honors colloquium class pieced together a collaborative research project that shares some similarities to our online book review project (Fischer et al. 2003). In one semester, Fischer's first-year honors composition students wrote individual paper-based research essays, a standard project for composition courses, but in a second semester students "patched" these texts together as a hypertext document with no restrictions on how papers could be connected. Rather than emphasizing the research and writing process as a solitary activity conducted by an individual author, Fischer justified the project by arguing that "among the kinds of academic writing we do, research should be the *most* shared and dialogic task we perform (interviewing experts, quoting other texts, arguing or agreeing with others, etc.), yet we pretend that is not a shared space" (2003: 172; emphasis Fischer's). Although the first online review did not have this initial genesis in individual paper-based projects, the students in Web writing chose to organize the hypertext review in such a way that each writer was responsible for a certain segment of the project (i.e., book chapters) and wrote these chapter segments as individual authors with no collaboration. As a result, this design also influenced the class to similarly patch together individual electronic texts despite the fact that students did see *C&CO* reviews organized in a variety of ways (by topic, section, criticism, and theoretical leanings). The students also felt that the project needed an introduction written by Tulley as well as links within each chapter synopsis and review to other chapters and to at least two associative concepts within each segment. These links to various concepts ranged from an outside Web page explaining a difficult concept Gee established to a gaming page or other item of relevance to that chapter.

After determining the general format of the review in one of our faceto- face sessions, students visually mapped how chapters could link together on the chalkboard. Based on their viewing of published reviews for *C&CO*, they decided on a splash page featuring the cover graphic of Gee's work and a menu of chapters to choose from. Nearly all of the other reviews posted in the journal at the time of our review included a menu of choices and a cover graphic of the work being reviewed, and students collectively decided to stay within this "norm" of the online book review, another rhetorical choice we explore in detail later in the essay.

In one face-to-face brainstorming session, students talked about font choice, background, and potential use of graphics. One student suggested using a background that looked "computer-ish," and so students, on individual computers, set out to find a free background that met this criterion with the understanding that they would share their choices at the end of the period. After several minutes of searching and saving backgrounds, another student suggested that each author (including Tulley) post a sample ground on-screen of his or her first choice, with a representative font and any graphics, and then students could walk around and vote for the backgrounds they felt worked best. The most popular background initially selected was a light gray background printed with a binary format and a dark blue font. Other backgrounds with spinning computers and bright or unreadable fonts were rejected for being too busy; because the class ultimately could not agree on graphics in addition to the cover graphic of Gee's text, the other graphics were scrapped.

Once the initial draft of the review was composed, Blair spoke with the class regarding the work and mission of *C&CO*. Blair focused on the students' intuition as readers and viewers of digital texts, first by sharing a sample Web text from the journal and asking the students for their reaction to the design. As they reviewed the text, Barclay Barrios's "The Year of the Blog: Weblogs in the Writing Classroom" (2003), students shared both strengths and weaknesses, concluding that even strong, innovative Web texts had drawbacks in terms of readability and navigability. From that point, it was somewhat easier for the 2004 students to apply a more critical eye toward color, font, text size, visual and textual integration, the amount of text on screen, and the role of links and other forms of navigation in contributing to rhetorical purpose. In this way, the students moved through Selber's continuum, establishing functional literacy through experimentation with the tools, critical literacy both through their collective analysis of the significance of Gee's work for readers of *C&CO* and through their critique of existing Web texts for both form and content, and finally rhetorical literacy through constructing a document that attempted to meet the needs and expectations of the journal's audience.

Because Blair talked about both theoretical as well as technical considerations of the journal, she invited students to evaluate the work they produced in the context of the discussion. For example, after students heard her speak about readability and took another look at already published reviews with her from an editor's eye for readability and design, they decided to scrap the serif font chosen in favor of sans serif and the grey background for a clean white background with dark blue text (fig. 1). They also spent more time exploring repercussions of Gee's chapters after revisiting previously published reviews and noted how other authors dialogued with, rather than summarized, the text under review. Though neither the editors nor Tulley restricted student choice, discussing the rhetorical implications of the identity of *C&CO* readers encouraged more audience-based choices.

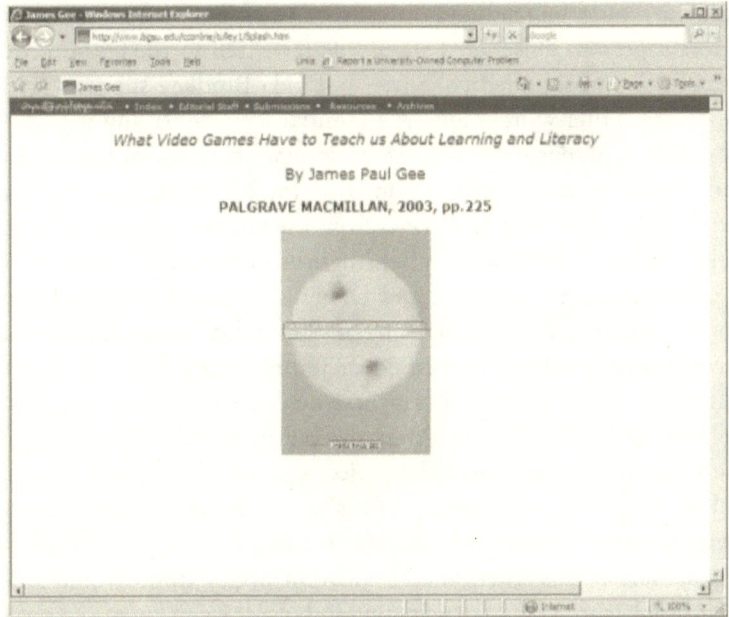

Figure 1. Cover page of student book review of James Paul Gee's *What Video Games Have to Teach Us about Learning and Literacy*

SHIFTING FROM PRINT CONSUMPTION TO DIGITAL PRODUCTION

Unlike Fischer's students, who felt strongly about using their own voices rather than adopting a standard "class," or neutral, voice in the process of composing their class Web text, Tulley's 2004 class was conflicted about the issue of voice. This juxtaposition is evident in the end product. For example, the students claimed to want a neutral voice that sounded more "academic" and one that "smoothed over" the differences in writing styles among the ten authors, but they also ultimately decided to attribute each chapter review to an individual student who did the initial writing on that segment. Several students argued that by "authoring" individual chapters, they all would get a share of the credit that they could list on their resumes in time for graduation and job hunting. By assigning Tulley one definite segment, the students felt that her presence in the text was equal to that of each student. Moreover, although individual voices were clearly present, during a peer review of segments, students also argued that each segment should be read and "parts that stuck out" (i.e., written in a different person, tense, etc.) should be rewritten so the entire review "matched" and sounded cohesive. As Linda Brodkey suggests (1987: 396), "the writer-writes-alone is a familiar icon of art and is perhaps most readily understood as a romantic representation of the production of canonical literature." Similarly, these English majors clearly had trouble distancing themselves from the notion that the individual author was privileged, as in other English courses single authors such as Jane Austin, Shakespeare, and Dante are studied as single voices. Understandably, they viewed any multivocality or disjuncture between review pages as unfocused or unprofessional despite the fact that digital formats often foster these qualities by encouraging commentary and collaboration. After the review by Blair in her role as editor, students determined the project should be evaluated for readability, rhetorical effectiveness of assigned segment writing (though these individually authored segments eventually become a plurality of voices, making this criterion for evaluation largely arbitrary and somewhat problematic), and participation in both the writing of the review and in class discussions in Blackboard (the content management software being used) about Gee's work in general.

Another complication of the joint review was the teacher-student hierarchy persistently present in the classroom. Although a teacher's authority is always present to some extent, we aimed to serve as technological guides or mentors on the project rather than masters of technology in our roles as teacher and editor (Haas, Tulley, and Blair 2002). Though Tulley did establish the review as the final project and assigned the grade, both of us invited students to have input as to how the project should be written and designed (though these choices at times were nixed by *C&CO* editors). Although it is unrealistic to presume that academic writers new to digital composing will get it just right, teachers must foster composing strategies that ensure that the final product will be more than print on screen, or the mere migration of a traditional text-based essay toward digital storage. To enable such strategies, we felt it was important to provide a process-based environment similar to that in print-based writing courses based on rhetorical principles, though clearly invention, drafting, revising, and editing will manifest themselves much differently in such digital contexts, as Honeycutt and McGrane (205: 102) argue.[5] We felt a project such as a digital book review enables reflection about the ways technology impacts both form and content, in addition to the process itself. Ironically, Gee's discussion of the connections between video games and a range of learning processes guides not only the content but also the larger philosophy of the collaborative book review in that the process of teacher and student working together to produce a hypertext or new media document helps to break down hierarchies between them. The hypertext environment fostered by this project opened a space to discuss why composing the collaborative online review required different thinking strategies than previously used in other English courses.

Still, the class insistence on having Tulley write the first chapter review, as well as the introduction to the overall project, countered the collaborative process fostered by multimodal composing to some extent. For example, on peer review days when Tulley's work was posted on screen and students spent time in front of the text ostensibly offering revision suggestions, they would find only the most minor comments regarding something "safe," such as punctuation, despite Tulley's best efforts at encouraging the deeper revision they offered their peers. As noted previously, students also felt the review should funnel through Tulley's introduction, thus her "Note about Our Project" is the first and only page readers can access from the initial splash page. Besides offering Tulley's voice as the first voice read in the text, this segment and the chapter 1 review are the most solo-authored, because the work remains largely in her words, untouched. Despite the more collaborative elements the digital review offered Tulley, Blair, and the students, the students never lost sight of the fact that Tulley would be assigning the end grade and that Blair could choose not to accept the review for publication. Thus, the teacher-student hierarchy never fully disappeared during our research and publication process, though, as the successes described indicate, the hypertext format made these issues transparent and students were aware of them. For instance, though Tulley chose to provide comments on each student's first draft of an individual page and participation points for individual students, these individual pages became a blend of voices under revision. Because the completed review was a collaborative effort woven together from fragments of each student's writing, Tulley chose to assign the final grade to the class as a group despite the fact that some students contributed more than others.

Editorial choices also reinforced the teacher-student hierarchy. Rather than place their resulting work in the Reviews section of the journal, Blair decided to place the piece in the Professional Development section, a space for innovative digital practice, interviews, and other forms of pedagogical reflection. Admittedly, in making this decision, Blair reinforced a hierarchy by privileging Tulley's voice as the teacher, allowing her metacommentary to shape and potentially portray the students' work as more novice than other reviews published in the journal. Rather than promoting the document as the review it was, this placement inevitably showcased the review as the typical "class project." Clearly, for professors of English to rethink how we teach multimodal composing in our classes, we need to rethink these studentteacher author relationships as well.

Engaging with the Text: Collaboration versus Cooperation

In Fischer's reflections on her project, she ultimately makes the distinction between *collaborative* and *cooperative* writing and argues that despite her best efforts to obtain a collaborative project, she ultimately ended up with a cooperative one. She notes that

> the first, I believe, is more multi-authored from the start, more shared, more successful in achieving a higher degree of shared authorship and revision. The latter involves teamwork and cooperation, but the work remains at once individual, although shared through "links." The writer's signature remains intact. (2003: 173)

Unlike Fischer's project, we argue that the jointly authored 2004 review was successful because it achieved a collaborative stance overall, despite the cooperative elements and the teacher-student hierarchy that emerges at points. Like Fischer's class project, our review clearly began as a cooperative effort where students decided through the democratic process how to organize and visually represent the review (for example, voting on a background). The division of writing responsibility where each student was assigned a chapter was also clearly cooperative, because students did need to refer to each other's chapters but could largely write the initial chapter voice drafts on their own and in their own voices.

Because of their own insistence on sounding like a solo-authored voice despite being individual authors, somewhat ironically the students ultimately ended up with more of a collaborative project than the published version might initially indicate. For example, on peer review days, students would post their chapters on screen, and every student would read everyone else's screen in a rotation with the agreed understanding that the peer readers could change and alter texts in any way they saw fit as they sat down at each station. This process was very similar to a process in Blair's graduate seminar in computer-mediated writing titled Studio Review (Denecker 2007), where students originally completed similar reviews that remediated the traditional peer-review procedures of meeting in a circle face-to-face to discuss a print-based document. The Web writing class engaged in this roundtable peer review/revision several times, and many "authors" of the chapters often returned to their screens to see altered or rearranged texts. As far as Tulley could tell, although there were not any cases where one student completely rewrote another's work, there was much debate over word choice, length, and tone for the review. Because students were free to type away at each other's texts, substantial revisions were made beyond surface-level concerns. Any disputes over the final version of each segment were again collectively voted on to decide "what sounded better" and what would make the most sense to *C&CO* readers.

One review design issue that offered students real instruction in the critical analysis of Web texts was how the presence of "thought-provoking" word links might function for a reader. Gordon (2005: 55) points out that links that only make sense to the composing authors essentially function as writer-based versus reader-based prose, and "composers of hypertexts should work hard to ensure that readers will find a document's hyperlinks genuinely helpful — a problem that Web designers have discussed a great deal lately as a matter of producing user-centered Web documents." After several peer review/revision sessions, students learned to ask questions about each other's hypertext document production, including a textual question ("what kind of wording is appropriate for a link?") and a navigational question ("where will this link take me?") (60). The peer review/revision sessions were thus very useful for sorting through these issues because each of the other nine readers in the class was likely to navigate a chapter page in a different way, including these links to sites outside the review. As a result, "highlighting these problems not only helps to foster the novice author's ability to build hypertexts that operate in ways that are familiar and accessible to readers, but it also lays the groundwork for developing the novice's linking creativity" (62). This is a skill that English majors desperately need as screen texts continue to gain scholarly legitimacy and even traditionally canonical works can be read online in multimodal formats. Finally, having students work within a peer review session allowed the students to discuss the purpose of these outside links, "to consider whether they want their links to be more prosaic or more poetic, more hierarchical or more associative" (62).

The class ultimately determined that the links within the review were navigational and hierarchical but that the outside links chosen for chapter pages were ultimately more associative. Students chose to include these links as a way of taking the reader outside of the *C&CO* context in a manner similar to the linking occurring in blogs that they had viewed earlier that semester (see Blood 2002 for more on blogs). They argued that linking to these associative concepts was one way of situating Gee's work, as well as their own review, in Web space and of developing a broader Web conversation about literacy and learning. Because the students had previously written blogs in the Web writing course, they were familiar with an associative structure. Surprisingly, many students did not seem to mind that their texts were altered and therefore jointly authored by classmates, particularly because every student had the power to revise every other student's text, including these hyperlinks to outside sites. One student argued, "It's not like I printed my paper already and turned it in so I don't feel that attached to what I wrote." We speculate that because Fischer's class started with solo-authored research papers to begin with, it was too difficult for students to let go of these solo-authored papers to allow a true multimodal collaboration, whereas for Tulley's students these ownership issues were felt to a lesser extent, if at all. Still, it is also clear that Tulley's students still wanted to retain initial credit for authorship over the chapters they started with, even though they realized these individual attributions became arbitrary in many of the chapters after peer review/ revision sessions.

The decision to reveal the collaborative process in constructing the first Web text was also one unexpected success. At our concluding design session, students decided to reveal the backstory as a necessary part of the book review, despite initial concerns about calling attention to their relative inexperience as writers by this inclusion. This backstory included not only a representative sample of one of our online chat logs about the project archived in Blackboard but also visual "snapshots" using the whiteboard within Blackboard to represent our process.[6] Although the whiteboard may have been secondary to our actual process of composing the book review, the reflection students demonstrated using the whiteboard did provide a visual/ textual accompaniment to the synchronous chat unfolding at that time as a work in progress. This choice to include the chat log provides a deeper look at our digital invention process while revealing student tensions about the multimodal format. Using Blackboard technology, Tulley took two "snapshots" to capture what was on the whiteboard at that time, though by no means is the archival process sophisticated enough to record the ongoing whiteboard process among students and teacher, and it does not demonstrate who posted what sketch or word. In addition, because voices were merged, it is not clear if every single person posted a word or drawing (which differs from the online chat function or a MOO, a text-based virtual reality forum, where individual actions are attributed to authors); students could potentially learn from the whiteboard postings of others even if they did not want to post. Beth Hewitt (2006: 8), in her own study of whiteboard conferences, emphasizes how the whiteboard actually fosters collaboration: "From a pedagogical standpoint, this viewing feature may engage the kinds of collaborative learning that typically occur in a traditional classroom because students who view others' conferences potentially can learn from the conference itself without active participation." The looser structure of this dialogic talk on the whiteboard, as well as in the synchronous chat, also allowed students to write in a space free from the concerns of appearing professional to *C&CO* readers as authors. Several students even argued that the backstory should actually be the front story, as their collaborative work and play on the review of Gee also supports his argument that video games (and, by association, much computer play, such as drawing on the whiteboard) lead to increased language and literacy processes, a development *C&CO* readers would likely take interest in (Gee 2003; see also Matthews-DeNatale 2000). This choice to include the messy work of the writing process reveals how the 2004 students moved beyond thinking of the hypertext review as a cooperative project with solo-authored components because they understood it ultimately to be a collaborative text, and they wanted to reveal how the final review developed.

Admittedly, some aspects of this collaborative authoring process could occur within print-based projects; however, in this context, students' experimentation with digital literacy tools levels the playing field because they inevitably apply strategies not necessarily part of the instructors' technological expertise or expectations. Similar to Blair's role in earlier collaborative reviews of *CyberReader* and *Nostalgic Angels*, the latter a process in which Tulley participated as a doctoral candidate, and in a more recent publication by graduate students in Blair's rhetorical theory class on the role of blogs in the rhetorical tradition, Tulley's role as a facilitator and coauthor is an important one. Although she provides a sense of context and maintains an instructional voice, this does not necessarily detract from the students' combined perspectives about the role of Gee's work. The resulting Web text (fig. 1), like any other published in *C&CO* and elsewhere, has its strengths, including ease and clarity of navigation in the form of yellow buttons and depth of commentary with sections for each chapter. Nevertheless, weaknesses include less attention to the visual design, especially considering the white background and yellow buttons, and the align-

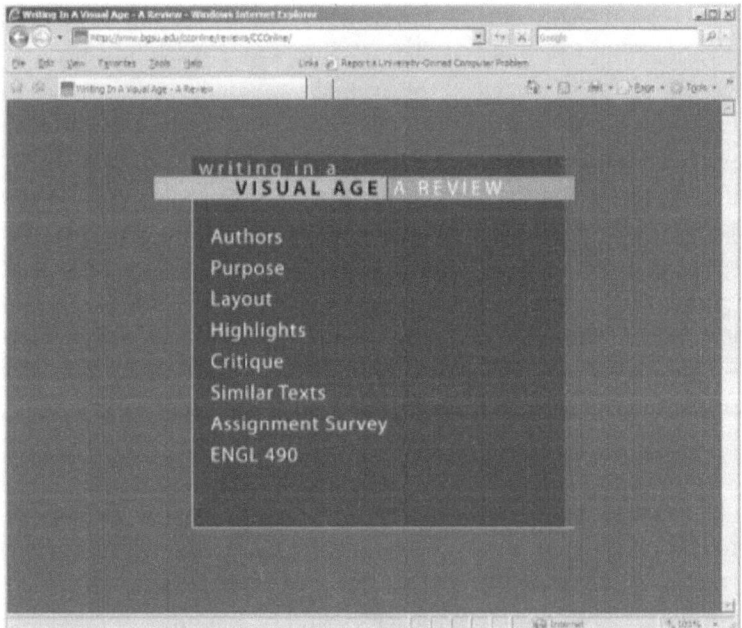

Figure 2. Review of Lee Odell and Susan Katz's ***Writing in a Visual Age***

ment between image and text, particularly compared with the quality of design and color scheme in the second review (see fig. 2). Yet in privileging some Web design features over others, the students address Emily Golson's (1995) concern that the emphasis on the postmodern, decentered authorial components in student hypertexts may ultimately lead to products that detract from audience awareness by privileging visual flash over rhetorical substance. By insisting that each author was credited for his or her chapter, the overall review does not read like a coherent whole. As we note earlier, this may not only detract from the Web text's status as a viable review worthy of publication but may also limit the role of technology in remediating the book review's potential as an experiment in multimodal literacy development.

In his article "Digital Natives, Digital Immigrants," Prensky (2001: 1) makes a distinction between students as digital natives and teachers as digital immigrants, claiming that the "single biggest problem facing education today is that our Digital Immigrant instructors, who speak an outdated language (that of the pre-digital age), are struggling to teach a population that speaks an entirely new language," which we argue has all too often been overlooked as a viable component of the English curriculum. Attempting to equalize the digital composing process through both reflection and collaborative skills sharing, as evidenced through Tulley's web Writing class, is one way to bridge the gaps between teachers and students and among the students themselves, some of whom may not be as native as Prensky presumes. That these pedagogical efforts have had an impact on students is apparent from a more recent review by a second Web writing class Tulley taught in spring 2007, a review that, in addition to improvements in design (fig. 2), suggests an equally prominent emphasis on critical and rhetorical literacy in their focus on the purpose and design of the book itself. Just three years later, students seem to have an awareness of effective design principles; this may be because the University of Findlay had recently enacted a multimodal initiative to encourage study of both print and multimodal texts as part of the English curriculum. As an editor, Blair once again met with this class, relying on a similar studio review process that focused on an analysis of several published Web texts, using a range of "intuitive" criteria and the following criteria adapted from Joan Huntley and Joan Latchaw's "The Seven Cs of Interactive Design" (1998: 129):

Context: What is the purpose?
Consideration: Who is the audience?
Clarity: How accessible is the form and content?
Conciseness: In what ways is the text and design to the point?
Coherence: How does the site function as a whole?
Correctness: Does the site conform to professional/academic standards of style and grammar?
Creativity: What makes the site fun, memorable, etc?

Section authors ultimately displayed their portions of the review for critique and revision suggestions in light of these criteria, and it is worth noting that most of these criteria, consistent with Judy Gregory's (2004) contention that digital and print texts are as similar as they are different, could apply to print documents as well. Although contributors to *C&CO* are often faculty or graduate students, in comparison with other reviews in both content and form, Blair notes that this second review is as strong as most of those the journal has published in the past five years. Unexpectedly, because of illness, Tulley was unable to attend class the day that Blair was scheduled to meet with the students about the review; we decided to go forward with this plan anyway. From Blair's perspective, a notable difference between classes that she attended was the sense of her own role: in the first class, she assumed a more hierarchical role that kept her in the front of the room the majority of the time; in the second studio review process, the students took more charge of the class session, relying not only on the seven Cs but also their own understanding of design issues, including navigation, visual theme, and amount of text on screen. The relative quality of these undergraduate projects is affected by a range of variables, including whole class and individual student motivation, not to mention the particular digital skills set of each class and access to more sophisticated Web-design software. Because the spring 2007 class seemed to be more familiar with analyzing Web texts in general, the choices they made more closely mimicked the reviews already published in *C&CO*.

Significantly, Tulley's commentary in this second review is blended within overall commentary about the English 490 class, a page in which several student voices contribute to the development of the page's content, suggesting a less hierarchical approach than in the first review (a hierarchy that may have been reinforced more by the students than their instructor). Certainly, the opportunity for students to publish in a real-world context with faculty as coauthors and editors rather than as teachers plays an important role in making their Web-based efforts more relevant than a traditional academic essay that may have only a classroom writing group and the teacher as an audience. Admittedly, there are other assignment contexts that enable a more authentic audience beyond the classroom and that do not involve the use of the Web, suggesting that success in Web-based writing courses involves careful consideration of the relationship between technology and pedagogy.

As evidence of the potential of integrating technology in such a rhetorical manner, in a course evaluation from spring 2007, Tulley received the comment, "I am excited that I finally got a chance to publish *something* after 4 *years* of reading famous ppl." Although this comment may reflect a lack of satisfaction with the English curriculum at the University of Findlay in general, it does appear to imply that there is a need to bridge the gap between the consumption and production elements inherent in the English major. Such a comment also suggests that English faculty need to do more to integrate multimodal composing opportunities — not to mention other more potentially authentic print and electronic audience contexts — within their courses, sustaining the knowledge that students develop in courses such as Web writing, even if that means simply allowing students to respond to traditional assignments and genres in a range of visual, verbal, and aural media. Although many faculty may consider themselves ill-equipped to evaluate multimodal responses to their assigned writing projects, a Web-based document may, as Judy Gregory (2004: 283) suggests, be judged by similar criteria even while we acknowledge that those criteria manifest themselves differently in digital formats. As Gregory concludes, "in our enthusiasm to embrace the new online medium, we have focused more on the differences between media rather than on their similarities," a point that is consistent with concepts of remediation and one that may provide a sense of comfort to English colleagues less comfortable with assessing multimodal texts. Interestingly enough, our students may be more able to embrace this concept, as one student comment on the project indicates:

> The class itself did impact my career path because I want to publish more works on the Internet, and use different techniques to write (like hypertext). I think it's important to note

what people are writing about isn't really changing; the way works are viewed is what is changing. There's blogging, hypertext, e-books and e-zines. More people can view others works than ever before. I believe the internet and technology in general is impacting the way people read and write (stylistically), and will continue to impact in the years to come.

Inevitably, what makes the second review successful is not only its visual design but also its status as a review, particularly in its organization around rhetorical principles that are more clearly privileged versus an organization based on actual identity of the student authors as a class as in the 2004 review. Though a link to that identity does exist from the opening menu, this contrasts significantly to the first review, in which the class identity is at the forefront. Despite our equal emphasis on the design components of the two reviews, another significant content difference is the shift away from the chapter-based organization of 2004 to more of an issue-based organization that represents a more sophisticated approach to the genre of the book review, whether it be print-based or Web-based.

Conclusion: Reflections on Successful Research and Publication Projects with Students

Although we believe the initial 2004 project was a relative success despite the complications described, our goal in the spring 2007 class was to get students to envision a review as a truly dialogic piece, not just with the readers of *C&CO*, but with each other. Because students viewed single-authored reviews posted on the journal site, they were very concerned that their review sound like one person wrote it and thus that they essentially all had to "agree" on the usefulness of Gee's argument, the focus of the book, and what this research means for teachers and scholars. This artificial single voice was not evident in the topically organized second review. Although the multimodal format actually works against such a read (for example, *C&CO* readers may read only a few chapters, read out of order, or read only the backstory), we wonder if a better use of the project would be to have students conduct an online debate about the book, while in the process still revealing the salient points of the text. This format may work against the traditional style of book review from scholarly journals, in which someone in the field critiques a recent book offering (closer to the format of the response pieces of journals such as *College Composition and Communication*), but might actually serve to be a more critically written review from a rhetorical standpoint, because it is unlikely that all ten authors read the book in the same way. For example, several students specializing in English education talked about changing lesson plan design in one of their other classes after reading Gee's work, while a creative writing student interested in gaming cited Gee as a reason why games should count as homework in classes. Still another, excited about publishing the review, expressed far less interest in the nuances of Gee's argument and ultimately failed to find that the text offered new light on the link between games and literacy. This commentary suggests that the process of remediating the review within a multimodal context can provide a catalyst to students across programs to consider the role technology plays within their own literacy processes as readers and writers. Indeed, one of the authors of the Odell and Katz review acknowledged that the collaborative review and writing process impacted her career by providing a broadened perspective of what constituted literate practice within the content of the English curriculum:

> When you think of English courses, you think of American and British literature, creative and technical writing. I think it's great University of Findlay is incorporating more Internet and technology classes into English, because it is the future of reading and writing. I am trying to take all the "E" literature and writing courses I can, because I know they will be vital in the future. I think that University of Findlay should have some kind of technological or web emphasis to the English major because more and more writers are going to use the web for publishing as well as using programs to change how their works are seen.

Ultimately, the reviews of both James Gee's *What Video Games Have to Teach Us about Learning and Literacy* and Lee Odell and Susan Katz's *Writing in a Visual Age* go beyond mere functional computer literacy to help students critically examine arguments about the impact of visual and multimedia literacy on academic texts and contexts and to engage in new media literacy practices to produce effective arguments. In this way, such projects have the potential to address each of the three literate practices Selber outlines and to test discussions of literacy by Gee, Odell, and Katz in their own multimodal composing processes. That a balance among these three aspects of multimodal literacy is important is most evident in the increasing numbers of students relying on social networking tools such as Facebook and MySpace, a reliance that calls for a range of rhetorical skills in developing an individual professional and personal identity, not to mention critical skills in communicating in these public social spaces. This increase in access to and use of social networking software is perhaps one factor in the overall increase in digital knowledge students bring to the classroom, a type of literate practice that many educators continue to ignore.

Like Fischer and her class patchwork of Internet essays, we hoped that Tulley's review projects invite students to "actually pull up their chairs to the table of scholarship and *contribute to* rather than simply *repeat* the conversations" (Fischer et al. 2003: 172). We argue that the reviews, while serving the very practical purpose of reviewing texts, also engaged students in a complex rhetorical process in which they needed not only to read and understand the texts but also to explore the usefulness of digital literacy research and pedagogy for *C&CO* readers. Because we were in the fortunate position of having the editor, Blair, talk face to face with Tulley's students, students completed both the 2004 and 2007 reviews under somewhat optimal circumstances in which they could actually discuss rhetorical choice with the editor prior to publication (an unlikely scenario for most student publication projects). Another student from the 2004 project claims,

> One of the most important things that writing the review did for me was give me some experience in collaborative writing. Although I am sure I read collaborative articles as an undergraduate, I didn't think about writing for publication, let alone what it meant to write something for publication with other people. The fact that as a class we had to compromise and work together really changed the way I viewed writing. Having Editor Blair come to our class and talk about the journal and the editorial process and getting the feedback from different readers made the writing seem a lot more authentic. Not only was I practicing a new type of writing in that class, specifically writing a book review, but writing for a potentially broader audience made me appreciate the concept of audience even more.

Since the completion of the Gee review, this student is now a doctoral candidate in the program where Blair teaches, and she will begin work as a section editor for *C&CO* in summer 2008, which suggests the potential for such collaborations to contribute to the development of future digitally literate faculty in English studies. She further contends, "I went in to the class with an interest in blogging, web design, and writing but I left the class seeing that there were people in the field [who] were combining these three things and making a career out of it. I was excited by the thought of being able to work within the field, and when I started graduate school the following semester it really helped me focus on how I could start incorporating technology into the classes I was teaching." This student's story perhaps serves as a fitting conclusion to an article advocating that multimodal literacy acquisition among students and faculty can best be achieved through collaborations on remediating traditional genres within the discipline, as it represents a generational shifting of hierarchies, beginning with teacher Tulley, who was once Blair's student and is now mentoring the next generation of multimodally literate teachers and colleagues.

Yet, as the DigiRhet.org group (2006: 247) concludes, "Even if students manage to find the most supportive, nurturing learning communities imaginable and even if students are well versed in critical, analytical approaches to digital writing and rhetoric, all the effort put forward helping students learning digital rhetoric is wasted if those same students aren't also able to see the relevance of digital rhetoric to their own lives once they leave the digital rhetoric classroom." Such a statement is inevitably a call for writing teachers not merely to integrate technology for its own sake but rather to consider real-world assignment contexts in which issues of audience, purpose, development, organization, and style call for a range of digital rhetorical choices. If, as Lisa Toner (2003: 254) argues, "a good writing class must be expanded to recognize students' hypertextual and casuistic construction of authority as a negotiation among course goals, projects, and assignments and activities of their public lives beyond class," then the multimodal book review, albeit with the complications noted throughout our discussion, essentially offered one way of conceptualizing this expansion. The composing process and ultimate publication of both reviews helped students see that relevance, a relevance that can and should be integrated within the entire English curriculum rather than relegated to a single course, a single assignment, or a single genre.

We acknowledge the collaborative multimodal book review as one example of the potential to remediate traditional print genres within English studies, and, of course, not every class will have access to an online journal editor to assist in the digital composing process. However, we agree with Jeffrey Grabill and Troy Hicks (2005: 306), who conclude, "English teachers should no longer have a conversation about literacy without considering technology." Although some faculty within English departments may continue to believe that curricular emphasis on the consumption of literary texts exempts them from teaching functional, critical, and rhetorical digital literacy, to shirk this responsibility risks reinscribing a curriculum in which future faculty in English studies fail to bridge the gap between the literate practices of the academy and the actual literacy practices of twenty-first-century students. Failure to recognize multimodal texts such as Web pages, podcasts, and digital movies also impacts the perceived relevance of the English major inside and outside the academy and limits the marketability of undergraduate students, particularly if they choose not to pursue advanced study in the discipline. Despite these constraints, English studies is well situated to implement the study of differences between print and Web texts and contexts, given that textual analysis along with the rhetorical tools of arrangement and delivery have long been hallmarks of the field and are what unite programs within English departments. As our own case studies illustrate, reconceptualizing a print genre in a digital space actually allows English majors to expand perceptions not only of critical reading and writing practices but also of the shifting modes and media in which they occur.

Notes

1. For example, the University of Southern Indiana offers a senior-level course titled Writing in a Digital Age (see www.usi.edu/LIBARTS/english/description.asp#ENG%20411) and the Ohio State University – Mansfield offers both Digital Media Composing (see www.susandelagrange.com/269/?page_id=3) and Digital Media and English Studies (see www.mansfield.osu.edu/courses/view.cfm?id=322).

2. This course was added at the University of Findlay for the first time in spring 2004 as an elective to enhance the multimodal literacy experience of English majors, and it meets both face-to-face and virtually in a hybrid course format. Class sizes in most 400-level courses at the University of Findlay are usually seven to fourteen students.

3. This course is normally taught on a two-year rotation, in the spring semester of evennumbered years. Because Tulley was on sabbatical in spring 2006 and there were no other faculty qualified to teach the course, the course was offered in spring 2007 instead. It will be taught again in 2009 with the revised title Digital Composing for English Majors to better reflect the emphasis on a variety of digital tools used in the course in addition to "Web" composing, such as audio recorders, digital filmmaking software, and art software.

4. Initially, we had offered students the choice of reading Gee's work before examining reviews, but students preferred doing a survey of reviews before reading to understand how reading Gee's work for pleasure might differ from reading it to compose a review.

5. In their essay "Rhetoric and Information Architecture as Pedagogical Frameworks for Website Design," Honeycutt and McGrane (2005: 103) argue that although it "benefits students to know the ever delicate interplay between logos, pathos, and ethos and how these elements are constrained by certain factors of the rhetorical situation," a rhetorical approach is somewhat limiting in digital contexts. Instead, they advocate "a broader, deliberative view of rhetoric that has as its goal ethical decision making within both public and private forums" and synthesizes both a rhetorical and information architecture approach.

6. Beth Hewitt (2006: 7) argues, "The most understudied of synchronous platforms in the context of writing instruction may be whiteboard technology." We found it interesting that students chose to have both a visual as well as a textual archive of our collaboration, and Tulley prompted whiteboard use regularly throughout the course to allow students to present ideas in a variety of media.

WORKS CITED

Alexander, Jonathan. 2002. "Digital Spins: The Pedagogy and Politics of Student-Centered E-zines." *Computers and Composition* 19.4: 387 – 410.

Balsamo, Anne. 2000. "The Virtual Body in Cyberspace." In *The Cybercultures Reader*, ed. David Bell and Barbara M. Kennedy, 489 – 503. London: Routledge.

Blood, Rebecca. 2002. *The Weblog Handbook*. New York: Perseus Publishing.

Bolter, Jay D. 2001. *Writing Space: Computers, Hypertext, and the Remediation of Print*. Mahwah, NJ: Lawrence Erlbaum.

Bolter, Jay, and Richard Grusin. 1999. *Remediation: Understanding New Media*. Boston: MIT Press.

Brodkey, Linda. 1987. "Modernism and the Scene(s) of Writing." *College English* 49.4: 396 – 418.

Denecker, Christine. 2006. "So You Want to Be an English Teacher? Technology, Literacy, and Language Arts." *CEA Forum* 35.2. www2.widener.edu/%7Ecea/352denecker.htm.

Dibbell, Julian. 1999. *My Tiny Life: Crime and Passion in a Virtual World.* New York: Henry Holt and Company.

DigiRhet.org. 2006. "Teaching Digital Rhetoric: Community, Critical Engagement, and Application." *Pedagogy* 6.2: 231 – 59.

Elbow, Peter. 1995. "Being a Writer vs. Being an Academic: A Conflict in Goals." *College Composition and Communication* 46.1: 72 – 83.

Fischer, Katherine, Chris Bailey, Aaron J. Brown, Jennifer Dondlinger, Joe Doolittle, Jacqueline Kerkeman, Rosemarie Schneider, Elizabeth Serflek, and Pam Smith. 2003. "Crazy Quilts: Piecing Together Collaborative Research." In Galin, Haviland, and Johnson: 171 – 84.

Galin, Jeffery R., Carol Peterson Haviland, and J. Paul Johnson, eds. 2003. *Teaching/Writing in the Late Age of Print.* Cresskill, NJ: Hampton Press.

Gee, James Paul. 2003. *What Video Games Have to Teach Us about Learning and Literacy.* Hampshire, England: Palgrave.

Golson, Emily. 1995. "Student Hypertexts: The Perils and Promises of Paths Not Taken." *Computers and Composition* 12.3: 295 – 308.

Gordon, Jay. 2005. "Teaching Hypertext Composition." *Technical Communication Quarterly* 14.1: 49 – 72.

Grabill, Jeffrey T. 2003. "On Divides and Interfaces: Access, Class, and Computers." *Computers and Composition* 20.4: 455 – 72.

Grabill, Jeffrey, and Troy Hicks. 2005. "Multiliteracies Meet Methods: The Case for Digital Writing in English Education." *English Education* 37.4: 301 – 11.

Gregory, Judy. 2004. "Writing for the Web versus Writing for Print: Are They Really So Different?" *Technical Communication* 51.2: 276 – 85.

Gregory, Marshall. 2001. "Curriculum, Pedagogy, and Teacherly Ethos." *Pedagogy* 1.1: 69 – 89.

Haas, Angela, Christine Tulley, and Kristine Blair. 2002. "Mentors versus Masters: Women's and Girls' Narratives of (Re)negotiation in Web-Based Writing Spaces." *Computers and Composition* 19.3: 231 – 49.

Harrington, Susanmarie, Rebecca Rickly, and Michael Day. 2000. *The Online Writing Classroom.* Cresskill, NJ: Hampton Press.

Hewett, Beth L. 2006. "Synchronous Online Conference-Based Instruction: A Study of Whiteboard Interactions and Student Writing." *Computers and Composition* 23.1: 4 – 31.

Honeycutt, Lee, and Karen McGrane. 2005. "Rhetoric and Information Architecture as Pedagogical Frameworks for Website Design." In *Technical Communication and the World Wide Web*, ed. Carol Lipson and Michael Day, 81 – 112. Mahwah, NJ: Lawrence Erlbaum.

Huntley, Joan, and Joan Latchaw. 1998. "The Seven Cs of Interactive Design." In *The Dialogic Classroom*, ed. Jeffrey Galin and Joan Latchaw, 106 – 32. Urbana, IL: National Council of Teachers of English.

Journet, Debra. 2007. "Inventing Myself in Multimodality: Encouraging Senior Faculty to Use Digital Media." *Computers and Composition* 24.2: 107 – 20.

Journet, Debra, Tabetha Adkins, Chris Alexander, Patrick Corbett, and Ryan Trauman. 2008. "Digital Mirrors: Multimodal Reflection in the Composition Classroom."

Computers and Composition Online, spring 2008. www.bgsu.edu/cconline/Digital_Mirrors/.

Joyce, Michael. 1990. *afternoon, a story*. Cambridge, MA: Eastgate Systems.

Krause, Steven D. 2000. "Why Should I Use the Web? Four Drawbacks and Four Benefits to Using the World Wide Web as a Pedagogical Tool for Writing Classes." In Harrington, Rickly, and Day: 105 – 24.

Kress, Gunther, and Theo Van Leeuwen. 2001. *Multimodal Discourse: The Modes and Media of Contemporary Communication*. London: Arnold.

Matthews-DeNatale, Gail. 2000. "Teach Us How to Play: The Role of Play in Technology Education." In Harrington, Rickly, and Day: 63 – 80.

Odell, Lee, and Susan Katz. 2006. *Writing in a Visual Age*. Boston: Bedford St. Martin's Press.

Prensky, Marc. 2001. "Digital Natives, Digital Immigrants." *On the Horizon* 9.5: 1 – 6.

Rice, Jeff. 2006. "What Should College English Be? Networks and New Media." *College English* 69.2: 127 – 33.

Romano, Susan. 1993. "The Egalitarian Narrative: Whose Story? Which Yardstick?" *Computers and Composition* 10.3: 5 – 28.

Selber, Stuart. 2004. *Multiliteracies for a Digital Age*. Carbondale: Southern Illinois University Press.

Selfe, Cynthia. 2004. "Students Who Teach Us." In Wysocki et al.: 43 – 66.

Stroupe, Craig. 2000. "Visualizing English: Recognizing the Hybrid Literacy of Visual and Verbal Authorship on the Web." *College English* 62.5: 607 – 32.

Takayoshi, Pamela, and Cynthia L. Selfe. 2007. "Thinking about Multimodality." In *Multimodal Composition*, ed. Cynthia L. Selfe, 1 – 42. Cresskill, NJ: Hampton Press.

Toner, Lisa. 2003. "Public Life and Rhetorical Ethos." In Galin, Haviland, and Johnson: 171 – 84.

Tulley, Christine, and Kristine Blair. 2002. "E-writing Spaces as Safe, Gender-Fair Havens: Aligning Political and Pedagogical Possibilities." In *Teaching Writing with Computers: An Introduction*, ed. Pamela Takayoshi and Brian Huot, 55 – 66. Boston: Houghton-Mifflin.

Turnley, Melinda. 2006. "Contextualized Design: Teaching Critical Approaches to Web Authoring through Redesign Projects." *Computers and Composition* 22.2: 131 – 48.

Tyner, Kathleen. 1998. *Literacy in Digital World: Teaching and Learning in the Age of Information*. Mahwah, NJ: Lawrence Erlbaum.

Wide Research Collective. 2005. "Why Teach Digital Writing?" *Kairos* 10.1. english.ttu.edu/kairos/10.1/coverweb/wide/index.html.

Wysocki, Anne, Johndan Johnson-Eilola, Cynthia Selfe, and Geoffrey Sirc. 2004. *Writing New Media: Theory and Applications for Expanding the Teaching of Composition*. Logan: Utah State University Press.

REFLECTIONS

Reflections is on the Web at http://reflectionsjournal.net/

Reflections, a peer reviewed journal, provides a forum for scholarship on writing, service-learning and community literacy. Originally founded as a venue for teachers, researchers, students and community partners to share research and discuss the theoretical, political and ethical implications of community-based writing and writing instruction, *Reflections* publishes a lively collection of essays, empirical studies, community writing, student work, interviews and reviews in a format that brings together emerging scholars and leaders in the fields of community-based writing and civic engagement.

"Engaging Community Literacy through the Rhetorical Work of a Social Movement" by Christopher Wilkey

"Engaging Community Literacy" represents the importance of extended and deep community/university partnerships that move beyond ameliorating the results unjust policies toward addressing the fundamental rights of a local community. In the process, Wilkey demonstrates the value of such work not only for residents, but for our students as well. The accompanying interview with Bonnie Nuemeier also represents *Reflections* commitment to providing space for all the participants of such partnerships to share their insights and beliefs with our readers. We believe that if the best community/university partnerships are truly dialogic and democratic, then scholarly journals must represent those values in its pages.

Engaging Community Literacy through the Rhetorical Work of a Social Movement

Christopher Wilkey

Abstract

This essay establishes a context for discussing how community literacy pedagogy can bene!t from critical engagement with the rhetorical actions of a grassroots social movement. Drawing from ongoing community literacy work in Cincinnati's Over-the-Rhine neighborhood, I detail the prospects of speaking truth to power in relation to composition studies' ongoing skepticism of rhetorics of social protest. I end by arguing that there are central aspects associated with oppositional rhetorics that can be encountered in community literacy initiatives and used to support forms of social change often excluded from conciliatory rhetorics.

> *I see the community literacy project as a seed to start recording our history, our efforts, and our perspectives. History leaves us out. If the truth of our experience is never told, then much is lost. Knowledge is power. It's not everything, but it's a piece of how we get left out. If the history of Over-the-Rhine only gets written by the dominant forces, then there is a lot of blank pages. We have always said in our effort, a step out of oppression is expression.*
>
> — Bonnie Neumeier,
> Over-the-Rhine People's Movement activist

Neumeier's words above reflect the power of literacy when courageous individuals on the margins of society decide to "speak truth to power."

For Neumeier and others like her, literacy has the potential to call attention to social injustices by enabling people to realize that "a step out of oppression" is indeed expression. And, these peoples' stories of oppression and exclusion are not without their opposites—liberation and inclusion. The very act of giving expression to lived experiences of hardship and struggle is an act of justice and redemption, one that helps assure that a people's history no longer goes unheard.

In the best of circumstances, speaking truth to power presents fundamental themes of tragedy and struggle aligned with genuine hope and possibility for the present and future. As antidotes to social injustice, hope and possibility are quite distinct from merely "wishing" or "dreaming." As Paula Mathieu points out, "To take on hope is to take on risk and responsibility while maintaining a dogged optimism" (17). In the context of a social movement, retaining what might be called a "critical hope" requires mobilizing actions that inspire and motivate while simultaneously calling out instances of social oppression and/or disenfranchisement. Literacy works to connect these actions associated with critical hope—actions expressing both a critique of the status quo and a progressive vision of the future—when communicating that the need for social change is necessary. It is at these moments, when speaking truth to power becomes much more than simply protesting on behalf of "truth" against those in power, that the work of a social movement becomes the work of literacy pedagogy.

The challenge for community literacy practitioners is to align our work with social movements and to use literacy and rhetoric to advance distinct causes. Community literacy practitioners can initiate pedagogical practices embodying critical hope which dramatize the interplay between critique and progressive social action, between social protest and a discourse of possibility. Locating the most opportune times to build strong working relations with social activists is not a straightforward task; the platforms for literacy associated with such a community are bound to differ in significant ways from the comfort many of us, along with our students, identify with the university classroom. Building productive alliances with social activists and the communities they represent is necessary to develop a pedagogical framework that utilizes a diverse set of literacy practices and to bring people together across radically different social standings and cultural backgrounds. Speaking truth to power requires exposing social injustices and directly calling out those who are responsible and holding them accountable. When considered side-by-side, these dual objectives—using literacy to bring people together to build community across difference while directly calling out others to expose their complicity with social injustices—may seem at odds. How, for instance, are we to reconcile the virtues of respect and reconciliation—the hallmarks of community-building—with a strident, confrontational rhetoric designed to target particular audiences deemed complicit in maintaining an unjust status quo?

This essay argues that community literacy projects can appropriately utilize the progressive rhetoric of community-building across difference, together with the provocative rhetoric often associated with speaking truth to power, when initiated within the context of a social movement committed to social justice. Drawing from rhetorical analyses and community literacy work in support of a local grassroots movement in the Cincinnati neighborhood of Over-the-Rhine, I show how social protest and community building—and by extension radical critique and direct social action—can function together as pedagogical activities that use public discourse to challenge dominant perceptions of inner-city life. In the community activism described throughout this essay, the seemingly contradictory poles of what Edward P.J. Corbett has identified as "the rhetoric of the open hand" and "the rhetoric of the closed-fist" are combined through the pedagogical work of a particular social movement, signaling the power of rhetoric and literacy to advance critical hope. Ultimately, I argue that classroom practices employing the oppositional rhetoric of speaking truth to power have key advantages over the conciliatory rhetoric usually associated with work in community literacy when it comes to engaging our students in social justice work.

In what follows, I establish a context for discussing the rhetoric of the Over-the-Rhine People's Movement, a grassroots movement in Cincinnati's Over-the-Rhine neighborhood. I continue to work with this movement in connection with introducing students to the value of speaking truth to power. I then provide a rhetorical investigation into the movement's approach to speaking truth to power in relation to composition studies' ongoing skepticism of rhetorics of social protest. I then turn to community literacy work in Over-the-Rhine that is being done in coordination with People's Movement activities. This work provides an example of how community literacy pedagogy can benefit from critical engagement with the rhetorical actions of a social movement. I end by arguing that there are central aspects associated with oppositional rhetorics that can be encountered in community literacy initiatives and used to support forms of social change often excluded from conciliatory rhetorics.

COMMUNITY ACTIVISM IN ACTION: RHETORIC AND THE OVER-THE-RHINE PEOPLE'S MOVEMENT

Cincinnati's Over-the-Rhine neighborhood is not unlike many inner-city communities across the nation where attempts at community development clash with the reality of economic disenfranchisement and social oppression. According to the *Over-the Rhine Community Housing* website, "In 1950 approximately 30,000 people resided in Over-Rhine, with whites constituting 99% of that population. Recent data show a population of about 7,600 residents, 80% black. Of the current residents, the median household income for four is less than $13,000. Of Over-the-Rhine's 7,500 habitable units, 3,000 are below housing code standards. About 300 buildings stand vacant." Over-the-Rhine continues to suffer from many of the typical problems associated with low-income urban environments, "including population decline, homelessness, increased segregation, building abandonment, high rates of unemployment and underemployment, and little access to political power" ("Over-the-Rhine, Our Community").

The professional class has long sought to rehabilitate this urban space, adhering to the belief that developing the area merely requires the free-market and entrepreneurial spirit to take center stage. This movement toward economic rejuvenation is very much underway. As described in an airing of National Public Radio's Weekend Edition Sunday, "The first time you come and drive through Over-the-Rhine, you'll focus on the street corner drug sellers. The second time, you'll notice the Italianate architecture, the bright colors. And then you'll see the coffee shop that sells used books, the art galleries, music clubs" ("Fighting Hunger in Cincinnati").

The neighborhood is currently being gentrified. The threat of further displacement continues, and the future viability of a long-term local grassroots movement to secure the livelihood of low-income residents and workers remains under siege. Over the past forty years, the Over-the-Rhine People's Movement, "a network of organizations based in social service, community education, the arts, welfare rights, and affordable housing development" ("Over-the-Rhine, Our Community"), has consistently addressed issues of racial equity and social justice as well as provided needed services for residents. The success of People's Movement activists over the years is most evident in their historical efforts to stave off economic development plans done at the expense of low-income people.

My ongoing work in Over-the-Rhine follows my deep conviction that recent corporate efforts to transform the neighborhood make it essential that the work of the community organizations affiliated with the People's Movement be supported to enhance equitable redevelopment. The rich history of community activism affiliated with the People's Movement through the years signals the power of literacy to effect change in the community. Even though the powerful have tended to downplay their point of view, these activists understand how their own voices are central to the movement toward community self-determination.

A People's Account of Over-the-Rhine: Then and Now

The history of the Over-the-Rhine People's Movement dates back to the late 1960s and early 1970s when neighborhood activists took it upon themselves to organize and advocate for direct services for an ever-increasing homeless and poverty-stricken population residing in the neighborhood. Very much a product of a time when radical social movements across the globe were flourishing, the People's Movement utilized a rhetoric that framed the conditions of poverty engulfing the neighborhood as local manifestations of broader, global structural injustices. And for these activists, remedying social injustices at the local-level was largely a matter of linking their work to social movements challenging the status quo more broadly. Specifically, arguments revolving around issues such as affordable housing, homelessness, welfare rights, and education in the neighborhood, employed direct appeals to struggles associated with movements advancing anti-imperialist, feminist, anti-war, and pro-labor agendas. A major forum for disseminating People's Movement rhetoric in Over-the-Rhine during the 1970s and the 1980s was *The Voices Over-the-Rhine Community Newspaper*, a neighborhood publication raising awareness of political and civic matters facing residents and workers. A predominant goal for

People's Movement activists and *Voices* writers during these early days was to directly connect the hardships of poor residents and workers in Over-the-Rhine to the plight of oppressed groups everywhere. For instance, at times, movement activists and *Voices* writers equated the social forces creating the poverty conditions in Over-the-Rhine with the imperialist practices spawning the forced removal of American Indians onto reservations:

> We recognize that Indian people are not alone in the fight to force the rewriting of history. Other "nations" of oppressed people are struggling to expose the truth of how they have been exploited by the American system—Black people, Appalachians, the Vietnamese. And we here in Over-the-Rhine, in our struggle for good living conditions, face some of the same oppressive problems American Indians face—and face the same small rich class of people who rule this land. Our struggles are the same. ... If we understand the true history of genocide of Indian people, we can better understand the many exploitations of the present American system." ("American Indian")

Putting aside the problem of validity in associating gentrification to Indian genocide, the target of protest for these activists was the American system itself and the interests it served. It is clear who they regarded as responsible for its maintenance and legitimization: "In America, where power is held in the hands of a small rich class of people, the present-day news and history is written to support the money interests of that small group; not all the masses of people" ("American Indian"). The workers and residents of Over-the-Rhine are portrayed as casting their lot with the masses of disenfranchised and exploited people, in opposition to the small group of people holding a disproportionate share of wealth, status, and power in American society.

The direct association of Over-the-Rhine with the historical struggles of disenfranchised and exploited people everywhere would find fuller expression in later accounts of the gentrifying process taking place in the neighborhood. In addressing the continuing gentrifying practices leading to the inevitable displacement of low-income people in the neighborhood over the last forty years, it has not become uncommon to characterize an individual working to "revitalize" Over-the-Rhine as the "modern 'urban pioneer'" who seeks to "wipe out native populations under the new manifest destiny—the promise of a bohemian culture, a vibrant business life, and bustling streets filled with walking consumers" (The Dean of Cincinnati).

Longtime People's Movement activist and well-established university citizen Thomas A. Dutton has been active in Over-the-Rhine since the early 1980s when, as an architect professor from Miami University in Oxford, Ohio, he began working closely with People's Movement activists in their efforts to secure low-income housing. Interested in investigating how the built environment and architectural design intersect with the lived experiences of low-income people in urban centers, he was initially impressed with the historical Italianate buildings and their place in the urban landscape of the neighborhood.

In 2002 Dutton founded the Miami University Center for Community Engagement in Over-the-Rhine, a university-community partnership organization with a strong "relationship with the Over-the-Rhine People's Movement and other important organizations within the inner-city of Cincinnati that struggle for human and racial rights, and social justice" (*Miami University*). As the Center's website further notes, "Accordingly, it is a site for learning and for producing knowledge that intersects with the needs and demands of a social movement. The Center privileges human and ecological needs as leading priorities in urban development, and challenges the profit motive as the dominant arbiter in urban social policy." (*Miami University*). The flagship initiative of the Center is their Residency Program where "university students, faculty members, and staff collaborate with community organizations and leaders to revitalize the neighborhood through a range of initiatives" ("Campus Compact"). Students in the Residency Program spend an entire semester taking all their courses at the Center and living in Over-the-Rhine. Dutton was recently honored by Campus Compact with the 2009 Thomas Ehrlich Civically Engaged Faculty Award, an annual national award given to a prominent activist teacher-scholar, which recognizes "exemplary leadership in advancing students' civic learning through public scholarship, commitment to service-learning and civic engagement, and community partnerships" ("Campus Compact").

Dutton has written extensively on how the gentrification taking place in Over-the-Rhine is emblematic of the larger global effort to control and dispose of entire marginal populations—many of whom reside in inner-city communities—in the name of urban revitalization and economic development. Fully aware of the stakes involved in calling out dominant portrayals of urban progress for their deliberate whitewashing of the actual social costs of gentrification, Dutton nonetheless holds nothing back in his indictment of those he views as responsible when he writes: "Is it really too extreme to suggest that white society never intended to fully include blacks and other people of color and shows no inclination to bring about such inclusion and equality?" (Dutton *Indian Reservations* 3). In asserting that history demonstrates the deliberate exclusion of peoples of color from the white narrative of "American progress," Dutton turns to historian Jeffrey Ostler for an account of how proposed arguments for the assimilation of the American Sioux Indians turned, in practice, into the takeover of their lands and near extermination of Sioux ways of life:

> Remarkably, as the Sioux began living on reservations in the late 1870s, many Sioux leaders genuinely thought they might be able to work out a relationship with the United States that would allow them to preserve some of their land and ways of life, while adjusting to new conditions and demands. By the late 1880s, however, as the United States relentlessly cracked down on Sioux ways of life and demanded further cessions of land, these hopes began to seem elusive. (qtd in Dutton *Indian Reservations* 4)

Drawing further from Ostler's portrayal of Sioux dispossession and near extermination, Dutton notes that many of the American officials and policymakers at the time were "undoubtedly sincere" in their "belief that assimilation for Indians was possible and desirable." And yet, the dark, unstated assumption that American Indians were "heathen and savage" worked to ultimately override the idea that they were capable of participating in American civilization as equals (4).

Referencing the contradictory nature of imperialist practices in efforts to assimilate American Indian populations, Dutton points to continuing attempts to revitalize Over-the-Rhine through gentrification: if the goal is to eradicate the cultural identity and practices affiliated with a marginal social group, what better way to do so than to convince members of that group that if they just follow your lead, they are bound to share in the prosperity you already enjoy. Then, to insure that they inevitably fail to live up to the standards established for inclusion, you banish all traces of their way of life—all reminders of their "inferior" cultural heritage—and with them, all the requisite resources for flourishing in the new environment you have just created for them. The net result is exclusion and displacement, the removal of a people not only from the land they had long occupied, but from that which has forever marked their identity as persons, as human beings living on their own terms.

In terms of speaking truth to power, what is most striking about Dutton's account of gentrification as essentially an imperialist project is the boldness—the utter lack of timidity—in its charge that there are those who remain directly complicit in the perpetuation of social injustices done at the expense of society's most vulnerable members. In this account of gentrification, the misery felt by Over-the-Rhine workers and residents calls attention to the suffering experienced by excluded and dispossessed peoples everywhere. "Displacing the poor and arranging their disappearance," Dutton writes, "is the game plan" (7). For Dutton and other People's Movement activists, calling out those in power for their deliberate efforts to legitimate fundamentally unjust actions is largely a matter of defending the oppressed from the assaults of the oppressor. Protecting the interests of the poor and the dispossessed is what motivates their outrage directed towards those they deem culpable.

The potential value that social protest holds for activist work in inner-city communities like Over-the-Rhine is something that I try and teach my students. Introducing students to the People's Movement history of social protest encourages them to explore the grittier side of community activism and take sides on issues of public concern. The fallout of the neighborhood Uprising of 2001, which brought national attention to the city of Cincinnati during a four-day period in April of that year, is a prime example of the kind of issues facing Over-the-Rhine residents and workers over the last decade. It all began in the aftermath of the police shooting of Timothy Thomas, a 19 year-old black man. Officer Steven Rouch shot Thomas in the back during an on-foot pursuit—several police officers were chasing Thomas because of old traffic violations ("The Trigger"). The incident ignited a storm of protest from the city's Black community in general, and Over-the-Rhine residents and workers in particular. Subsequent rioting that followed the shooting drew local and national media attention. A *Cincinnati Enquirer* article sub-heading read: "Violence tears open the city, and it takes a curfew to bring calm. Bodies, property and the city's reputation are damaged in the worst urban unrest here in 30 years..." ("The Riots Explode"). Buried in news reports from media outlets across the city and nation focusing on the violence, were acknowledgements that peaceful protests were organized over the four-day period of civil unrest. Protests expressed the deep-seated anger and frustration with, among other things, the fact that fifteen African-Americans had been shot to death by city police officers during the preceding six years ("The Trigger"). While looting and property destruction took place in a number of Cincinnati neighborhoods, Over-the-Rhine activists organized peaceful protests that sought to explain why many of the "rioters" felt under-siege by the city establishment. "If you're fine when things are normal, then you want things to stay normal," said protest organizer Rev. Damon Lynch III. "If you're not, then normal is an uncomfortable place to be" (The Trigger").

Through extended inquiries into the Uprising of 2001 and the peaceful protests, including the subsequent civil unrest and its aftermath (which has both renewed efforts to improve race relations in the city and emboldened efforts to gentrify Over-the-Rhine), students in my Writing for Social Change are encouraged to locate meanings that express something other than the uncritical view that "these people" were simply "immoral rioters" searching for an excuse to create mass havoc and chaos. Furthermore, students are asked to situate the violent acts of looting and property destruction in relation to the well-organized and peaceful demonstrations calling the city officials and police force into account for their ongoing discriminatory policies and practices against the poor and people of color. In doing so, students complicate ready-made assumptions regarding the nature of organized social protest and the value of using discourse to confront a culpable establishment head-on.

Rather than viewing proclamations of indignation—expressed through such slogans as "Stop Killing Us, or Else!" and "Don't Shoot!" ("Photo Timeline")—as the mark of an "uncivil" or "unreasonable" response to an unfortunate situation, students come to question the all-too-easy identification of the direct challenge to authority such slogans clearly represent with any subsequent acts of violence that may eventually be wielded against that authority. Rather than viewing the confrontational rhetorics of social protest on display in the organized streets demonstrations as *the cause* of much of the violence that was to ensue, students consider if the real culprit might actually be the unjust and oppressive living conditions forced on communities like Over-the-Rhine. Students inquire into the possibility that governmental policies that do little good for the poor, virulent racism, and a capitalist economic system increasingly assure that entire communities in our inner cities are left off the map. In this context, protest placards proclaiming "Cincinnati Cops: Stop Killing Black People!" ("Photo Timeline") do more than lay blame at the feet of Cincinnati police officers; such discourse positions the police officers as agents of the State who have a responsibility to resist the oppressive and domineering charge to control, and make submissive, black bodies on the streets. Speaking truth to power, students learn, involves articulating a "truth" that those in power may not be comfortable hearing but that nonetheless prioritizes the necessity of expressing indignation directed at an unjust system that perpetuates the indignant conditions many are forced to live under.

Some students decide to speak truth to power directly in their own writings. After an entire semester of regular class meetings in Over-the-Rhine—meeting and interacting with street activists and learning about various People's Movement activities from the past and present—members of one Writing for Social Change class participated in an Open-Mic gathering at InkTank, a community writing center in the neighborhood. At this monthly event, writers of all stripes share writings with the broader community. Many of the writings address community issues and concerns, inviting audience members to reflect on perceptions of Over-the-Rhine and ongoing struggles taking place in the neighborhood. The writings take many forms, such as poems, short stories, and commentary essays. Some presenters engage in slam poetry and rap. One student from the Writing for Social Change course performed a rap he had written that encouraged the audience members from Over-the-Rhine (OTR) to stand up and take notice of ongoing gentrifying efforts and to organize to confront the establishment. The following is an excerpt from his rap:

OTR, OTR

You really, really ain't bad as they say you are
Equal rights under the law is all we asking fa'
And if you ain't gon' give 'em to us then we grabbin' 'em
We grabbin' 'em

> Man you know I'm getting kinda mad
> They fighting us so we need to start fighting back
> All power to the people, they ain't liking that
> But I could really care less 'cause it's a righteous act
> I'll bet ya that
> And I can tell you that gentrification
> Will lead to OTR's disintegration
> So basically what I'm saying
> Is that corporatized development's inherently racist
> They've got the nerve to call themselves philanthropists
> A better word that they could use is cancerous
> They're undeterred, they're deceitful, and they're mannerless
> The cheddar swirls, greed swallows evenhandedness
> So to my people, now's the time to get our mind right
> 'Cause if we don't, we'll regret it in our hindsight

The performance of these lyrics resonated powerfully with audience members, many of whom had been living and working for years in Over-the-Rhine and were experiencing first-hand the negative effects of gentrification and the prospects of displacement. The fact that a white college student was taking on the role of an Over-the-Rhine resident and activist through this performance did not seem to bother them; in fact, it could be argued that they truly appreciated that someone from outside the neighborhood appeared to "get it." In rather dramatic fashion, by invoking the People's Movement ongoing struggle to stop gentrification, this text takes the side of "the oppressed" while encouraging an organized opposition against the "oppressor."

This student's text also suggests that, like countless other social justice activists, People's Movement activists have always been just as concerned with holding themselves responsible for the welfare of their community as they have been critical of those holding them down, standing in the way of their own liberation: "We believe that our struggles here in OTR [Over-the-Rhine] are part of that struggle of people all around this country (and world) for decent living and working conditions and control over their own lives. . .We believe that individual people—in words and actions—must fight against injustice, discrimination, poor living and working conditions ("Why We Print" 13). For People's Movement activists, calling out the oppressor and motivating the oppressed to work toward self-determination are akin to identifying the warden while moving the prisoner to unchain himself.

Speaking Truth to Power: Hands, Fists, and Social Protest

The approach to speaking truth to power described above suggests a distinct conception of political rhetoric. As an expression of political rhetoric, being competent in naming the oppressor and systems of oppression is not all that is required for People's Movement activists to effectively call into question unjust actions. Rather, what is needed is a rhetorical framework to critically interrogate the unjust activities enacted by those who wield power over the oppressed and to hold them accountable. At the same time, the oppressed must use discourse to challenge each other to "unchain themselves," and in so doing, build community for the purpose of coming together for self-determination.

In proclaiming who and what are actively working against the interests of the poor in Over-the-Rhine, People's Movement activists complete only one half of the equation necessary to speak truth to power. The other half entails convincing others that their critique, or protest, is worth engaging. However, the rhetoric deployed by the People's Movement must contend with a number of obstacles, the most obvious being the tendency to be labeled by audiences as "extremist" or "coercive." In this sense, the People's Movement shares much in common with the rhetorical legacy of American radicalism. According to James Darsey, American radicalism is best exemplified by "its concern with the political roots of a society, its fundamental laws, its foundational principles, its most sacred covenants" (9). Subsequently, its rhetoric might be characterized as "a steadfast refusal to adapt itself to the perspectives of its audience," and as a result, be perceived by the majority as "uncivil" or "extremist" (5-6). The backdrop for establishing what might come to be stigmatized as an incendiary rhetoric is the promotion of its opposite: a civil, conciliatory rhetoric. Nonetheless, the form and content of a "civil discourse" is wholly dependent on the rhetorical situation from which it derives. In the case of the People's Movement's employment of social protest, it is useful to examine the form of "civility" it is in response to.

In "Corbett's Hand: A Rhetorical Figure for Composition Studies," Richard Marback examines composition studies' continuing disavowal of confrontational rhetorics in favor of the humanist rhetorics associated with our professional discourses, which are portrayed as conciliatory, civil, and effectively reasoned. Turning to Edward P.J. Corbett's 1969 article, "The Rhetoric of the Closed Fist and the Rhetoric of the Open Hand," Marback traces composition's inability to effectively engage the public on issues of justice to the field's response to the turmoil of the late 1960s, when numerous protest movements centering on issues of race, class, and gender were ultimately positioned as "coercive" by the broader culture. Drawing from the classical rhetorical figure of the "open hand and the closed fist," composition studies constructed "the humanizing, liberating potential of the writing hand in opposition to the externally and physically enforced violence of the closed fist" (189). Corbett argued that composition studies needed to side with the "reasoned, sustained, conciliatory discussion of the issues" of the open hand, in contrast to the "non-rational, non-sequential, often nonverbal, frequently provocative means [of persuasion]" of the closed fist "prevalent in the late 1960's" (qtd. in Marback 181). According to Marback, however, the uncivil attributes ascribed to social protest concealed the actual violent and coercive dynamics of certain rhetorics marked as "civil" or "progressive." It is this privileging of a civil discourse, in opposition to the "unseemly" confrontational discourse of social protest, that composition studies has inherited.

While the People's Movement clearly operates in a different context from composition studies, its positioning as a movement on the margins of the broader culture suggests that much of its work remains a response to dominant rhetorical modes and styles. In the case of composition studies in the late 1960s, the rhetoric on society's margins that presented the biggest challenge to the field's conception of itself as promoting the democratic ideal of the open hand was the closed-fist rhetoric associated with Black Power. Through the discourse of civility marked by the open hand, stood its opposite—the Black Power fist, made emblematic of the exact kind of discourse that was understood to be an anathema to a democratic polity. "From the perspective of liberal democracy," Marback writes, "the image of the conciliatory open hand gives expression to the most significant opportunities for discursive mediations of civic life, while the closed-fisted refusal to engage in a discussion in these terms signals all that is opposed to democratic values and civic participation" (182). On the other hand, "In a society where racial identity correlates with power and privilege, the Black

Power fist gives expression not only to belligerence, but to the feelings of anger and frustration with systemic indifference to discrimination and segregation" (184).

In the same way that the anger at the white establishment and the moral indignation expressed through the clenching of fists stood as a justified response to racial oppression and discrimination, the People's Movement's targeting of Over-the-Rhine "urban pioneers" as "colonial rulers" (See Dutton "Colony Over-the-Rhine") signals an appropriate response to the real-world violence of gentrification. As an Over-the-Rhine developer recently put it in describing his great fortune to expand and develop his area of operations to revitalize the neighborhood, "We're having a lot of success. This area is like a low-hanging fruit" ("Private Firm Renovates"). The People's Movement use of social protest is a response to precisely this kind of "open hand" rhetoric, which in actuality operates as a coercive, imperialist project disguised in the cloak of "civility" and "conciliation."

As Marback demonstrates, the rhetoric of civility embedded in the image of the open hand has provided composition studies with an idealized version of writing to intervene in public affairs to challenge social injustices, and contribute to social change. Insofar as the "open hand" pits the expression of a privileged group in opposition to an "unreasonable" and "coercive" closed-fist rhetoric, teachers can imagine students getting training in a privileged discourse that will give them access to public audiences. However, when communicating effectively means using a discourse to "move out of the realm of the disenfranchised into the realm of privilege" (191), then it is difficult to imagine how that same discourse might address the concerns of a socially disenfranchised group, other than to say that one is providing critical insights from a position of privilege entirely divorced from the discursive exchanges and material conditions giving rise to the social injustices in the first place. The capacity of teachers and students, then, to use public discourse in ways that matter is severely contained because the mere expression of critical insights purporting to challenge the system is understood as equal to actually *changing* the system.

Unlike this idealized image of an open hand, for those speaking truth to power it is precisely the discursive exchanges and material conditions determining the everyday lives and concerns of the socially disenfranchised that mark the terms of engagement with systems of privilege and oppression. Rather than using rhetoric to fashion a critical-distancing from issues as a way to direct social change from above, speaking truth to power confronts power head on to *critically engage directly with issues*, and in so doing, upends the figure of the open hand raised up and the closed fist clenching. Turned downward, the open hand is now envisioned as moving down grasping, engulfing, and smothering everything within its reach; while the closed fist rises up from the ground, and asserts itself, disrupting attempts made by the open hand to hold it down. In this sense, the closed fist rhetoric of the People's Movement finds ways to disrupt the established symbolic order so as to call attention to a new social order, one that re-thinks everyday perceptions of inner-city life.

It is exactly at this point of discursive disruption where we can theorize that the operation of the hand and fist ultimately becomes paradoxical: the disruptive movement of the closed fist pushing upward becomes enmeshed in the open hand, but rather than smothering the closed fist, the open hand now works to embrace it. Combining fist with hand, the new figure links the power of critical assertion with the receptiveness of listening—the capacity of the fist to assert itself becomes an act of self-determination which is nevertheless dependent on the good will of the embracing hand to give full recognition to the capacity of oppressed peoples to express their own self-worth and dignity on their own terms.

Fists and Hands as Gifts and the Work of Critical Hope

The figure of the closed fist critically asserting and the open hand embracing finds expression in a guest column by Thomas A. Dutton appearing in the *Cincinnati Enquirer* entitled "The Gift of the Drop Inn Center." This piece deals with the ongoing controversy in Over-the-Rhine involving the Drop Inn Center, a homeless shelter that stands as a founding member organization of the People's Movement. The debate centers on how the Drop Inn Center, the region's largest homeless shelter, should fit into plans to revitalize the neighborhood. The Drop Inn Center has been in its present location in Over-the-Rhine for over thirty years, and powerful interests have long sought to re-locate the shelter outside of the neighborhood to make room for upscale economic development. Much more than a homeless shelter, the Drop Inn Center has consistently addressed issues of racial equity and social justice as well as provided needed services for residents. Furthermore, the organization has always worked to document and promote a fuller understanding of the struggles and hopes of low-income folks.

In this guest column, Dutton addresses the tendency to portray the Drop Inn Center as a hindrance to community renewal. Shifting gears away from directly comparing gentrification in Over-the-Rhine to the colonial project of dislocating American Indians, Dutton now pushes the fist upward toward the hand collapsing by taking issue with those who suggest that the Drop Inn Center attracts an "undesirable" population and arguing that the homeless shelter actually epitomizes the empathy required to "restore a person's humanity." In a direct indictment of those who would suggest that the Drop Inn Center should move out of Over-the-Rhine, Dutton asserts that the homeless shelter is "a place of compassion, a place of redemption in peoples' struggle to overcome addiction to drugs and alcohol, a healing place. And it is out of this base of interpersonal dynamics that we can see the contribution of the wider political mission of the Drop Inn Center and the Over-the-Rhine People's Movement: to restore Cincinnati's humanity". The kind of empathy Dutton has in mind challenges us all to make connections between the hardships of inner-city living and the relative wealth of many middle-class suburbs—the struggle to make ends meet and the comfort that comes with securing a roof over one's head. For Dutton and the People's Movement, as long as Greater Cincinnati fails to substantively cultivate this sense of civic awareness amongst its citizens, segregation across racial and class lines is certain to continue. As long as the voices of the powerful predominate over the voices of socially and economically disenfranchised citizens, social injustices will remain a reality in the region.

In the final analysis, Dutton challenges his readers to perceive the homeless as "gifts"—inviting fellow citizens to revitalize their own capacities to show deep compassion through civic engagement. In doing so, his words disrupt established hierarchies between hands and fists "where homeless folks are typically not seen, indeed, they are scorned, reviled, denounced [and] rejected." In their place he puts the fists enmeshed with hands as "gifts"—the source of empathy deriving from assertions of dignity spawned initially under conditions of extreme hardship and pain.

The linking of fists with hands also testifies to the capacity of speaking truth to power and calls attention both to the political importance of directly engaging extreme duress not of one's own choosing, and to the possibility of remaining hopeful as one works toward a more just society nonetheless. Identifying with suffering one did not cause while remaining hopeful is a dual impulse best summarized by Cornel West in his articulation of prophetic pragmatism, a philosophical account of progressive political activism:

> Prophetic pragmatism, as a form of third-wave left romanticism, tempers its utopian impulse with a profound sense of the tragic character of life and history. This sense of the tragic highlights the irreducible predicament of unique individuals who undergo dread, despair, disillusionment, disease, and death and the institutional forms of oppression that dehumanize people. Tragic thought is not confined solely to the plight of the individual; it also applies to social experiences of resistance, revolution, and societal reconstruction. Prophetic pragmatism is a form of tragic thought in that it confronts candidly individual and collective experiences of evil in individuals and institutions—with little expectation of ridding the world of all evil. Yet it is a kind of romanticism in that it holds many experiences of evil to be neither inevitable nor necessary but rather the results of human agency, i.e., choices and actions. (228)

West's explanation of prophetic pragmatism describes tragedy in terms of the individual and social experiences of suffering that are ultimately attributable to the consequences of living in an unjust society. Confronting and coming to terms with this sense of the tragic in modern society requires identifying with human suffering and working for social change despite the recognition that such efforts will yield imperfect results. At the same time, the utopian impulse of prophetic pragmatism holds that because many experiences of suffering and social oppression are not "natural" and are the consequences of human intent and actions, there are substantive opportunities for articulating a politics of possibility, inspiring people to be hopeful in working for radical social reform and transformation.

West's description of suffering within a utopian impulse is a variation on the theme of critical assertion and receptiveness epitomized in my account of the revised figure of fists and hands. For prophetic pragmatists, this dynamic of critically asserting oneself while depending on the good will of others to join in the struggles to transform the status quo is cast as the limitations and possibilities of progressive political action. The tragic understanding of modern society calls for critical attention to the limitations of progressive political action, or the "human impossibility of paradise," yet also impels individuals to work for social change by making critical assertions out of "moral outrage and human desperation in the face of prevailing forms of evil in human societies and lives" (229). At the same time, the utopian impulse of prophetic pragmatism highlights the possibilities of inspiring people to join in the struggle to work for social change and to remain hopeful regarding progressive political struggle by virtue of the fact that social "evils" are often the result of collective human action, and are thus transformable. The interaction between fist and hand—between critical assertions regarding the status quo and the hopeful response that works to build community across difference—creates the conditions necessary for enacting critical hope in the People's Movement's ongoing efforts to speak truth to power.

IMPLICATIONS FOR COMMUNITY LITERACY PEDAGOGY

Speaking truth to power has significant pedagogical implications for the prospects of initiating community literacy projects in tandem with the work of a social movement. Before describing my community literacy work in alliance with the Over-the-Rhine People's Movement, it is helpful to clarify the role of community literacy pedagogy as a form of action sustained by the work of a social movement that supports the kind of rhetorical dynamics outlined in the previous section. When it comes to creating a pedagogical framework, my account of speaking truth to power suggests that simply mobilizing critical resistance on the part of students as a solution to the problem of community disempowerment disengages the work of community literacy projects away from local communities Simply having students provide academic critiques as a literate strategy for countering social injustices in a local inner-city neighborhood like Over-the-Rhine has consequences not unlike what may happen in a writing classroom on a university campus if the discourse used remains largely disengaged from the real-life rhetorical situations of the everyday lives of people residing in that community. While emphasizing that the solution to social injustices is actualized in students' use of literacy to *identify*—and perhaps theoretically challenge—the work of hegemony, all too often community literacy pedagogy fails to consider ways in which literacy might be used as an *activity* for combating social injustices keeping the status quo in place.

This opposition between critical insight and structural change marks the gulf between engagement and rhetorical action in community literacy projects that simply ask students to write critically *about the social injustices they observe in the community*. For community literacy projects to work toward structural solutions to systemic problems, they need to take into account the necessity of using writing as a tool for *collectively critically engaging*. For community literacy projects to fulfill their promise of social change, proposing solutions is not enough. Implying that when individuals simply identify the work of hegemony this automatically satisfies the conditions for acting more justly in the world draws attention away from structural solutions. The stark divide between critical insight and social action inherited from the broader discipline of composition studies helps explain why community literacy practitioners interested in social change often find it so difficult to provide an institutional framework for effectively challenging the status quo in the local communities in which they work. Whenever community literacy pedagogy solicits individual students to articulate critical insights at the expense of genuine social reform in partnership with local grassroots movements for change, the possibility of instituting actions that work for social justice is greatly compromised.

Positioning community literacy pedagogy within the context of a movement for social change requires finding ways for literacy education to provide opportunities for learning what is at stake in activist work. This pedagogy brings students and teachers into dialogue with community members and activists to critically engage issues and to disrupt established hierarchies across systems of privilege and oppression. In the process, community building across difference is initiated by providing material space for critical assertions that challenge structural injustices. In this sense, speaking truth to power operates as a literacy practice that provides opportunities for enacting critical hope by grounding writing in the material conditions giving rise to the most pressing issues facing a community while bearing witness to the possibility of enacting genuine transformation in the service of social justice. Going beyond merely identifying and critiquing social injustices, inviting students to work with community members and activists to use writing critically to speak truth to power can be a genuine act of civic engagement.

COMMUNITY LITERACY WORK WITH THE OVER-THE-RHINE PEOPLE'S MOVEMENT

My involvement with community literacy work in Over-the-Rhine began when I first made contact with a few People's Movement activists and heard them express a strong desire to document and publicize the long history of community activism in Over-the-Rhine. I had already engaged in a number of social justice related activities in the neighborhood during the previous four years and was viewed as a credible partner because I had earned, as a People's Movement activist once told me, the required "community credits." Furthermore, I had already internalized much of the vocabulary and ideological dispositions of the People's Movement. This ability to "talk the talk" of the movement gave us a shared language for discussing issues that mattered and provided me with an entry point for learning more deeply about the people, including their struggles, hopes, and fears.

I eventually established a working relationship with Thomas A. Dutton at the Miami University Center for Community Engagement in Over-the-Rhine. I teach my Writing for Social Change course at the Center. Students in this class meet regularly at the Center and interact with Over-the-Rhine community residents and activists as a way of examining how an actual social movement and everyday people use rhetoric and writing to work for social change. Significantly, the university where I teach—largely a commuter campus with many first generation college students—is in the suburbs across the river from Cincinnati. My students are very familiar with "how Over-the-Rhine, within the cultural imagination of the entire Cincinnati region, has become so symbolic of all the negative images and things that are supposedly wrong with the city: crime, blight, dirtiness, general poverty, etc. . ." (Wilkey qtd. in Dreese et al). Most of my students come from suburban environments and many claim "to know" Over-the-Rhine, although their familiarity with the neighborhood often comes "from watching the crime reports on the 11 o'clock news." It is not a stretch to say that many students are often "afraid to visit the neighborhood" (Wilkey qtd. in Dreese et al).

As an example of community literacy emphasizing public writing, this Writing for Social Change course culminates in an "Over-the-Rhine Campaign Project" in partnership with People's Movement activists. Over the course of the semester, students are introduced to ongoing activist campaigns in Over-the-Rhine to assist low-income individuals and the homeless. Students have numerous face-to-face interactions with community activists and take on many critical investigations into media and community texts dealing with Over-the-Rhine. Students also have substantial opportunities to participate in the formation of actual campaign projects through interactions with these community activists. The components of a given campaign can take many forms, including: designing and producing a "street newsletter" or "'zine," creating a Display Board based on oral history interviews of Over-the-Rhine residents and workers, and working with Over-the-Rhine residents and workers on their writing. The basic requirement is that the project be done in consultation with our community partners.

As part of their Over-the-Rhine Campaign Project, a recent class of students designed and produced a 'zine entitled *The People's Friend*, in recognition of their support of the Over-the-Rhine People's Movement. One of the students, Dana Divine, had the opportunity to read a poem that he wrote which was published in this 'zine at an Open Mic gathering at InkTank, the previously mentioned community writing center in Over-the-Rhine. Writers and poets from the Men's Recovery Program at the Drop Inn Center homeless shelter direct this event. I facilitate a weekly writing group at the Drop Inn Center with these men, who use writing as a tool for recovery from drug and alcohol abuse. Central to my pedagogical approach in facilitating this writing group is to make connections with the broader social issues in Over-the-Rhine as a way of strengthening their work through the recovery progress.

The poem Divine wrote for the 'zine and Open Mic is entitled "Gentrification—a.k.a. Get the Fuck Out!". During one of my meetings with the Drop Inn Center writing group, I passed out my students' 'zine to the men. I asked them to write in response to the pieces in the 'zine. One of the men, "The Mad Poet," wrote a poem in direct response to Dana's poem. The Mad Poet's poem, entitled "Serfication—a.k.a. I am One With the Land," completes a textual interaction that demonstrates the capacity that speaking truth to power has in using social protest to build community across difference. Below, I present both poems in their entirety:

GENTRIFICATION—A.K.A. GET THE FUCK OUT!

by Dana Divine

Out with the tired, old, poor,
we want something easy on the eyes.
How about a nice café,
Maybe some upscale clothing shops.
The people need better living conditions,
I'm for some new condos (market rate of course!)
Why don't these people get their shit together,
Pull themselves up from their bootstraps?
Turn that frown upside down,
make those lemons into lemonade.
Try getting a goddamn job,
make a contribution to society.

This community is growing, expanding,
we're trying to rebuild and reinvent.
We don't want to kick people to the curb,
maybe they can just scoot out of the way.
Let's not allow anyone to slow us down,
change must be painless and quick.

This world is forever changing,
Only the strongest can keep up,
it's a Darwinian thing,
the survival of the richest.
There is no progress without casualties,
it's the American way by God!

***

Serfication—a.k.a. I Am One With the Land

By The Mad Poet

I am tired, old, and poor,
I line up twice in soup kitchens for more.
Can you see that I am down but not out,
Why must I get the fuck out?

I am one with the land,
You must seriously reconsider your plan.
Please grant me more time to pay,
I am currently learning the right way.

By simply taking it day by day,
I know what they say.
I am society's so-called ill,
Lost my job, can't pay the bills.

No matter what the sun always shines,
Today I opposed a sip of wine.
Instead I drank cold lemonade,
Things not perfect, but soon I'll have it made.
My pain is sometimes un-bearing,
Upscale society is so uncaring.
A smile gets me through the pain,
I do this even in the rain.

The community is growing and expanding,
I am taking vocational classes through understanding.
The poor cannot compete with the riches,
Does Darwin's theory mean I must sleep in ditches?

Is your community redevelopment approved by God,
Or should I march and scream a Christian Jihad?
Unnecessary causalities is so unkind,
What happened to no man left behind?

> Can you see that I am down but not out,
> Why must I get the fuck out?
> I am one with the land,
> You must seriously reconsider your plan.

Speaking in the voice of the Over-the-Rhine market-rate developer, Divine uses sarcasm to highlight the dangers unfettered market-rate development holds for low-income individuals in communities like Over-the-Rhine. A culmination of what he learned through his critical inquiries into the rhetoric surrounding the historical and contemporary struggles in Over-the-Rhine, the poem reaches back against systems of privilege and oppression to make space for an alternative perspective to be heard. In the process, the poem invites an encounter with difference as an opportunity to learn more about the lived experiences of the "other." The Mad Poet accepts Divine's invitation by speaking in his own voice and on his own terms, proclaiming boldly the true impact that gentrification has on the lives of the most vulnerable in society. Taken together, both poems illustrate how speaking truth to power calls direct attention to unjust political arrangements and holds the oppressor accountable—all the while providing the material conditions necessary for encouraging community ties across difference.

CONCLUSION

Much of the recent scholarship in community literacy centers on finding ways to use literacy to bring students together with community partners for the purpose of transforming relations between self and other across sites of radical difference in ways that are both ethical and just (see Flower; Long). Linda Flower justifies engaging students in this kind of community-building work by contrasting it with a critical discourse that encourages students to "*speak against something*—against the media and ideology, against their own assumptions and inclinations as well as against institutions, oppression, and power" (78). For Flower, while critical approaches to composition clearly help students become aware of issues of oppression and domination and marginalized "others" in society, they do not make readily available the kind of literacy tools necessary for involving students in the "difficult art of dialogue" that is necessary for participation in "the culturally diverse public forums that materialize in dorm rooms, fraternity meetings, or professional courses and later in policy-drafting sessions at the office and decisions at the PTA" (79). Flower further clarifies her preference for teaching community literacy as civic dialogue when she asks:

> Where do we learn how to *speak with* others? How could we develop an intercultural rhetoric that supports dialogue, deliberation, and collaborative action across differences? Our current paradigms . . . prepare us well to *speak against* forces that diminish and oppress, to deconstruct, critique, and resist. They let us stand without compromise, outside and above. But they often fail us when we face the much more difficult practice of *speaking for something*—in ways that actually make a difference. (79 italics in original)

The terms established for civic dialogue posed above are set in direct opposition to the rhetoric of social protest I have outlined in this essay. I have argued that as a tool for speaking truth to power, critical approaches to social protest can actually transform relations across systems of oppression and privilege and thus open up opportunities for building community across difference. In the process, I have attempted to show how an oppositional rhetoric might be utilized to directly engage social injustices, and in doing so, hold accountable those who are perpetuating an unjust status quo. Instead of asking, "How do we teach the rhetorical art of ongoing inquiry versus position taking (even when that position is inspired by a liberatory ideology)?" (Flower 79), I would have us ask, How do we work with students to show that position taking is essential and that the "art of ongoing inquiry" is not limited to the conciliatory acts of a "civic dialogue"? How do we teach that the oppositional rhetoric of speaking truth to power is an important dimension of many effective organized efforts to collectively inquire into social injustices and confront directly head-on those entities responsible for maintaining unjust political and economic arrangements? How, in other words, do we confront a conciliatory rhetoric that would have us believe that building a community of individuals to organize and express outrage directed at an establishment that clearly perpetuates social injustices is at best rather impotent and at worse reactionary, even violent?

In her recent book *Living Room: Teaching Public Writing in a Privatized World*, Nancy Welch makes a strong case for the value of inviting students to consider how activist rhetorics that are oppositional might be employed in their own writings. In doing so, Welch turns to what activist writer Arundhati Roy has termed a "rhetoric from below," which stems "not from official policy makers but from and to those who feel the daily effects of official policy" (71). In presenting to students a series of activist confrontations with official policy makers, governmental entities, corporate bosses, and university officials, Welch highlights how the creation and use of slogans such as "Money for the classroom/Not for the boardroom" and "Part-Time America Doesn't Work!" are examples of "the art of practical discourse . . . the search for the available means to move a recalcitrant boss, to deter a bellicose presidential administration" (72). Bringing such texts to class can demonstrate to students "the motivation for mass resistance by people who are bound together in, and potentially against, the same 'race to the bottom'. Solidarity rhetoric has in these moments a material, not only a moral, basis" (15). I would add that instances of such organized mass resistance also counteract a common debilitating effect of conciliatory rhetoric, namely, its tendency to downplay the extent to which a "just anger," at times, might very well be a legitimate rhetorical grounding for campaign organizing. Furthermore, the fact that such organized attempts to use discourse to directly oppose a targeted establishment has at times been proven necessary to enact social change stands in stark contrast to the taken-for-granted notion that simply inquiring into injustices with others through civic dialogue leads to just actions.

Community literacy projects such as the one I have outlined in this essay offer one way for students to learn the links between writing and social change through direct engagement with an actual social movement on the ground. Students in my Writing for Social Change course become first-hand witnesses to oppression, as they come to experience—both dramatically and vividly—ordinary people organizing efforts to fight social injustices. Through practices of both collective inquiry *and* collective position taking, students learn that sometimes placing demands for change on established audiences is the only alternative available for people who have been historically marginalized and disenfranchised.

As community literacy practitioners, aligning our work with social movements committed to progressive social change can introduce us, along with our students, to rhetorical strategies that have the potential of transforming community relations. At the same time, oppositional rhetorical strategies that speak truth to power have the potential of disrupting power relations in the context of community-building while also calling attention to the legitimacy of critical assertions and receptive listening in the more general, global debates involving issues of social justice. While creating an atmosphere of productive discursive engagement across racial, class, and gender lines may prove extremely challenging in public spheres where dominant voices effectively work to silence those on the margins, engaging grassroots social movement activities on the ground is more likely to provide substantive opportunities for discursive exchanges that challenge dominant conceptions of the lives of the socially disenfranchised and dispossessed. As an invitation to encounter people's organized efforts to challenge social injustices, engaging community literacy through the rhetorical work of a social movement holds the promise of encouraging us, along with our students, to experience writing and rhetoric as tools for genuine social change.

Acknowledgements

I would like to thank Over-the-Rhine People's Movement activists Bonnie Neumeier, Thomas A. Dutton, and Pat Clifford for their feedback on an earlier draft of this article.

Works Cited

"American Indian Special Issue." *Voices Over-the-Rhine Community Newspaper* 7.2
(1975): 1-2.

"Campus Contact Honors Miami University Professor for Aiding Impoverished Neighborhood While Enriching Education." Campus Compact. 7 Jul. 2009. 10 Sept. 2009 <http://www.compact.org/ news/press-releases/campus-compact-honors-miami-university-professor-for-aiding-impoverished-neighborhood-while-enriching-education/7336/>.

Darsey, James. *The Prophetic Tradition and Radical Rhetoric in America*. New York: New York University Press, 1997.

Divine, Dana. "Gentrification—a.k.a. Get the Fuck Out!" The People's Friend. 1.1 April (2009).

Dreese, Donelle, and Thomas A. Dutton, Bonnie Neumeier, Christopher Wilkey. "A People's History: Teaching an Urban Neighborhood as a Place of Social Empowerment." Transformations: The Journal of Inclusive Scholarship and Pedagogy 19.1 (2008): 38-53.

Dutton, Thomas A. "Colony Over-the-Rhine." The Miami University Center for Community Engagement in Over-the-Rhine. Miami U. 1 Aug. 2007 <http://www.fna.muohio.edu/cce/_pdf/Colony%20Over%20 the%20Rhine%202.pdf>.
---. "Indian Reservations, Trojan Horses, and Economic Mix." The Miami University Center for Community Engagement in Over-the-Rhine. Miami U. 24 Mar. 2007 <http://www.fna.muohio.edu/cce/_pdf/indian_res. pdf>.
---. "The Gift of the Drop Inn Center." Cincinnati Enquirer 19 Jan. 2008: C7.
"Fighting Hunger in Cincinnati." Podcast. Weekend Edition Sunday. 24 Dec. 2006. National Public Radio. 10 May 2006 <http://www.npr.org/ templates/rundowns/ rundown.php?prgId=10&prgDate=12-24-2006>.
Flower, Linda. *Community Literacy and the Rhetoric of Public Engagement.* Carbondale, IL: Southern Illinois University Press, 2008.
Horn, Dan. "The Riots Explode: A City's Dark Week." Cincinnati Enquirer 30 Dec. 2001. 24 Aug. <*http://www.enquirer.com/unrest2001/race3.html*>.
---. "The Trigger: Shooting 'Ignites Furious Response'." Cincinnati Enquirer 30 Dec. 2001. 24 Aug. <*http://www.enquirer.com/unrest2001/race2.html*>.
Long, Elenore. *Community Literacy and the Rhetoric of Local Publics.* West Lafayette, IN: Parlor Press, 2008.
Marback, Richard. "Corbett's Hand: A Rhetorical Figure for Composition Studies." *College Composition and Communication* 47.2 (1996): 180-198.
Mathieu, Paula. *Tactics of Hope: The Public Turn in English Composition.* Portsmouth, NH: Boynton/Cook, 2005.
"Over-the-Rhine, Our Community." Over-the-Rhine Community Housing. 10 May 2009 http://www.otrch.org/otrcommunity.html.
"Photo Timeline." *Cincinnati Enquirer* 30 Dec. 2001. 24 Aug. <*http://www. enquirer.com/unrest/unrestphotos.html*>.
"Private Firm Renovates 3 Sites in Over-the-Rhine" *Cincinnati Enquirer* 31 Jan. 2009: A4.
The Miami University Center for Community Engagement in Over-the-Rhine. Miami U. 2 May 2009 <http://www.fna.muohio.edu/cce/>.
The Dean of Cincinnati. "Walkability v. The Homeless." 29 Feb. 2009. Weblog post. *The Cincinnati Beacon.* 20 May 2009 <http://www.cincinnatibeacon.com/index.php/content/comments/walkability_v_the_homeless/>.
Welch, Nancy. Living Room: *Teaching Public Writing in a Privatized World.* Portsmouth, NH: Boynton/Cook Publishers, 2008.
West, Cornel. *The American Evasion of Philosophy: A Genealogy of Pragmatism.* Madison, Wisconsin: University of Wisconsin Press, 1989.
"Why We Print." *Voices Over-the-Rhine Community Newspaper* 7.2 (1975): 12.

Interview with Bonnie Neumeier

Christopher Wilkey

Chris: Can you discuss your early years in community activism? What brought you to the neighborhood and what led you to want to become a community activist?

<u>Bonnie</u>: I know that when I first came to Cincinnati I probably didn't call myself a community activist. I was born and raised in a small [Ohio] northwestern town, fifth daughter of 20 children. Even in our small town there were haves and have-nots, so my parents always taught me to look out for the underdog and when I was looking for a school to go to I happened to choose Cincinnati. It was the furthest place I had lived from home. My freshman year of college was turbulent. It was the year that MLK was shot, the Vietnam war was going on, and a lot of issues that I didn't feel I was well prepared to handle, and from my past and background I think I became really curious and cared about what was going on.

An upper classman asked if I wanted to go to Eastern Kentucky. I had never been to Kentucky and that is where I really saw, for the first time, rural poverty that impacted me a great deal. We worked with Brothers of Charity down in David, Kentucky. I saw families living in shacks, children without proper clothing, and I was disturbed by this. A lot of them had been working in the mines and were suffering from black lung, not getting all of their benefits, just raw poverty. [I saw where] they were living and where the mine owners were living and the disparity between the two was just stark! I came back and started to ask questions in my economics class and didn't get a lot of good answers. But I was very interested in wanting to make a difference so I went back, about two weekends out of every month that I was at college, and got really interested in what happened to mountain people when they came to the city.

That is when I discovered Over-the-Rhine. It was here in Cincinnati so I started to do volunteer work in the neighborhood, and all my 4 years of college I started to do a lot of reading and writing on Appalachian culture. I came to my major in social science and requested that I do my placement here in Over-the-Rhine. I ended up doing home visits which I loved because it got me out into the community, meeting people, seeing issues that the community was faced with here, and just learning as much and I could. They offered me the director of the Contact Center [a social service agency].

I had never read about organizing people to work, but I learned that from [other activists in the community]. This neighborhood was going through a major change and a lot of federal dollars were coming in as a result of the civil rights movement and a lot of the housing was being renovated; we called it the project rehab days, and a lot of people were sitting out on the street while their building was being fixed. I then learned about the *Voices Community Newspaper* (*VCN*). It use to be like a mimeograph sheet where people would talk about community meetings and recipes to share, but what the housing activists were wanting to do was advertise the address where people had been relocated to so they could be aware that we could help them with benefits. It was in that era where I was taught that you needed to give service to the people before becoming any part of a concrete organizing effort because you have to build trust with the people, put in your time, get to know them, so in the early years I did a lot of support work.

Eventually I became the coordinator of the *VCN*, and I was reading a lot of stuff on liberation theology. My eyes and mind were being challenged, and a lot of what I thought about the world was being shook up. I was learning about how power works, and at that point I was questioning everything that I was brought up with. It was in that era that we were trying to develop a poor people's movement. What we had in common, both black and white, were issues of oppression because of the amount of money they had in their pockets, and I think that I really connected with that because of my own working class background; my parents struggled to makes ends meet, they raised a big family, and it wasn't until I got here that I got challenged to look at my issues of white privilege, my oppression as a woman, and as a working class woman, and this all happened through working on the streets.

Eventually I had to resign from the Contact Center because I was rocking waves. I was out all night helping to move people. I wanted to be out in the streets helping people. I understood my position of power as a director and [had a problem with] asking people to go to city hall about issues we were organizing around. I was asking my neighbors to go do it for free while I got paid, and so [after I quit as director of the Contact Center] I got involved with odd jobs to keep myself busy.

Housing, from the beginning of my time here, was a key organizing cause, because if you didn't have the people here, then what was the sense of fighting for anything else? A lot of people had a lack of affordable housing and substandard conditions. We were organizing rent strikes. Our movement was instrumental in creating the first tenant/landlord law here in the city because we were learning a lot about tenants and things like that. It was here in this neighborhood that I was taught that you have to be concerned about symptoms of oppression, but that you needed to also walk with that foot of justice. [I was learning that if] we come together collectively and organize around an issue that impacted us, we could make a change.

And it was that one important ingredient [to have those most impacted by the injustices to speak out on their own behalf]. [Those most] effected by the system would be best to talk to city hall. Or homeless people on the street, they would go down and have things to say to city hall to speak on their own behalf. The tenants that we were housing had the right to have a voice. Parents who were living here and losing their schools, they have a right to speak out. So I was learning about all of that, and I was learning that education was very important but not everyone we were working with had that educational background. They had a lived experience and that gave them the credentials to speak about what was happening to them. I learned that it isn't just people with a degree behind their name. It was about experience, and over the years I have learned so much from older African American women, black and white folks with little income but [who] had a keen knowledge about what was happening to them. [They understood how they] were oppressed, and with some encouragement and being brought together, they were not suffering from oppression in isolation, [which] helped them to feel that it was not their fault.

I don't remember what year we coined the Over the Rhine People's Movement, but it was that poor people's movement thing that we realized we were doing. We were creating this wheel that was the hub for fighting for basic human rights, and people who lived in the community that were from the Deep South or the Appalachian Mountains had the right not to be shoved out because someone else thought that land was valuable. Through these organizing efforts grew these grassroots organizations in the community. So that is how I grew and got involved and saw what can happen when people stand up for their rights. There was very little money and what we have been able to do with low budgets is amazing. I now call myself an activist, and I was trained here from the people in the community and not any academic book.

People in the community showed me that even with great odds they can still have a fighting spirit or hope, and through that effort we can lobby city council, do petitions, talk to people who have landlords, and that is where I learned about protest. There are times in an effort, after you have tried everything else, and if they finally say no, then sometimes you have to use your body, put your body on the line for what you believe in. So we started doing human service work at the same time we were organizing and that is how I see the two as linked. I grew up being impacted by that and so glad that I walked with, paraded with, laughed with, sang with, the spirit that is here. I think that is something that the city over looks sometimes. They don't see the asset that is here and will walk over people, make them invisible. There is a thing about being a victim of poverty, but I have seen people decide that they are going to turn that around and be actors in their own history. It's not just sitting and moping about the cards you have been dealt. It's about standing up and people wanting to work hard for what they believe in. That we have a voice and that is the asset that we have.

Chris: You talk a lot about the history and your experiences. How do you see things now in the neighborhood? What are the issues?

What needs to be accomplished?

Bonnie: Well, it has changed from when I first came because [back then] there were a lot more people and everyone here were on a fixed income. I feel that by declaring it a historic district, we knew back then that a change by way of gentrification would occur, and anyone knows across the country that when an area near the downtown becomes a historic area that things will change. Sometimes it does feel that the gentrification feels like we are being occupied or taken over. I think it is because of our efforts that we still have an amount of community control over housing. In the early years we knew this was going to happen so we bought our property in the different sections so that you wouldn't have your pockets of poverty and pockets of rich. People say that it should be a mixed community, and there are advantages to living with diversity, but it takes a certain kind of person to live with difference and not have that attitude like we are just going to take control.

I do think we have to be careful not to be silenced or afraid to challenge those who have money and power. We knew that someday this avalanche of gentrification would be here and that what we were trying to do was have a piece of that pie. Early buying of the property was not to just board up the homes to keep people out, but to board them up so that we could have money for the time in which we could renovate them to ensure affordable housing. This is tough to have a loss of population, and have seen the avalanche, that scares people. Times have changed. You can challenge city hall back in the 70s and 80s and not be thrown into jail. We use to bring cardboard signs. You can't do that anymore. I remember being at city hall and not liking something, so I stood up on my chair. Now you do that and you are escorted out. I think we have lost, through more authoritarianism and elitism, that we don't have public spaces to put our views out without the powers at be saying to get those people out of the way; it has become a lot rougher. Some of the city council people back then I thought were not for the poor, but look at the people now…[back then] they were at least moveable. You could count the votes and lobby them and get them on your side because they saw the determination and you could reason with them, not now because of the forces of power that are against the neighborhood. I don't think they know how to work with difference or to maintain equitable difference. That is why we are important. If there is going to be equitable difference in this neighborhood, they need to start valuing the presence of the people's organizations that kept this neighborhood alive. There would not be housing out there had it not been for us going to city hall and saying to not tear things down.

Chris: Could you talk a little bit about the Miami University Center for Community Engagement in Over-the-Rhine and their Residency Program, a university-community partnership that provides, among other things, college students with the opportunity to live, work, and take coursework in the neighborhood for a semester?

Bonnie: I think that the Residency Program grew out of our movement's work in the community. We believed in speaking out in what we believed in, and they reached out to us to share about our stories and our struggles. How people got consciousness raised by our work, so we have always entertained civic groups, churches, schools, and stuff like that. After all those years of success and engaging college campuses, they now think about sending students to Over-the-Rhine. Some places will send them to Central America, Africa, Asia, and we were saying hey right in your backyard there is a really good experience that students can have that is not so far way. We know that they can gain things by going to other countries, but what we have experienced here can be a challenge too. So what happens is in the fall semester, primarily the students are architecture students, students come for an orientation weekend and stay in housing provided by Over-the-Rhine Community Housing and then they take 3 different classes. They study here at the center and the architect students engage in a design/build project. The other students that are from other disciplines, I am responsible for placing them in other community organizations where they can do community service.

The whole thing about this is that we would only do it if the neighborhood could benefit from this; this is not only about what students can learn or help us with, but what we can gain as well. I do think that there have been some exciting things occurring. I like it because I know I was a college student when I became enlightened, and I kind of wish someone had nurtured or mentored me on the things I had to do. I remember my experience and how mind and eye opening it was, how much I learned, how rich and expressive and rich my life had become because of my attitude and social analysis of the world. I believe if we can pass that on, they can take that and become more sensitive to neighborhoods that are oppressed, if they are in positions of power in the future that [they] can change the world by their activism when they leave here. Some have chosen to stay here. Obviously some do leave because we can't employ everyone here, but hopefully they take this where ever they go and I see that it is a ripple effect. Our movement towards engaging students and having them help benefits our work here. We all win in the end.

Chris: What are the most important educational goals when working with college students in Over-the-Rhine? What do you want them to get out of the experience?

Bonnie: One of the students from last semester took the summer course, stayed on and just left this week, and I was amazed by her. She was from an area close to mine in northwest Ohio, and we always start out with story telling. When you have to interact with a culture different then your own, and seeing that student grow from where she came to where she is at now as a justice seeker, this happened through having a mentor along the way, being challenged about race and class. She had never had that before. All the students have this experience, but I know that all the things she learned will benefit her wherever she lands. She was an architect major, but by being involved with Over-the-Rhine she saw how architecture impacts a neighborhood. She lived here with us, and that is the part about the Residency Program that is special; you are walking the streets with us, you have to see the world through the neighborhood's eyes, and what you see is going to be very different. Building those relationships is really cool. I believe that everyone grows from where they came. You don't see it in everyone, but I think there is a willingness to be challenged and accept change, and I have heard more students say that this experience changed their lives. They have an opportunity to look at the world differently, and that's pretty cool. It's neat to see people out there raising awareness, and it also gives our own people in the neighborhood the opportunity to share their struggles. A lot of times we tell people about the things that go on here and people don't believe us.

Chris: What kind of teaching strategies do you use to create empathy in the students towards the residents? What role does empathy actually play?

Bonnie: I encourage a lot of journal writing and reflection. I have a writing session each week, and I will ask them to pay attention to what I call "Abiding Images". They can be a song, graffiti on the wall, an image, a sound, and they take that and writer and go deeper with that. I also encourage them to engage with the people, i.e. . . . out in the park, sitting on the stoop, just engaging people in conversation. Also, whatever is happening on the ground, we will invite students to go with us, like going to city hall, and it is there when they hear the people plead for the little benefits that they want, people can connect more emotionally. They are experiencing it along with us, they feel the anger of the people, they know how many times we have to go and say the same things and seeing that we don't get anything back. There is one thing that is common so far in the four years this has been going on. About a month into it they become totally frustrated with it. They question how people can be treated this way. It is total disbelief that the world is really this unfair. You're supposed to just go to city hall, tell them the truth and then you get what you want. So there is a deep frustration, but they can see the hard work and they can get into it then too right along side of us, because it is about being beside one another, not on top or doing it for others. They witness the frustration, and it takes a while for students to find out how to put their just anger into action. I think the work of the students, their skills and energy, they enhance our work, and then they earn something with us and then fall in love with us. That helps for people to not see us as the statistics anymore, or the poor people. They actually will have an educational conversation with some struggling with addiction or homelessness and as real, live people who are visible. The relationship building, seeing the world through our eyes, is what really brings it to life.

Chris: You mentioned writing. Could you talk about that a little more?

Bonnie: I love poetry and the whole idea of prompts; I give prompts. I'll bring a poem and take a line out of that poem, and I ask students to fast write and have them relate it to their experience, so they are always writing about what they are seeing and doing, how they are feeling. I think that sometimes the role as an educator is to set the environment where they can be encouraged to express themselves, and if they have that safety, anything can come out of it. I put them in a circle, I might use candles, we might do a chime, but they do fast write so that they are not editing themselves, and it allows them to just write. Even with the videos we have done, they listen to them and I will say to jot down some thing that you hear in that video, then I'll come back and we will do a fast write using that prompt. I'm using writing more with groups to help process their experience. Some take the guidance, some not, but I think women really understand about journaling. Men tend to just say that it is not their thing, and I think that is a big loss because if you have a journal, you can go back to that first page and read that initial responses and then see where you have evolved, and even if you don't have that, you can at least record your growth. I have students from previous years tell me how glad they are that they have this, even thought when they first start they may say that we don't have time or data to do this, but we encourage them to do it. It doesn't have to be a long paper. It can be just your thoughts on the week, what are your highlights, what was disturbing about it, what did you see different or the same from your own life, what images when you lay down at night, what comes to mind, did someone call you a name, these are all crucial.

Chris: What is the connection between your local community work, and that which would be labeled as the work of a social movement?

Bonnie: I think that what goes on in Over-the-Rhine is a microcosm of what is going on in the world. It is very important, no matter where you are at, to be able to ask those critical questions about power; whose agenda is being served, who has the power to do what, who is benefiting, who sets the standards of behavior. Right now there are areas of this country and abroad where you have to ask who is allowed on what lands. I have always seen this neighborhood as a land struggle and depending on who has the power to own it say what can go on here. The people at the very bottom get shoved off land, and that is happening in Central America, Israel, and the Middle East. I often talk to students about the sense that poor people are getting the biggest portion of federal dollars, where do they get that idea? There is such a minute piece of money that comes from the government. You can learn that a lot of things that happen globally is going on here, unemployment, loss of jobs to foreign countries. I guess I started making the connection with imperialism and the use of power by seeing it in the local struggle, but if we make connections we see it isn't about blaming the poor for there problems. You have to have a broader view, and if you don't it just leads to despair faster. Over-the-Rhine is dealing with issues that have global impact. I think that we have to do better about linking up social struggles across the country. We are communities of resistance, challenging the mainstream value systems that pit poor against the rich, people of color against white, making divisions, and we need to change that. Part of working with the students is raising awareness, and I feel we need young people to get out there. What we are doing is a poor people's movement and that is going to grow because of the economy; the middle-class are the ones who are going to be suffering.

Chris: So with students, it is about creating awareness, that this is a time where they can find out where they stand.

Bonnie: Yes, but they struggle. They feel like once they have their eyes opened, they can never shut them again and forget about what they saw. They have had to think and wrestle through a lot of stuff about themselves and their backgrounds. I have to tell them that there is a place for them. You can be rich, or middle class, or poor and still contribute to the work that we have going here. The people in our neighborhood are smart, though they may not have the resources, all of the things we have done with limited budget, not living beyond our means. I see people come in day-in and day-out going to city council and asking the same question every week. There is a sense that maybe you only have one voice and that you have to keep using it. By using this I think we can [gain] the solidarity of the students. They are the future.

WRITING ON THE EDGE

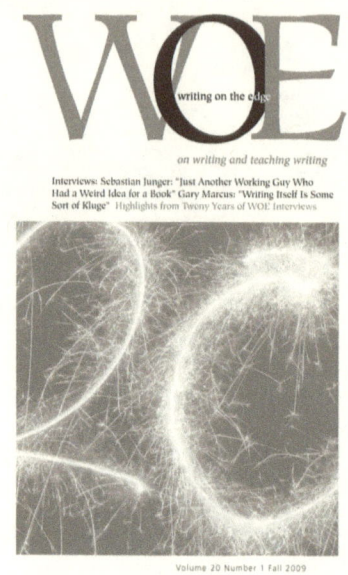

Writing on the Edge is on the Web at http://woe.ucdavis.edu/

Writing on the Edge, now in its 21st year, is a University of California at Davis sponsored journal about writing and the teaching of writing. We publish articles, essays, creative nonfiction, cartoons, short stories, poems, collages, and whatever else. In each issue we also publish interviews with writers (e.g. Toni Morrison, Calvin Trillin, John McPhee) and writing teachers (e.g. Peter Elbow, Linda Flower, David Bartholomae). We think writing about composition does not have to be boring, that it can be interesting and lively. We are a journal to be read for pleasure rather than duty. We give annual $500 prizes for the best interview and the best anything else.

"Everything Was Going Quite Smoothly Until I Stumbled on a Footnote" by David Bartholomae

David Bartholomae's "Everything Was Going Quite Smoothly Until I Stumbled on a Footnote" was originally a lecture in honor of David Osborne (1930-1996), Professor of English at Ohio Wesleyan University, where David was an undergraduate. The piece perhaps naturally then has a strong voice and a personal as well as an intellectual point of view. While structured like a traditional essay, the piece has many of the elements of a collage, full of poems and quotations (some of them quite lengthy), with even the title coming from an early chapter of the Ph.D dissertation by David's student, Richard Miller. Finally the piece shows as well as tells how scholars actually work.

Everything Was Going Quite Smoothly Until I Stumbled on a Footnote

David Bartholomae

From a lecture in honor of David Osborne (1930-1996), Professor of English at Ohio Wesleyan University

> *The grand work of literary genius is a work of synthesis and exposition, not of analysis and discovery; its gift lies in the faculty of being happily inspired by a certain intellectual and spiritual atmosphere, by a certain order of ideas, when it finds itself in them; of dealing divinely with these ideas, presenting them in the most effective and attractive combinations,—making beautiful works with them, in short. But it must have the atmosphere, it must find itself amidst the order of ideas, in order to work freely; and these it is not so easy to command.*
>
> —Matthew Arnold,
> "The Function of Criticism at the Present Time" (1865)

1.

I came to Ohio Wesleyan as a freshman in 1965. To most of you this probably seems like a long time ago (to me, it seems a *very* long time ago), and I was prompted by the occasion of this lecture to think back to where I was--where I was in my life, where I was in history (in the period we call the 60s), and to where I was, in Matthew Arnold's terms, within a certain order of ideas.

In 1965, we were the last freshman class to wear dinks, little multicolored beanies you wore to remind you of what you already knew—that you were foolish and awkward and stuck out on campus like a sore thumb. Women had to be in the dorms by 10:30 on week-nights, 1 am on the weekends, and they locked the doors if you were late. Women could not wear pants unless the temperature fell below freezing. We went off to "barn" parties, driving home at night with dozens packed into the back of rented trucks, everyone loaded to the gills with 3.2 beer, loaded to the gills or unloading—and to save us from the dangers of drinking on campus.

We were either the last or among the last class to have compulsory chapel. Once a week, with a lecture or presentation, more Unitarian in spirit than Methodist, our attendance was recorded through the new technology of the IBM punch card. As a freshman, I would carry stacks of them hidden in my jacket to stuff into the box to record the presence of the absent upperclassmen in my fraternity house. At our first chapel meeting, we were greeted by the President (I think) who welcomed the class of >69. One young women, Liz Dumbleton, shouted out from behind her program: >69 is not a class; it's a position. And I thought to myself: "Wow. I am now in the big leagues."

By the time we graduated, drugs had come to Delaware, Ohio; women had to be in by 5 AM (five AM, go figure); and the senior who recruited me during fraternity rush, Jack Dawson, was killed in action in Vietnam. We came clean for Gene McCarthy and took leaflets to unsuspecting Ohioans. I was working as a waiter at Bunn's restaurant when the news came through that Martin Luther King had been shot, and I was stunned by what I heard spoken over the breakfast tables.

I had some truly wonderful teachers. Anna Macias, who taught Latin American history and whom I got to know again years later, since she was a close friend of a colleague of mine at the University of Pittsburgh. Ben Spencer, who was the very image for us of the scholar—silent and kind, confident of what he knew, which seemed to be everything, and with the ability to read American literature out loud to us in manner that was, itself, a form of criticism—the pace and inflection, the phrasing and emphasis, all did as much for us as the critical essays we read. Ron Rollins, who led us into a passion for Joyce and for Irish literature and who had the ability, which I cannot imitate, to speak for minutes at a time in alliterative phrases: Bloomsday, June 16th, a dismal day in dear dirty Dublin.

And David Osborne, in whose name we are gathered today. The most vivid classroom memory I have of David are of those moments when he would suddenly sing in class, with a dear, true voice; he would do it without warning—a period song, a ballad, a song from the Victorian stage would interrupt a lecture or discussion to illustrate a point-Cor, perhaps just to remind us that there was more there than we knew. He was a surprising teacher; his classroom was a quiet place where we learned to listen carefully and the reward was a surprising insight, a Victorian moment that suddenly made vivid sense of the present. I was inspired to memorize Arnold's "Dover Beach," thinking it would be a good way to impress my girlfriend, Joyce Dunlop, a Tri-Delt.

These teachers and their colleagues, this lovely and historic campus, these old buildings and the memories they contain, all provided a certain intellectual and spiritual atmosphere, a certain order of ideas—and it was here that I found myself in 1965. I first read Arnold as a student of David Osborne, my copy of "Essays in Criticism" is heavily marked and annotated; I can remember struggling to read these long, strange sentences. And the passage I used as my epigraph is one of the passages I had heavily marked on its first reading: The gift of literary genius "lies in the faculty of being happily inspired by a certain intellectual and spiritual atmosphere, by a certain order of ideas, when it finds itself in them."

2.

Well--Nostalgia is the blank check issued to a weak mind. I waxing nostalgic and it is time to stop and to get this lecture moving.

I love that line: "Nostalgia is the blank check issued to a weak mind." It comes to me from a poem by a friend and former colleague, Tony Hoagland, in a book with a wonderful title, itself a small poem: *What Narcissism Means to Me*. This is the opening of the poem:

> That one night in the middle of the summer
> when people move their chairs outside
> and put the TVs on the porch
> so the dark is full of murmuring blue lights.
>
> We were drinking beer with the sound off,
> watching the figures on the screen—

> the bony blondes, the lean-jawed guys
> who decorate the perfume and the cars—
>
> the pretty ones
> the merchandise is wearing this year.
>
> Alex said, I wish they made a shooting gallery
> using people like that.
>
> Greg said, That woman has a Ph.D. in Face.
> Then we saw a preview for a movie
>
> about a movie star who is
> having a movie made about her,
> and Boz said, This country is getting stupider every year.
>
> Then Greg said that things were better in the sixties
> and Russ said that Harold Bloom said
> that Nietzsche said Nostalgia
> is the blank check issued to a weak mind,
>
> and Greg said,
> They didn't have checks back then, stupid,
> and Susan said It's too bad you guys can't get
> Spellcheck for your brains.

Russ said Harold Bloom said Nietzsche said—this is my theme today, transitions, legacy, the way things are handed down over time, how words and ideas are used and reused, and what schooling and teachers might have to do with that process.

Hoagland's poem draws its language and inspiration from the poet's lively, critical, mean-spirited engagement with both academic and popular culture. You hear the poem and you hear Cheers and Friends (and maybe Bordo and Baudrillard). You think of all those shows where people are prettier and wittier than we ever get to be in our everyday lives. Carl Dennis, in his book, *Poetry as Argument*, categorizes Hoagland as a political poet; he says Hoagland's poems are all about America as she shapes and determines who we are, what can be said, thought and done. And that's how this poem ends, with a reference out to America and to the people, and not only the pretty ones the merchandise is wearing this year:

> and we sat in quiet pleasure on the shore of the night,
> as a tide came in and turned and carried us,
> folding chairs and all,
>
> far out from the coastline of America
> in a perfect commercial for our lives.

You hear Cheers and Friends and then Real World or MTV reality shows (where bored kids watch bored kids complain about being bored). Stepping back you can hear Frank O'Hara or even Robert Frost. I also hear two other friends and colleagues, two other Pittsburgh poets.

This is Tony Petrosky, from his last book, *Crazy Love*. The poem is titled "In Sophia" and it is set in a café in Lithuania. It makes characters of Nietzsche and Proust and turns on slogans, setting them against a bleak Eastern European background:

> In the café in Sophia:
>
> Nietzsche loves to eat here with Proust on Tolbulchin
> in the nameless restaurant in the dimness and smoke,
> unnerved through the representations of time,
> contesting life right back to its lack of sense.
>
> ....
>
> Nietzsche nods
> and picks at the bread.
>
> Proust sighs.
>
> The trees grow distant shaking their arms.
> The birds disappear and all the creatures
> fold up into the magician's books.
>
> And as for happiness, Proust broke in,
> it has almost a single usefulness—

to make unhappiness possible.

Suffering almost all the more deeply hollows out the heart.

The next is Lynn Emanuel from her book, *Then, Suddenly*—. It has the meanness of Hoagland's poem and also the move to slogan and to dialogue and to literary criticism, and it, too, has the one great line, the one you wish you had thought of:

> I am giving a lecture on poetry
> to the painters who creak like saddles
> in their black leather jackets; in the study,
> where a fire is burning like a painting of
> a fire, I am explaining my current work
> on the erotics of narrative. It is night.
> Overhead the moon's naked heel dents
> the sky, the crickets ignite themselves
> into a snore, and the painters yawn
> lavishly waiting for me to say Something
> About Painting, the way your dog, when
> you are talking, listens for the words Good Dog.
>
> "Your indifference draws me like horses draw flies,"
> I say while noticing in the window the peonies
> throbbing with pulses, the cindery crows seething
> over the lawn. "Nevertheless," I continue, "I call
> your attention to the fact that, in this poem, what was
> once just a pronoun is now a pronoun talking about
> a peony while you sit in a room somewhere unmoved
> by this...."

I hear Frank O'Hara again, and Tony Hoagland; in the capital letters, turning clichés into allegorical dragons, I see the work of Bill Coles, a former colleague of ours and a legendary teacher of composition, and through him the now legendary Freshman course at Amherst College and then to Robert Frost, one of Amherst' presiding spirits. This is the order of ideas, the atmosphere I find myself in when I sit at my desk or enter a class in Pittsburgh. These poems, these lines, are in the atmosphere, as are others, and when we are attentive, when we are taken by them, when we find ourselves there, we make each others' work possible. This is one of the things I want to say. Even when the footnotes aren't there, there are footnotes.

All of these poems think about poetry's affection for the epigrammatic line, for the slogan, and they do so in a climate that is suspicious of sloganeering. (These poems have a certain resonance during the presidential primary campaigns.) And all of these poems think about the relationship of literary theory to everyday life and everyday language. I'm not saying that these poets agreed upon a common theme or set of concerns. Influence is much more subtle than that. And if asked about influence, my guess is that they all would be quick to deny making use of the others. And I am not talking about either theft or plagiarism but about paying attention—about how our work as writers and thinkers is always, even when we don't know it, even when we don't want it to be, how it is always informed by what has come before, by what sticks, by what shapes the way we speak and think--and what sticks sticks because the words matter—the work enters our lives and we are shaped and, hopefully, shaped for the better.

This was one of the great hopes of David Osborne in his teaching, and it was articulated for him a century before by his great hero, Matthew Arnold, in the essay I spoke from earlier, "The Function of Criticism at the Present Time." Arnold said that the purpose of criticism (choosing what to read and preparing others to read it) was to "learn and propagate the best that is known and thought in the world." And later, "Simply to know the best that is known and thought in the world, and by in its turn making this known,---- to create a current of true and fresh ideas."

3.

Sentences that echo sentences. The presence of the past in the work of the present. A current of ideas. I love to see this in my students' work. Several years ago Richard Ford came to our campus to read from his new book, *Men Without Women*. I was teaching a group of first year students, and I assigned the book so that they could be prepared for the visit. And I assigned a recent *NYTimes* review by Michael Gorra and I asked my students to write a book review, one that spoke from the perspective of their generation, its reading and its values.

Here was the opening of the published review:

> Richard Ford is among the most traditional of contemporary American writers and also among the most original. Original because traditional: in the sense that T.S. Eliot meant when he wrote that "not only the best, but the most individual parts" of a writer's work "may be those in which the dead...his ancestors, assert their immortality most vigorously."
>
> Ford's sinewy and distinctively American voice contains the echoing tones of many ancestors....And Ford's title does indeed signal an allegiance to the Hemingway legacy, or at least a part of it—his fascination with a world of male rituals that has, in the past, led him to write about duck hunting and car theft and fishing and football.

Here is the opening of the student essay I reproduced for class discussion—you will hear it rework not only the idea but the syntax of Gorra's review; and it keeps the performance moving along quite convincingly until, with the last sentence, it comes undone, and the student reminds us that he is a student:

> Richard Ford's *Women with Men* speaks in a strong, unrepentantly male voice enriched with a smoky sense of Americana and a slanted, self-deprecating wit. Ford's intelligent yet unassuming prose wraps around his characters and places them in the timeless sensibility of classic American writers like J.D. Salinger or Ernest Hemingway. The short stories "Jealous" and "Occidentals" both focus on male protagonists and decidedly male issues...Together, the two characters and stories serve up a diner-sized heap of commentary on knowledge, wisdom, experience and growing up.

The other students in my class were furious over this essay. It was cheating; it was copying; the writer wasn't playing fair. The writer, on the other hand, was completely floored by these accusations. It had never occurred to him that there were parallels; he thought of the opening as his, he thought the gesture toward literary history (Salinger added to Hemingway) was an achievement, and he thought of the review as one of his very best pieces of writing. He was proud of it.

As he should have been—it was his, as much as any of us every own our writing, and it was smart (a gesture toward the kind of thinking we think of as smart), it was stylish and voiced, and it was the best thing he had done all term. And, I said to the class, it was the first paper of theirs I had read that sounded like writing rather than the dreadful standard issue of the English class: "When one reads the short stories of Richard Ford, one can be transported to other worlds, the worlds of nature or the modern city...." That language, too, is prepared, learned, available; it is just that it is not the language of adults speaking about things that matter and so it is not a language I want to encourage. And the reason the students all felt so angry, so betrayed, although I didn't say this to the class, was that one of their own had broken out and tried to do something more interesting—not more original, that's not my claim for it, but more interesting. The grand work of literary genius, says Arnold, is synthesis and exposition, not analysis and discovery.

If there is a lesson here, and I believe there is, it is that you have to be ready to be taken by the words of others—learning, including learning to write, is not about invention, about being creative, it is not about having ideas on your own; it is about finding yourself in relation to the work of others, having a voice in intense conversation with other voices, learning to listen and to read in ways that allow the rhythms and cadences of other people's prose to dance at the ends of your fingers while you type away at the keyboard.

4.

I came Ohio Wesleyan the year after Alfred Ferguson left to teach at the University of Massachusetts, Boston. I was told that I missed out on a great teacher. He left, as I later came to learn, because this university, like most universities in the 60s, had difficulty finding room in the faculty for women, especially wives with PhDs. His wife was Marianne Ferguson, and their daughter, Jean Ferguson Carr, is now my colleague and good friend.

It is a small world. Marianne Ferguson became the chair at Umass; she was also one of the first women in the country to bring women's studies into the curriculum, and because women's studies has always been concerned with who has access to knowledge and authority, that English department has always had a strong interest in composition. While he was teaching as an adjunct in an academic support program at Umass/Boston, Richard Miller decided he wanted to work for a PhD with a focus on composition and pedagogy. Our faculty were well known to the faculty at UMB, one of our students, Judy Goleman, was teaching there, and Richard applied to Pittsburgh, where I became one of his teachers and the director of his dissertation. Richard is now the Chair at Rutgers, where I completed my PhD. There is a circle here—OWU, Pitt, Umass, Rutgers, and I want to the loop to return to David Osborne, who was hired by Al Ferguson, and this turns out to be surprisingly easy, although you will have to allow me a few minutes of what might seem like a digression.

5.

Richard Miller's dissertation began as a study of the ways in which several educational initiatives, like the Great Books program in the US or the Open University in Britain, imagined and represented the student—or the position that would be occupied by a young person who would then take on the role of the student. The dissertation became a book, published by Cornell University Press in 1998, and it is titled *As If Learning Mattered: Reforming Higher Education*.

In the opening chapter, Richard tells the story of the early stages of the research project, the dissertation, when he was thinking about Matthew Arnold, since Matthew Arnold had become the fall guy or the punching bag for those interested in radical educational reform, as Richard was. Arnold became the punching bag largely because of the broad circulation (and misreading) of his statement that the function of criticism and education should be to "learn and propagate the best that is known and thought in the world." This had come to stand as the representative slogan of elitism, and Arnold as spokesman for colonial power; his essays had come to stand as an argument for closing the canon to the work of emerging writers, or minority writers; for Edward Said, in *The World the Text and The Critic*, it rationalized the hegemony of "an identifiable set of ideas, which Arnold honorifically calls culture, over all other ideas in society"--and Matthew Arnold came to stand for the English (and western) desire to colonize the world and to impart strict controls over thought, speech, and writing.

Here is Richard telling the story of his dissertation project. I am going to read a lengthy passage, since it tells a story of scholarship that I take to be representative:

> [W]hen this research began, I had meant for Matthew Arnold to figure, as he does throughout much of the academy, as the whipping boy whose whipping would inaugurate my own "oppositional" project. I would identify him as a book-

ish elitist, out of touch with the world, blind to the needs of real students. All that remained for me to do was connect the dots and move on to the next exercise in critical historiography. And, as it happened, I discovered there was no shortage of evidence to support such a project: opening Culture and Anarchy to almost any page effortlessly provided me with all the damning quotes I would ever need; contemporary work that decried Arnold's influence, such as Chris Baldick's *The Social Mission of English Criticism* and Edward Said's "The World, the Text, and the Critic," was everywhere ready to hand. Everything was going quite smoothly until I stumbled on a footnote that brought my developing argument crashing to the ground.

As it turns out, Arnold was not the wealthy aristocrat I assumed him to be. Rather, he spent his life as one of Her Majesty's inspectors of schools, traveling the country to visit the nation's poorest schools and to inspect the often gruesomely disappointing results. This unwanted discovery led me to read in parts of the Arnoldian corpus that originally had held no interest for me--Arnold's book-length reports on foreign education, his annual inspection reports on British schools, his anonymous tracts concerning the Revised Code. In order to understand these works, I had to move to other parts of the archive altogether: parliamentary papers, histories of popular modes of instruction, handbooks describing the duties of school inspectors....

To be confronted with how little I knew about the history and the mechanisms for disseminating mass education was embarrassing, and my failure even to consider these matters important to my study was a further sign of the "conceptual crudity,@ as Silver would put it, of my original approach to these materials.

With this insight in mind, I realized that I could use my own ignorance and expectations as signs of a state I shared with many others. This, in turn, enabled me to historicize the connections between what I knew and didn't know and the areas of thought I had and hadn't been introduced to in school, as well as the teachers, writers, and ideas that I had and hadn't been given access to through the educational system; the autodidactic pursuits that that system had and hadn't given rise to; and, most important, the ways I had and hadn't been taught to define, think about, and respond to ignorance.

There is a way in which this is a conventional story. A scholar heads out with a fixed idea, a thesis, but stumbles on a footnote (or a document in the archive, or a line in a book) and, if this is a good scholar, a serious one, everything stops and the project reorganizes itself and the scholar realizes how unprepared she is for the work that must be done. She has to teach herself (to become an autodidact) to read things he is unprepared to read and to think things he has not yet thought. It is an exciting; it is necessary; it is conventional and predictable; and it must be staged (and experienced) as a surprise. Richard found himself in a position to make the most of what he didn't know rather than to avoid the unknown or to skirt the unmanageable. As I often say to freshman--the problem with the thesis is that it often comes before you know what you are talking about. More than anything else, you need to learn to think of ideas as provisional and strategic; of the opening as a way of getting started with a topic; of the summary as a point to push off from. If you are lucky, you will find that the thesis doesn't hold, that you have come upon counter-examples or side-tracks too interesting and too compelling to ignore.

Richard says, "Everything was going quite smoothly until I stumbled on a footnote that brought my developing argument crashing to the ground." As I remember the progress of the dissertation, he didn't stumble on a footnote; I put something in his path—or, to be precise, I put a book in his hands. The book was Fred Walcott's *The Origins of Culture and Anarchy: Matthew Arnold and Popular Education in England.* This was a book that was given to me by Dave Osborne, who had worked for years with the letters Arnold wrote as a school inspector. In the late 70s, in fact, when I was a brand new Assistant Professor at the U of Pittsburgh, David had written to see if I would be interested in editing these letters with him. He turned to me, I think, as a gesture toward a young person in his profession, a profession that requires research projects and publications; and he turned to me, I think, because I was young and because I was at a large research university, with collegial and travel and library resources that are not available to scholars working at the smaller, liberal arts colleges. He was a brilliant teacher but he was not a published (or publishing) scholar, and he felt this as burden. We never did collaborate on this project; but over the period of half a year we did share notes and books and one of those books made its way into the path of Richard Miller, who stumbled on a book that passed from my teacher to me and from me to him. The third chapter of Richard's book is about the importance of considering Arnold's career as a school inspector—it is a direct extension of David's Osborne's work.

It is appropriate, even essential, that Richard and I would tell the "footnote" story differently. One is a teacher's story; the other a story of scholarship and writing, of discovery and initiative, where the work is Richard's and not mine and not David Osborne's. I'm not concerned with who has the better memory; I am concerned with the necessity of memorial, and there is no dearer memorial that to see a student write himself (or herself) into the narrative of scholarship. And in the narrative of scholarship, the teacher must disappear and become silent. In his dedication to my copy of his book, Richard wrote:

> For Dave, my mentor, my most trusted advisor, and my dear friend, who made this book and my unlikely academic career possible by teaching me how to invent a place for myself in the community.

His was the act of invention and Richard, in homage, is echoing the title of an essay of mine, "Inventing the University," an essay that talks about learning in just these terms.

6.

The first time I read Walt Whitman was at Ohio Wesleyan in a junior seminar. I was sitting next to Ben Spencer in a small room with a round table. While he was talking, I was watching his face and trying in my mind to compose a poem (which I'm afraid I often did in lieu of taking notes). This was going to be a poem about his thick skin, which was coarse and freckled and whiskered, and that folded as it broke over his tight shirt collar. ("Elephantine," was the word I was stuck on, and I was trying to think about how to make it honorific.) I was captured by Ben Spencer's voice when he read and spoke, by the look of his skin and the hairs sticking out of his ears, features I had not yet seen in my own father and that, of course, I now see in the morning when I look into the mirror to shave—or that I see if I have my glasses handy.

He read,

> I am the teacher of athletes,
> He that by me spreads a wider breast than my own proves the width of my own,
> He most honors my style who learns under it to destroy the teacher.
>
> I teach straying from me, yet who can stray from me?
> I follow you whoever you are from the present hour;
> My words itch at your ears till you understand them.
> I do not say these things for a dollar, or to fill up the time while I wait for a boat;
> It is you talking just as much myself....

And in the famous final lines, Whitman says:

> You will hardly know who I am or what I mean,
> But I shall be good health to you nevertheless,
> And filter and fiber your blood.
>
> Failing to fetch me at first keep encouraged,
> Missing me one place search another,
> I stop some where waiting for you

For me and for many, more than we could know or number, David Osborne has been good health and filter and fibre, central to me to the order of ideas; I think of him when I think of the desire for the best that is thought and known. I wish everyone the opportunity of such teachers.

About the Editors

Steve Parks is Associate Professor of Writing at Syracuse University. He is author of *Class Politics: The Students' Right To Their Own Language* and *Gravyland: Writing Beyond the Curriculum in the City of Brotherly Love*, as well as co-editor/publisher of over fifteen community press publications. He has also served as editor of *Reflections: A Journal of Writing, Service-Learning and Community Literacy* and is currently Executive Director of New City Community Press (www.newcitycommunitypress.org).

Linda Adler-Kassner is author, co-author, or co-editor of seven books and over thirty-five articles and book chapters, including *The Activist WPA: Changing Stories About Writers and Writing*, which won the Council of Writing Program Administrators' Best Book Award in 2010. Her research focuses broadly on the ways that audiences inside and outside the university understand writing and literacy; on how people act on those understandings (in the past and in the present); and on the implications of those actions for writing programs and institutions.

Brian Bailie is a PhD candidate in the Composition and Cultural Rhetoric program at Syracuse University. Bailie's work focuses on the intersections of technology and activism, transnationalism and rhetoric, identity and media, and the ways activists exploit, expand, resist, and utilize these intersections to their tactical advantage. Bailie has served as contributor, associate editor, and special issue editor for *Reflections: A Journal of Writing, Service-Learning, and Community Literacy*. His most recent publications have appeared in the *KB Journal* and *Composition Forum*.

Collette Caton is a PhD student in the Composition and Cultural Rhetoric program at Syracuse University. Her research interests include feminist rhetorics, digital writing, media studies, and working-class rhetorics. She has presented conference papers at CCCC, Computers & Writing, and Feminisms & Rhetorics, and she has served as a contributor, associate editor, and special issue editor for *Reflections: A Journal of Writing, Service Learning and Community Literacy*.

www.ingramcontent.com/pod-product-compliance
Lightning Source LLC
Chambersburg PA
CBHW030131240426
43672CB00005B/98